Taxcafe.co.uk Tax Guides

# How to Save Inheritance Tax

By Carl Bayley BSc FCA

# Important Legal Notices:

Taxcafe®
TAX GUIDE – "How to Save Inheritance Tax"

**Published by:**
Taxcafe UK Limited
67 Milton Road
Kirkcaldy KY1 1TL
Tel: (01592) 560081
Email address: team@taxcafe.co.uk

Sixteenth Edition – May 2020

ISBN  978-1-911020-57-8

# Disclaimer

# About the Author

Carl Bayley is the author of a series of 'Plain English' tax guides designed to help families, landlords, and other business owners understand the taxes they face and make savings through sensible planning and by having the confidence to know what they are entitled to claim. Carl's particular speciality is his ability to take the weird, complex and inexplicable world of taxation and set it out in the kind of clear, straightforward language that taxpayers themselves can understand. As he often says himself, "my job is to translate 'tax' into English."

Carl enjoys his role as a tax author, as he explains: "Writing these guides gives me the opportunity to use the skills and knowledge learned over more than thirty years in the tax profession for the benefit of a wider audience. The most satisfying part of my success as an author is the chance to give the average person the same standard of advice as the 'big guys' at a price everyone can afford."

Carl takes the same approach when speaking on taxation, a role he frequently undertakes with great enthusiasm, including his highly acclaimed annual 'Budget Breakfast' for the Institute of Chartered Accountants.

In addition to being a recognised author and speaker on the subject, Carl has often spoken on taxation on radio and television, including the BBC's 'It's Your Money' programme and BBC Radio 2's Jeremy Vine Show.

Carl began his career as a Chartered Accountant in 1983 with one of the 'Big 4' accountancy firms. After qualifying as a double prize-winner, he immediately began specialising in taxation.

Carl worked for several major international firms until beginning the new millennium by launching his own tax and accounting practice, Bayley Miller Limited, through which he provided advice on a wide variety of taxation issues; especially property taxation, inheritance tax, and tax planning for small and medium-sized businesses, for twenty years, before selling the practice to focus on his favourite role as an author and presenter.

Carl is a former Chairman of the Tax Faculty of the Institute of Chartered Accountants in England and Wales and a member of the Institute's governing Council. He is also a former President of ICAEW Scotland and member of the ICAEW Board. He has co-organised the annual Practical Tax Conference for the last 17 years.

# Dedication and Thanks

## *A Special Dedication*

Normally, as regular readers will know, I like to dedicate my books to my family, past, present... and those who will brighten my future.

This time, however, I would like to dedicate this book to the heroes working for the NHS, in care homes all over the UK, and elsewhere on the front line helping to keep our country running, and to keep us all safe: you have my thanks, my eternal gratitude, and my deepest admiration.

With your help, let's all make sure this guide remains, as it is meant to be, about long-term planning.

As for my family, past, present and future, you are of course all still in my thoughts.

Lastly, I could not close this dedication without mentioning my partner Linda, who is one of those heroes. Bless you princess, I'm so proud of you.

## Thanks

Thanks are due to:

The Taxcafe team, past and present – for their help in making these books far more successful than I could ever have dreamed

My old friend and mentor, Peter Rayney – for his inspiration and for showing me that tax and humour can mix

Rebecca, Paul and David – for taking me into the 'fold' at the Tax Faculty and for their fantastic support at our Practical Tax Conference over many years

Gregor – for the 'brain-storming' sessions and those amazing ideas that sprang from his lateral thinking

Jane Evans – for some useful practical insights

And last, but far from least, thanks to Nick for giving me the push!

**C.B., Roxburghshire, May 2020**

## To Our Readers

At this difficult time, the author and Taxcafe would like to offer our very best wishes to all our readers and their families and friends.

# Contents

# Foreword

This sixteenth edition of *'How to Save Inheritance Tax'* comes at a time of great difficulty, uncertainty, and stress to us all. At the time of writing (May 2020), the Coronavirus crisis is at a critical stage and we are in lockdown. If you are reading this guide many months, or even years, from now, you may therefore be puzzled by the odd comment written in the context of the current situation. Hopefully, from your point of view, it is all just a bad memory.

I will be honest, I have always found this a difficult subject to write about: not because of the undoubted technical complexities – that is something I am well and truly accustomed to dealing with as a tax author. No, I find this particular tax to be difficult to write about from an emotional perspective, because it is, inevitably, largely about death. My first introduction to the topic, as a young accountancy student, came within weeks of my own mother's death and that, perhaps, may be why I have always found the subject somewhat distasteful.

Nonetheless, as a professional tax writer, I have always tackled this subject to the best of my abilities and strived to give readers the quality of advice they deserve, just as in all my guides. I am confident I have succeeded in this aim and I believe the guide you have here is as comprehensive and detailed as anyone could wish for.

But to help me, and I hope you too, deal with the emotional aspects of the subject, I have, in previous editions, tried to inject some levity and humour into the topic. Now, with the crisis we currently face, there might be an argument to say this humour is inappropriate and perhaps I should re-write the guide to be more reflective of the present situation. I considered this approach but, in the end, I still believe in trying to put a smile on people's faces (including my own), even when tackling such an emotive issue. So, the humour, such that it is, has stayed. If I offend anyone, I sincerely apologise, but I hope most readers will simply smile at my efforts.

When it comes to tax, I believe you should never pay more than your fair share, and you have every right to undertake sensible planning measures to legitimately reduce, or delay, your tax bills; especially to protect your family.

However, when all is said and done, the reason we pay tax is to fund vital public services, something that is now more important than ever. Tax is the hallmark of civilisation and, while I will help you pay no more than your fair share that is still something we should all remember.

# Chapter 1

# Introduction

## 1.1 THERE ARE TWO CERTAINTIES IN LIFE

Generally speaking, I find the oldest sayings are the truest. One old saying is, 'There are only two certainties in life: Death and Taxes'.

At the point where these two great 'certainties' meet lies 'Inheritance Tax', and it is through the medium of this tax the Government will aim to get its final pound of flesh from you, just as you have departed this life.

Most people spend their lifetime trying to accumulate a reasonable amount of wealth, to take care of themselves in old age and then pass on any remaining surplus to their children. Much of the Government's fiscal policy is aimed at encouraging this behaviour.

It is somewhat unfair then, that without careful planning and a great deal of pre-emptive action, many families will ultimately face a huge Inheritance Tax bill. Unchecked, this tax bill will rob your family of a significant proportion of their rightful inheritance – up to 40% of it, in fact.

Most people are absolutely appalled at this prospect, which, of course, is where Inheritance Tax planning comes in!

Inheritance Tax, as we know it today, arrived in 1986, the brainchild of Margaret Thatcher and her then Chancellor, Nigel Lawson. The tax is actually little more than a re-branding of its predecessor, Capital Transfer Tax, which, in turn, had replaced the earlier and rather more Draconian Estate Duty that, in its day, had played a major part in turning many of Britain's stately homes into amusement parks!

It is quite ironic that Inheritance Tax should have such a long lineage because it is, of course, one's descendants who will suffer its effects.

The principal difference between Inheritance Tax and its predecessors is the fact there is a general exemption for most lifetime transfers to other individuals. This is part of the reason behind accusations the Labour Party made to a previous Conservative Government that they had allowed Inheritance Tax to become a 'voluntary tax', paid only by the unwary, ill-advised and unprepared taxpayer, while wealthier taxpayers took expensive professional advice and avoided the tax.

Certainly there was, and still is, an element of truth in this accusation. In recent years, however, it has become increasingly difficult to avoid this hated 'grave-robber's tax', with a host of measures introduced by Governments of all persuasions designed to block many of the popular methods used by families attempting to plan for the inevitable.

As we will see later in the guide, some Government attempts to block Inheritance Tax planning suffer from their well-known tendency to 'use a sledgehammer to crack a nut'. In fact, the scope of one particular charge (the 'pre-owned assets charge') is so wide many innocent taxpayers are completely unaware simple domestic arrangements like buying a house together may have led to a charge being technically due.

Not satisfied with getting this quite absurdly Draconian measure on the statute books, Gordon Brown turned up the heat even further in 2006, with a savage attack on trusts.

Help seemed to be at hand the following year when the Conservatives proposed a massive increase in the nil rate band exemption to £1m. Although this did not materialise for many years and, even then, it had been watered down beyond all recognition by a host of 'ifs', 'buts' and 'maybes', it did at least prompt the old Labour Government into making nil rate bands transferable between spouses.

Suddenly, overnight, it seemed almost every married couple, civil partnership, widow, widower and surviving civil partner had effectively doubled their nil rate band.

Since then, however, things have taken a turn for the worse: as it seems all our politicians are happy to break their promises when it comes to Inheritance Tax.

Alistair Darling kicked off the 'season of broken promises' in 2009 when he announced the planned increase in the nil rate band set for the following year would not go ahead. Worse still, he went on to announce a five year freeze in the nil rate band at its 2009 level of £325,000.

Soon afterwards, Labour were ousted and the Conservatives became the 'senior partner' in the Coalition Government. Sadly, their promised increase in the nil rate band was swiftly shelved and Labour's five year freeze was adopted and eventually extended to twelve years!

So, despite our change of Government, we are now stuck with a nil rate band of just £325,000 until at least 2021. Furthermore, as we will see later, in Section 3.2, there may now be a strong chance the freeze will continue into the foreseeable future.

At the time of writing, inflation has already severely eroded the value of the nil rate band. A bout of high inflation in the near future would reduce its value even further and could undo most of the benefit of the transferable nil rate band regime introduced in 2007 (and those who are single or divorced never had that benefit in the first place).

Make no mistake about it; the twelve year freeze in the nil rate band is a significant tax-raising measure. As the value of the band decreases in real terms due to inflation, the Government's Inheritance Tax take is steadily increasing.

On top of all the broken promises about the nil rate band, the 2013 Budget brought yet more misery, as George Osborne announced a raft of new rules to restrict the deduction of liabilities. As one might expect, these have blocked a number of popular planning techniques. However, what will be less apparent to most people is that the rules will also lead to some astonishingly unfair results, especially when a family business is passed on to the next generation.

We will look at the impact of these rules in more detail later, but it is clear to me they severely undermine the original intention of helping small and medium-sized businesses survive their owner's death. The additional Inheritance Tax burden placed on many families will inevitably reduce many businesses' chances of survival.

In the July 2015 Budget, Osborne finally returned to that promise of a £1m nil rate band. And what a mess he made of it!

Instead of the simple £1m nil rate band he had promised, he created an additional 'residence nil rate band'. Claiming the new relief amounted to the equivalent of a £1m nil rate band: "Promise Made, Promise Delivered!" he said; was somewhat disingenuous, since getting the required level of exemption necessitates a complex combination of circumstances.

What Osborne did was rather like me promising to give one of my children £1,000 tomorrow – no strings attached, to do with as they please; but, instead of doing as I said, waiting eight years and then telling them I would give them £1,000 in another five years' time, but only if they got married and bought a house. That's what I call: "Promise Made, Promise Broken."

Despite the many changes to the Inheritance Tax regime, what still remains true to this day is the fact that it is the moderately wealthy members of society who suffer the greatest proportionate burden when compared with their overall wealth. In fact, it seems to me the restrictions on deduction of liabilities are likely to further exacerbate this tendency.

The problem for many people in the middle wealth bracket is they face a fundamental dilemma. On the one hand they have, on paper, sufficient wealth to leave their family with a substantial tax burden. On the other hand, they do not really have a great deal of disposable income, despite leading reasonably modest lifestyles. This means the simple expedient of just giving all their surplus wealth away is, in practical terms, simply not an option.

Recent trends have added to this problem. Increases in property values in some parts of the country have pushed more and more people into the Inheritance Tax bracket, especially in London and the South East, and other 'hotspots' like Edinburgh or Bath. We may see some reversal of this trend in 2020, but property values are still likely to remain the number one cause of many people's Inheritance Tax burden.

The second factor adding impetus to the 'asset rich/cash poor' situation, which many people find themselves in, is the current poor level of return on investments. In short, what this means is a lot of capital produces only a modest income, leaving a great many people with very little real wealth today but serious Inheritance Tax problems for tomorrow!

As ever, there remain two effective ways to avoid Inheritance Tax:

- Die poor, or
- Plan ahead

Most of us find the first option somewhat unpalatable and also quite difficult to achieve without a remarkable sense of timing!

Until recently, 'planning ahead' has also been seen as the prerogative of the very wealthiest members of society, leaving the moderately wealthy to pick up the bill. However, my aim in this guide is to help put an end to this situation.

If the Government is still prepared to allow Inheritance Tax to be even partly 'voluntary', albeit to a far lesser extent than previously, then why should anyone volunteer?

Early and careful planning is the key to reducing the eventual Inheritance Tax burden on your family and you don't need to be a millionaire to do it. Or to need to do it either, for that matter!

Besides which, a great many people are surprised to discover when they add up all their assets they are, in fact, millionaires anyway – on paper, at least.

While some tax can still be saved through 'last-minute' planning, a great deal more unnecessary tax can be avoided by planning for death and taxes throughout your lifetime. Read on and I will show you how.


## 1.2    GUIDE OVERVIEW

In this opening chapter, we will start by taking a brief look at some background issues important to an understanding of the rest of the guide.

Following that, in Chapter 2, we will cover some of the basics, including how the tax is calculated and who pays it. All of this comes under the general heading of 'know your enemy', because it is important to understand what you're up against before you start to make plans to combat it.

We then move on, in Chapter 3, to look at the main exemptions available at any time, both during your lifetime and on death; as well as those only available on death.

Chapters 4 and 5 look at the area of lifetime transfers, including the additional exemptions available and how to maximise them.

The first five chapters prepare us for Chapter 6, which is devoted to Inheritance Tax planning for married couples, widows, and widowers (including civil partners). The changes introduced in 2007 fundamentally altered the Inheritance Tax planning landscape for married couples. In many cases, something that was the best advice before is now the very last thing you should do!

Married couples therefore need to consider everything contained in the rest of this guide in the context of the issues and advice set out in Chapter 6. The chapter also includes a detailed analysis of the position facing widows and widowers, with advice on crucial tax-saving action that needs to be taken by the recently bereaved.

Even those who are currently single or divorced will benefit from Chapter 6 as it includes vital advice on the potential Inheritance Tax benefits of marriage.

Chapter 7 covers the important area of business property relief, perhaps the most valuable piece of equipment in our Inheritance Tax planning armoury; as well as agricultural property relief, which can also be highly beneficial.

We then move into the realm of trusts in Chapters 8 and 9 and we will see what powerful tools these vehicles can provide in the battle against Inheritance Tax.

Chapter 10 reminds us there is a 'bigger picture' than merely saving Inheritance Tax and here we will widen our sights to take in other aspects of estate preservation. This is reinforced in Chapter 11 with a look at the interaction between Inheritance Tax and Capital Gains Tax.

In Chapter 12, we look at the all-important issue of the family home. Here we will take a detailed look at some of the practical implications of the residence nil rate band, as well as some of the other planning techniques available to shelter the family home from the Government's most despised form of taxation.

Chapter 13 focuses on the powerful long-term planning strategy of family investment companies, which has the potential to save landlords and other investors millions of pounds in Inheritance Tax. After that, in Chapter 14, we look at some other more advanced planning techniques.

In Chapter 15, we cover perhaps the most drastic of all planning techniques, with a guide to emigration, as well as a look at the advantages available to those who have already done it.

Chapter 16 provides a useful 'whole life' timetable for effective Inheritance Tax planning, which puts everything else we have learned into context and also reassures us that, while it's never too early to start planning, it's never too late either!

Chapter 17 covers the planning a bereaved family can still carry out even after someone has died. While this is not the ideal time for truly effective Inheritance Tax planning, it is surprising how much can still be achieved if the deceased's family acts quickly.

Finally, Chapter 18 takes a look at the future of Inheritance Tax by examining some ideas currently under consideration within government circles. These ideas are not yet at the stage of becoming Government proposals, and may, in fact, never see the light of day. For this reason, I have not taken them into account in the rest of the guide. However, since Inheritance Tax planning is very much about looking at the long-term, it is worth us looking at these ideas as, ultimately, they may affect your family.

This expanded guide fully updated for the drastic changes introduced over the last few years, and the latest planning ideas available today, has something of value for everyone and provides a valuable tool in the battle against the Government's most controversial form of taxation.

## 1.3    TERMINOLOGY AND ABBREVIATIONS

Throughout this guide, you will see me refer to 'married couples' and 'spouses', as well as 'widows' and 'widowers'. In each case, the tax treatment applies equally to married couples of all types and to civil partners.

Any references to 'married couples' should be taken to also include registered civil partnerships; any reference to the taxpayer's 'spouse' will also include their civil partner where relevant; and any reference to 'husbands' or 'wives' will include spouses of the same gender and civil partners. Similarly, any reference to 'widows' or 'widowers' includes surviving civil partners.

For the avoidance of doubt, I would, in particular, point out the spouse exemption covered in Section 3.3 and all the planning issues covered in Chapter 6 apply equally to same sex spouses and civil partners. However, it remains important to remember, unless specified to the contrary, the tax treatment being outlined applies to legally married couples and legally registered civil partners only.

Inheritance Tax, like many other UK taxes, is administered by reference to the UK tax year, i.e. the period of twelve months ending on 5th April. Thus, for example, the 2020/21 tax year is the year ending 5th April 2021. Any references to the 'tax year' in this guide should be construed accordingly.

Other periods are also important for Inheritance Tax purposes and a reference to 'seven years' or 'more than two years', for example, means a strict period of calendar years rather than tax years.

Trust concepts and terminology are key to an understanding of Inheritance Tax planning. As well as the various types of trust, we will encounter important concepts such as 'interest in possession' and 'life interest'. A full explanation of the trust terminology will be given in Chapter 8.

Generally, at Taxcafe, we don't like using jargon because we want to keep our guides as simple as possible. To save some space, however, we have allowed ourselves a few abbreviations. We think they are fairly obvious, so they should not cause any confusion. We will explain what each abbreviation means the first time we use it and they are set out again in Appendix D for ease of reference.

## 1.4 WHY WORRY?

Of course **you** won't actually have to pay the Inheritance Tax ('IHT') on your own estate. Furthermore, for many people, everything can safely be left to their spouse free from IHT.

And if you have no other dependants or potential beneficiaries but simply resent paying any unnecessary tax, you can simply leave it all to charity.

But most people **do** have someone they care about. Usually they have children or other family or friends whom they want to see benefit from the assets they have built up in their lifetime and they don't want to see the Government taking 40% of it away.

Even if, in the first instance, you are leaving everything tax free to your surviving spouse, your accumulated wealth will eventually be hit by IHT if you don't plan ahead.

As we will see later in the guide, you need to take action **now** to safeguard your family's future prosperity. Alternatively, you may be the potential beneficiary yourself, trying to get an elderly relative to plan for the preservation of **your** inheritance. Either way, there is plenty to worry about!

### But Am I Wealthy Enough to Worry?

Most people are quite surprised to discover just how much they are actually worth. How often have you heard someone say, "I'm worth more dead than alive"? Very often, especially as we get older, it's true (in pure financial terms only, of course).

This is basically because it takes an enormous amount of capital just to support one person. When that person dies, the capital that was previously tied up in supporting them is freed. (After the Government gets its share!)

Hence, although you may not feel particularly wealthy, you may still find you have a large potential IHT bill. You'd be amazed just how many 'paper millionaires' there are these days. Take a look at this example:

### Example
*Rosemary is a divorcee with no children of her own: although she is very close to her two younger sisters and their children. She owns a fairly average sized detached house, which her ex-husband transferred to her under the terms of their divorce settlement. The house is bigger than she really needs, but she has fond memories of the many holidays her nephews and nieces spent there, so she is quite attached to it. She has been advised that its current market value is £450,000.*

*Rosemary is retired and lives off her savings and an investment portfolio she managed to accumulate after her divorce. Although these produce an income of only £19,500 per annum, their total value is approximately £535,000.*

*Rosemary also has some jewellery, some silver and a few antiques. Altogether, these are worth £10,000. Lastly, she has a small car, worth £5,000.*

*Nobody would call Rosemary rich by any stretch of the imagination. She's living off only £19,500 a year. But add it all up and you will find she is a millionaire! This means Rosemary's family has a potential IHT bill of £270,000!*

And you don't need to be anywhere near as 'wealthy' as Rosemary to have an IHT problem. Once your estate is worth over £325,000, you have a potential exposure to tax at 40% on the excess (subject to any transferable nil rate band: see Chapter 6; and any available residence nil rate band: see Section 3.4). £325,000! What's that these days? A house, a car, a few savings and you're there!

So, yes, generally speaking, if you can afford to buy this guide there is a strong chance you are wealthy enough to worry about IHT!

## 1.5    PROPERTY TAXES

IHT planning often involves the transfer of UK property. This will sometimes lead to tax charges arising on the transfer in the form of some variation of Stamp Duty. The type of Duty arising will depend on which part of the UK the property is located in, as follows:

| | |
|---|---|
| England: | Stamp Duty Land Tax ('SDLT') |
| Scotland: | Land and Buildings Transaction Tax |
| Wales: | Land Transaction Tax |
| Northern Ireland: | Stamp Duty Land Tax ('SDLT') |

The rules applying under each form of Duty are broadly similar. There are some variations in the rates, however. Details of the rates applying to all UK property are included in the Taxcafe.co.uk guide *'How to Save Property Tax'*.

For the sake of simplicity, I will refer only to SDLT throughout the rest of this guide, but similar charges will arise on property in Scotland or Wales, except the Duty will have a different name and will be charged at different rates.

## 1.6    A GUIDE TO EFFECTIVE INHERITANCE TAX PLANNING

All tax planning needs to be undertaken carefully and in full knowledge of the circumstances of the taxpayer's individual situation. This is probably never more true than in the case of IHT, where a detailed review of the individual's situation is vital.

I have dealt with all the recent changes to IHT law on the basis of our current understanding. It is important to remember that further changes or restrictions could be introduced at any time and the precise meaning of some areas of law will only become apparent when tested in court: possibly many years from now.

IHT law is constantly changing. This means no one can be sure of having avoided the tax until they are safely tucked up in their grave! In addition to taking professional advice when putting your plans into effect, you should also commission a regular professional review to determine whether your planning remains effective.

I have highlighted some of the more popular planning techniques currently being used successfully by taxpayers wishing to protect their wealth from the scourge of IHT, or which are at least currently believed to work.

HM Revenue and Customs ('HMRC') does, however, have very wide powers to enable it to closely examine any IHT planning technique and will do its utmost to overturn any planning strategy when the law permits it to.

The associated operations rules and general anti-abuse rule covered in Section 10.19 are both particularly wide-ranging in this regard.

Please note that life expectancies and other statistics quoted in this guide are based on normal circumstances, prior to the Coronavirus outbreak.

Finally, the reader must bear in mind the general nature of this guide. Individual circumstances vary and the tax implications of an individual's actions will vary with them. For this reason, it is always vital to get professional advice before undertaking any tax planning or other transactions that may have tax implications. The author and Taxcafe UK Ltd cannot accept any responsibility for any loss that may arise as a consequence of any action taken, or any decision to refrain from action taken, as a result of reading this guide.

## 1.7 ABOUT THE EXAMPLES

This guide is illustrated throughout by a number of examples. Unless specifically stated to the contrary, all persons described in the examples in this guide are UK resident and domiciled for tax purposes.

In preparing the examples I have assumed the UK tax regime will remain unchanged in the future except to the extent of any announcements already made at the time of publication. However, if there is one thing we can predict with any certainty, it is that change **will** occur. The reader must bear this in mind when reviewing the results of the examples and it will be worth a look at Chapter 18 to see some of the changes that may lie ahead.

All persons described in the examples in this guide are entirely fictional characters created specifically for the purposes of this guide. Any similarities to actual persons, living or dead, or to fictional characters created by any other author, are entirely coincidental.

# Chapter 2

# Inheritance Tax Principles

## 2.1    TRANSFERS OF VALUE

"Inheritance Tax is payable on death. Everyone knows that, don't they?"

Like so many things 'everyone knows' (like 'man will never fly' and 'an iceberg will never sink a ship'), this is **WRONG**!

Now, admittedly, it is true that by far the biggest part of the IHT the Government collects arises on the occasion of someone's death. Furthermore, most of the remainder arises due to attempts to offload some wealth before then. However, what actually triggers IHT is not death but a 'transfer of value'.

In principle, IHT is chargeable on any 'transfer of value' made by any person at any time. Thankfully, however, there are a number of exemptions and these help ensure we don't have to pay the Government 40% every time we give the kids their pocket money.

The reasons we tend to think of IHT as applying mainly on death are threefold:

   i)    On death, we are inevitably forced to transfer our entire wealth to others, thus causing, for most of us, the biggest 'transfer of value' of our lives
   ii)   Most lifetime transfers to other individuals are exempt, or at least only become chargeable in the event of death within seven years
   iii)  The name of the tax implies (falsely) that it is only related to death

**What is a 'Transfer of Value'?**

A transfer of value occurs whenever you dispose of something and, as a result, your total net wealth is reduced. Your 'total net wealth' is referred to as your 'estate' and we will explore this concept further in Section 2.6.

What you are 'disposing of' may be money or any other asset with monetary value. Furthermore, it is the reduction in your own net wealth that generates the 'transfer of value', not necessarily the value of the asset disposed of. We will see an example of this a little later.

Any disposal of wealth by way of a 'transaction at arm's length' between unconnected persons is not treated as a 'transfer of value'.

Hence, the most basic transactions in life, such as buying the weekly groceries, will not be classed as a 'transfer of value', even though your total net wealth is inevitably reduced. Furthermore, when dealing at arm's length with unconnected persons, merely striking a 'poor bargain' will not be a transfer of value.

### Example

*John buys a car for £5,000 from Alexei, a second-hand car dealer. It turns out, however, that the car is an absolute wreck, worth at best around £800!*

*Poor John! However, at least there is no 'transfer of value' here, since John and Alexei are not connected.*

*If, on the other hand, John had bought the car from his sister, Janet, there would have been a transfer of value, as they are 'connected persons' (see Appendix B).*

Nevertheless, a transaction with a connected person will still not give rise to any transfer of value, as long as it is carried out in the same way as it would have been if it had been an arm's length transaction with an unconnected person.

### Example

*Mick wants to buy his father's house. His father, Keith, obtains an independent valuation on the house, which indicates it is worth £300,000. He therefore sells the house to Mick for this amount.*

*Unbeknown to Mick, Keith, and the valuer, plans for a new bypass are just about to be announced, as a result of which the house's value will increase dramatically.*

This may look like a 'transfer of value' but it isn't because Mick and Keith have struck the same bargain as would have been struck between unconnected persons.

### The Amount of the 'Transfer of Value'

As stated above, a 'transfer of value' occurs whenever you make a disposal that is not at arm's length and, as a result, there is a reduction in your total net wealth (your estate). The simplest type of 'transfer of value' is therefore a straightforward gift.

If you give someone £10,000 in cash, that is a 'transfer of value' of £10,000, if you give someone a painting worth £5,000, that is a 'transfer of value' of £5,000.

A 'transfer of value' also occurs when sales take place between connected persons at an undervalue, or an overvalue. If you sell your son a painting for £2,000 when it is, in fact, worth £10,000, that is a 'transfer of value' of £8,000. If you buy a car from your daughter and pay her £5,000, when the car is worth only £1,000, then that is a 'transfer of value' of £4,000.

But what is important to remember is that it is the reduction in the value of your overall estate that gives rise to the 'transfer of value'.

### Example
*Bjorn has a set of six antique chairs worth £20,000. He gives his son, Benny, one of the chairs. The value of a single chair, which is not part of a complete set, is only £1,500.*

*However, the 'transfer of value' here is not the value of Benny's single chair.*

*No, the 'transfer of value' is the reduction in the value of Bjorn's overall estate. Previously, he had a set of chairs worth £20,000. After the gift to Benny, he has five chairs worth £1,500 each, a total of £7,500.*

*Hence, the reduction in the value of Bjorn's estate, and thus the amount of the 'transfer of value', is £12,500.*


## 2.2     WHO IS LIABLE FOR INHERITANCE TAX?

For UK domiciled individuals, IHT arises on the net value of their entire estate (see Section 2.6) at the time of their death, wherever situated, less:

- i)   The 'nil rate band' ('NRB'): £325,000 for deaths occurring between 6th April 2009 and 5th April 2021
- ii)  Any transferable nil rate band ('TNRB') available (see Section 6.3)
- iii) Any other applicable exemptions & reliefs (see Chapter 3)

IHT also arises on certain lifetime gifts and other transfers (Chapter 4)

### What Does 'Domiciled' Mean?

Broadly speaking, 'domicile' is a concept similar to nationality and for most people it will be obvious whether or not they are UK domiciled. Nevertheless, this analogy is not entirely accurate and 'domicile' can sometimes be a highly complex matter. We will therefore return to a detailed examination of it in Chapter 15, where I will also explain the terms 'domicile of origin' and 'domicile of choice' referred to below.

The important thing to understand for UK tax purposes is that we first have to decide whether someone is UK domiciled under the general principles that we will examine in Chapter 15 and then also consider whether they are deemed UK domiciled under the principles outlined below.

### Deemed Domicile

From 2017/18 onwards, non-UK domiciled individuals who were resident in the UK for at least 15 of the previous 20 UK tax years are generally deemed to be UK domiciled for *all* UK tax purposes for the current tax year (even if they are no longer UK resident). However, this does not apply unless the individual is also UK resident:

a)      In at least one of the four tax years made up of the current year and the three previous years, and

b)      At some time after 5th April 2017 (but see further under 'Emigration' below)

Prior to 2017/18, an individual was deemed to be UK domiciled for IHT purposes if they had been tax resident here for at least 17 out of the last 20 UK tax years. Before 2017/18, this did not affect their position in respect of Income Tax or Capital Gains Tax ('CGT').

From 2017/18 onwards, individuals born in the UK, with a UK domicile of origin, but who have acquired a non-UK domicile of choice, and who were UK resident in either of the previous two UK tax years, will be treated as UK domiciled if they remain UK resident in the current tax year.

From 2013/14 onwards, an individual's tax residence is determined under the statutory residence test. In some cases, this may effectively hasten, or prolong, their deemed UK domicile. See the Taxcafe.co.uk guide *'How to Save Property Tax'* for further details of the statutory residence test.

## Immigration

An 'excluded property trust' may be used to exclude from UK IHT any foreign property held for the benefit of a person who originally had foreign domicile but later becomes either UK domiciled or deemed UK domiciled. See Section 9.13 for more details.

## Emigration

An individual who ceases to be UK domiciled under general principles will continue to have deemed UK domicile for IHT purposes for a further three years thereafter.

Both the old and new rules explained above effectively mean an individual with deemed UK domicile prior to emigration may retain it for up to a further three years thereafter.

Emigration is covered in more detail in Chapter 15.

## Non-Domiciled Individuals

If you are neither UK domiciled, nor deemed to be UK domiciled, as explained above, then IHT will generally only arise on any UK assets you hold, including land and buildings situated in the UK. Again, this liability arises on death or in the event of certain lifetime transfers which we will cover later in the guide.

Foreign currency bank accounts held by a non-UK domiciled individual at the time of their death are generally exempt from IHT, even when held with a UK bank or the Post Office. For the purpose of this exemption, the deceased must also be non-UK resident at the time of death.

Assets which are exempt from IHT by reason of a person's non-UK domiciled status are referred to as 'excluded property'.

UK residential property held indirectly by non-UK domiciled individuals (e.g. through a company, trust or more complex structure) is subject to IHT. Minor interests in UK residential property that amount to less than 5% of the individual's worldwide property interests are disregarded however.

The following countries have Double Tax Treaties with the UK covering IHT: France, Irish Republic, India, Italy, Netherlands, Pakistan, South Africa, Sweden, Switzerland, and the USA. These may affect your position (including the issue of 'deemed domicile') if you are domiciled in one of these countries.

## 2.3    WHO ACTUALLY PAYS THE TAX?

Despite my comments in Section 2.1, most IHT does still arise on death and, naturally, the deceased is not around to pick up the bill. So who actually has to pay the tax?

Subject to the points below, the usual default position is the liability for IHT arising on death falls on the personal representatives (see Section 2.4), who must settle the tax out of the general assets of the deceased's estate.

It is, however, possible for the Will to direct that a beneficiary should bear the tax on a legacy themselves. This can be useful to avoid the extra cost of 'grossing up' (see Section 2.9).

A beneficiary becoming entitled to a life interest in property under the terms of a Will must generally bear the tax arising on their legacy.

For property already held in trust, but which is included in the deceased's estate for IHT purposes (as explained in Chapter 8), the tax may fall on the trustees or on another beneficiary of that trust, depending on the exact circumstances.

### Lifetime Transfers

The primary responsibility for any IHT arising immediately on lifetime transfers falls on the transferor. It is possible, however, to stipulate that the transferee should bear any IHT arising (see Memorandum 2 in Appendix C).

Additional IHT liabilities frequently arise when the transferor dies within seven years of a lifetime transfer. These liabilities usually fall on the transferee.

IHT on lifetime transfers is examined in more detail in Chapter 4.

## 2.4    WHO ARE THE PERSONAL REPRESENTATIVES?

Where the deceased has left a Will, their executors are their personal representatives. In the case of a person dying intestate (i.e. without a valid Will), the person applying for a grant of representation (i.e. probate), or confirmation in Scotland, will be the personal representative.

Where no personal representative has been appointed by the court within twelve months after the end of the month of death then the deceased's beneficiaries will be required to fulfil the obligations regarding payment of IHT, delivery of accounts, etc, which would normally fall on the personal representatives.

## 2.5    HOW MUCH TAX IS PAYABLE?

On death, IHT is levied, generally at one single rate of 40%, on the entire value of your estate, less certain exemptions. The most important exemptions are the NRB, which is £325,000 for deaths occurring between 6th April 2009 and 5th April 2021, the exemption for transfers to spouses (see Section 3.3) and the residence nil rate band ('RNRB') (see Section 3.4).

Personal representatives of widows or widowers may be able to claim up to double the current NRB and RNRB where the first spouse to die did not fully utilise their own NRB or RNRB. We will cover this subject in detail in Chapter 6.

### Lifetime Transfers

Where a lifetime transfer gives rise to an immediate IHT charge, the rate applying is 20%, sometimes known as 'the lifetime rate'. Extra tax will often become payable on lifetime transfers in the event of the taxpayer's subsequent death within seven years and we will look at this in detail in Section 4.5.

Transfers made directly to spouses are usually tax free. Furthermore, the £325,000 NRB can be deducted from the total value of transfers made in the last seven years. As we shall see in Chapter 4, this is very important because it means tax-free transfers equivalent to the NRB can be made every seven years.

## 2.6    WHAT IS YOUR ESTATE?

Your 'estate' means everything you own, including land and property, shares and securities, savings accounts, cash, antiques, jewellery, paintings, your car, your furniture and anything else with any monetary value whatsoever.

Income arising up to the date of death must also be included (e.g. unpaid pensions or salary, accrued bank interest, etc.). Also included in the deceased's estate will be:

i)    The net value of any assets held on their behalf in certain types of trust (see Chapter 8),

ii)   The value of any relevant 'gifts with reservation' (see Section 4.9), and

iii)  The value of any assets they elect to have included in their estate in order to prevent an Income Tax charge on a deemed benefit in kind (Section 10.21)

For the purposes of IHT, any non-exempt transfers of value made in the seven years prior to death will also effectively be brought back into the deceased's estate. Reduced IHT rates do, however, apply to transfers of value made more than three, but less than seven, years prior to death.

Any liabilities, such as your mortgage, overdrafts, bank loans, credit card bills, outstanding utility bills, etc., may generally be deducted; although restrictions may sometimes apply (see Section 2.11). You may even deduct outstanding Income Tax and CGT liabilities!

'Reasonable' funeral expenses may also be deducted. What is 'reasonable' depends on your standard of living. (In one extreme case, the expense of a private army providing a funeral honour guard was deemed 'reasonable'.)

Sadly, the costs of obtaining UK probate and administering your UK estate may **not** be deducted; although the costs of obtaining foreign probate and realising the value of foreign assets (e.g. selling them) may be deducted up to a maximum of 5% of the value of those assets, where these are subject to UK IHT (see Section 2.2).

### Tax Tip
All other things being equal (although they seldom are), you may be able to save IHT by holding foreign assets instead of UK assets: even when you are UK domiciled. For example, the IHT on an estate worth £1m made up entirely of UK assets will be £270,000, even if your estate suffers more than £50,000 in probate and administration costs.

The IHT on a similar estate made up entirely of foreign assets would be £250,000, producing a saving of £20,000.

(I have assumed there are no exemptions or reliefs available, other than the NRB. I have also ignored any foreign tax implications: in practice, it is vital to consider these.)

In summary, subject to a few adjustments, your 'estate' is basically your total net worth. All the property transferred on your death is subject to IHT in the same way, whether it transfers under the terms of your Will, by intestacy, by survivorship (for jointly held property), or by any other means.

**Tax Tip**
Many people take out insurance policies to cover outstanding liabilities, such as credit card bills or bank loans, if they should pass away unexpectedly. The result of this is that these liabilities would not be deductible from the value of the estate as they were automatically settled on the taxpayer's death.

It would be far better to make provision for such liabilities by other means (see Section 10.12) and thus ensure they are deducted from the value of your estate for IHT purposes. As we shall see in Section 2.11, it remains important that the liability is actually settled out of the assets of the estate.

**Wealth Warning**
Many people assume tax-advantaged products, such as Individual Savings Accounts (ISAs) are exempt from IHT because they are supposedly 'tax-free'. Unfortunately, this is not the case and *ALL* assets have to be included in your estate, regardless of their treatment for Income Tax or CGT purposes.

**Practical Pointer**
Household personal effects are generally overvalued, resulting in unnecessary overpayments of IHT. The valuations most people have on their personal effects (jewellery, antiques, silverware, etc,) tend to be insurance valuations. However, the amount on which IHT is payable should only be the open market value of the assets and this is often considerably less.

## 2.7     THE BASIC CALCULATION ON DEATH

To illustrate the basic IHT calculation, let's take a look at a simple example:

*Example*
*Arthur has been very careful with his money all his life. At the time of his death in December 2020, his estate amounts to £3m.*

*Arthur has been divorced for many years and his Will leaves his entire estate to his son Tony. Hence, there are no exemptions available, other than the NRB.*

*The first £325,000 of Arthur's estate is exempt from IHT, as it is covered by the NRB. The remaining £2.675m is charged to IHT at 40%, giving rise to a tax charge of £1.07m!*

The tax is of course reduced (or even eliminated) where there is an 'exempt beneficiary', such as the deceased's surviving spouse or a charity. These exemptions are explored further in Sections 3.3 and 3.5 respectively.

The example above is about as simple (and painful) as it gets. In other cases there will be more than one beneficiary. This will not alter the total amount of IHT payable (unless any of them are an 'exempt beneficiary'), but it may affect who ends up bearing the tax.

### *Example*

*John dies with a total estate worth £1m. He leaves his nephew Paul, a house worth £300,000 on condition he settles any tax arising. He leaves his eldest son George, the sum of £250,000 in cash, stating in his Will that this sum should be free of all taxes, and he leaves the remainder of his estate to his younger son, Richard.*

*There are no exemptions available apart from the NRB. (By leaving his house to his nephew, John is unable to claim the RNRB: see Section 3.4. We will also assume there is no TNRB available: see Section 6.3.) Hence, the IHT arising is £1m – £325,000 = £675,000 x 40% = £270,000.*

*This amounts to 27% of the total value of the estate, so this is the effective rate applying in this case, sometimes known as the 'estate rate'.*

*As Paul has to settle the IHT on his bequest directly, he will therefore pay IHT at the 'estate rate' of 27% on the value of the house, giving him a liability of £81,000 (£300,000 x 27%).*

*As George's bequest is free of tax, John's personal representatives must pay the remaining £189,000 (£270,000 – £81,000). This means John's estate is effectively divided up as follows:*

| | |
|---|---|
| *Paul:* | *£300,000 (the value of the house)* |
| *George:* | *£250,000 (his tax-free legacy)* |
| *Richard:* | *£261,000 (£1m – £300,000 – £250,000 – £189,000)* |
| *HMRC:* | *£189,000 (with a further £81,000 payable by Paul)* |

The £261,000 received by Richard after dealing with specific legacies and paying the IHT due is often referred to as the 'residue'. In effect, as the recipient of the residue, Richard is suffering the IHT on both George's legacy and his own.

In Section 2.9 we will see what happens when there is also an 'exempt beneficiary'.

### 2.8    MAKING THE PAYMENT

IHT arising on death is normally due six months after the end of the month of death. Hence, in the case of Arthur who died in December 2020, it will be due by 30th June 2021. Personal representatives may sometimes have to pay the tax earlier, however, as the liability is triggered when they deliver their accounts for probate or confirmation purposes.

This same payment date applies to all IHT arising on death; both on the deceased's estate and gifts made within the previous seven years (Section 4.5).

The personal representatives may elect for any tax on land or buildings within the deceased's estate to be paid in ten equal yearly instalments, commencing six months after the month of death.

If the property concerned is subsequently sold, however, then the remaining unpaid IHT relating to that property becomes payable immediately.

Interest is normally charged on, and added to, payments made by instalments. Interest is also charged on late payments.

Since 2009, the interest rate applying has fluctuated within the range 2.75% to 3.25%. It is currently 3.25%: the same as for most other major taxes. (Clearly, the Government has no sympathy for bereaved families suffering from both financial turmoil and emotional distress!)

At the current interest rate, the cost of paying a 40% IHT bill by instalments is increased to a total effective rate of 45.85%.

When interest arises on either instalments or other late payments of IHT, there will be no Income Tax relief for it.

The beneficiaries could perhaps borrow the money to pay their IHT bills. Sadly, however, the IHT is regarded as a personal liability and the interest on such borrowings would generally be ineligible for Income Tax relief.

**Tax Tip**
There is a potential way around this dilemma if the beneficiary re-mortgages their own home to pay the IHT bill. If they subsequently move out of the house and turn it into a rental property, they will be eligible for Income Tax relief on the mortgage interest against their rental income. The beneficiary could then move into one of the inherited properties and adopt it as their new home.

Alternatively, the beneficiary may be able to obtain Income Tax relief by re-mortgaging one or more rental properties up to the level of their market value at the time of introduction into the rental business.

The obvious step might therefore seem to be to re-mortgage an inherited property, use this to pay the tax and then rent that property out. The problem, however, is that the IHT may have to be paid before the beneficiary can take title to the property. The beneficiary's own home may provide the answer to this problem once more.

***Example***
*Cheryl inherits her Aunt Sarah's house but has an IHT liability of £100,000 to settle. Cheryl therefore re-mortgages her own home and uses this money to pay the IHT. After taking title to Sarah's house, Cheryl mortgages that property and uses the funds to repay the mortgage on her own home. Cheryl then rents out Sarah's house and is able to claim her mortgage interest against the rental income.*

### Wealth Warning 1

If an inherited property is already a rental property, interest relief will only be available on borrowings against the property up to its value when it was first rented out.

### Wealth Warning 2

Interest relief for borrowings on residential rental property is now restricted to basic rate only for Income Tax purposes.

Furthermore, HMRC sometimes takes the view that no relief at all should be allowed on interest arising on additional borrowings used for personal purposes (including paying IHT bills). While this is contrary to many tax professionals' understanding of the law (including mine), this does mean the techniques described above carry a degree of risk.

Subject to these issues, the techniques described above may still remain useful: after all, relief at the basic rate of 20% is a lot better than no relief at all!

For a full discussion on the issues surrounding interest relief on rental property, see the Taxcafe.co.uk guide *'How to Save Property Tax'*.

### Selling Inherited Properties

If it becomes necessary to sell one or more inherited properties in order to pay IHT, there is one crumb of comfort in the fact there is unlikely to be much CGT to pay, as we shall see in Section 11.2.

### Paying Tax on Lifetime Transfers

Where IHT becomes payable on a lifetime transfer, it is due as follows:

i)   Gifts made between 6th April and 30th September – IHT is due on 30th April in the following year.
ii)  Gifts made between 1st October and 5th April – IHT is due six months after the end of the month in which the gift is made.

From a pure cashflow point of view, therefore, the best day to make a chargeable gift is 6th April. (This may not always fit in with the rest of your planning though!)

### Repayments

Where there is an overpayment of IHT, the rate of interest applying to the repayment of the excess is just 0.5%. This effectively means the Government is making an additional profit of 2.75% from the many bereaved families who are forced to make estimated IHT payments in an effort to meet the Government's deadlines! (Underpayments are charged with interest at 3.25%, whilst those who overpay receive a mere 0.5% in compensation.)

## 2.9     GROSSING UP

The amount of IHT payable on a specific asset or bequest may be affected by whether it is paid by the personal representatives. This is due to the procedure known as 'grossing up'. The rationale behind 'grossing up' is that where the personal representatives are bearing the tax, this effectively represents an additional 'transfer of value'.

However, 'grossing up' can only apply to the IHT arising on death where there is also an exempt beneficiary (see Section 2.7). It is that exempt person, or body, often the surviving spouse, who will ultimately suffer the impact of the 'grossing up'.

Hence, we are ***only*** concerned with 'grossing up' (on death) where there is a mixture of exempt and non-exempt beneficiaries and the personal representatives are bearing the IHT on one or more bequests to a non-exempt beneficiary.

The 'grossing up' process is rendered more complex where there are any exemptions available. This will apply in the majority of cases since the NRB is usually available for a start. However, for the sake of illustration, I will start with an example where there are no exemptions available, apart from the spouse exemption. This might occur, for example, where the deceased has made gifts in excess of the NRB within the last seven years (see Section 4.5).

### Example
*In 2018, Winston made a gift of £400,000 to his son Stuart. Sadly, Winston dies in March 2021. The total value of his estate is £2.5m. He has no TNRB entitlement and the RNRB will not be available due to tapering (see Section 3.4). Hence, in summary, the only exemption available is the spouse exemption.*

*Winston leaves a property worth £100,000 to his nephew Pete on condition he settles any tax arising. He also leaves his daughter Julia the sum of £480,000 in cash, stating in his Will this sum should be free of all taxes. He leaves the remainder of his estate to his widow, Cynthia.*

*As Pete has to settle the IHT on his bequest directly, he will pay IHT at a straightforward rate of 40%, i.e. £40,000.*

*The IHT on Julia's bequest will, however, be paid by Winston's personal representatives. This brings 'grossing up' into play. In other words, Julia's bequest must be grossed up to account for the IHT being paid out of Winston's estate.*

*The 'grossing up' factor is two-thirds. Hence, an additional two-thirds must be added to Julia's bequest, producing a grossed up amount of £800,000 (£480,000 PLUS two thirds of £480,000, i.e. £320,000).*

*The IHT due on this bequest is therefore £320,000 (£800,000 x 40%). As can readily be seen, this is equal to the amount of the 'grossing up' meaning the personal representatives can now give the original sum of £480,000 to Julia free of any further tax liabilities.*

In this example, it is Cynthia who effectively ends up bearing the tax on Julia's bequest since it reduces the amount remaining to be distributed to her. Furthermore, as the tax is paid by the personal representatives, it is increased from the £192,000 it would have been if Julia had paid it, to £320,000 instead. The rate of IHT on the bequest has effectively increased from 40% to 67%. If the family are in agreement, this outcome can be avoided by using a 'Deed of Variation' (see Section 17.1) to alter the terms of the Will so the beneficiary bears the tax and it is thus reduced back to 40%.

The two thirds rate of 'grossing up' shown in the above example is very much the 'worst case scenario'. Where any exemptions are available, these are taken into account first, before applying 'grossing up', meaning the overall effective rate can be much reduced. To see how this applies in practice, let's return to the example with a couple of modifications.

### Example Revisited
*On further investigation, it turns out Winston's gift to Stuart was actually made in 2010 (this is why it is so important to document gifts properly: see Section 4.3), so Winston's NRB is available after all. A later Will is also found in which Winston states that his personal representatives should bear the tax on the property left to Pete. Hence, grossing up will now apply to both legacies.*

*The total of Pete and Julia's legacies amounts to £580,000. From this, the personal representatives can deduct Winston's NRB of £325,000, leaving the sum of £255,000 subject to 'grossing up'. As before, the 'grossing up' factor is two thirds, producing a total IHT liability of £170,000 (£255,000 x 2/3).*

*Winston's estate is therefore distributed as follows:*
| | |
|---|---|
| *Pete:* | *£100,000 (the value of the property)* |
| *Julia:* | *£480,000 (her tax-free legacy)* |
| *Cynthia:* | *£1,750,000 (£2.5m – £580,000 – £170,000)* |
| *HMRC:* | *£170,000* |

*If the personal representatives wish to pay the IHT on Pete's property by instalments (Section 2.8), this element can be calculated on a simple pro rata basis, as follows:*

$$£170,000 \ x \ £100,000/£580,000 = £29,310$$

*The amount of IHT the personal representatives can apply to pay by instalments is therefore £29,310.*

As before, it is Cynthia, the exempt beneficiary, who effectively ends up bearing the cost of the 'grossing up'.


## More Complexity

Some readers may be wondering why I changed the example so that the personal representatives were bearing the tax on Pete's legacy. This was done purely for the sake of illustration. Where, in addition to there being exemptions available, there is also a mixture of legacies on which the beneficiary is bearing their own tax and legacies on which the personal representatives are bearing the tax, the 'grossing up' calculations become extremely complex. Nonetheless, the principles remain that: IHT being borne by the personal representatives must be 'grossed up' to account for the additional 'transfer of value'; and the exempt beneficiary ultimately suffers the consequences.

### Lifetime Transfers

'Grossing up' can also apply to lifetime transfers, although a lower 'grossing up' rate of one quarter applies. See Section 4.2 for further details.

## 2.10    COLLECTION OF TAX

As we saw in Section 2.3, liability for IHT may fall on any of:

- The transferor,
- The transferee,
- The deceased's personal representatives, or
- The deceased's beneficiaries

Naturally, HMRC will, in the first instance, attempt to collect the tax from the correct party. However, if they encounter difficulty in collecting the tax, they will look to any other party to the relevant transfer of value.

Hence, in the case of IHT arising on death, if a beneficiary is required to pay their share of the tax under the terms of the deceased's Will, but is unable to do so, HMRC will collect it from the personal representatives out of the remaining assets of the estate. Furthermore, the tax may then have to be grossed up (see Section 2.9).

Conversely, a beneficiary who should have received a bequest free from IHT could end up having to bear part of the IHT arising when there are insufficient liquid funds left in the remaining estate.

Transferees should usually bear any extra tax arising when the transferor dies within seven years of making a gift (see Section 4.5) but this rule will also be overridden if HMRC finds it necessary.

### *Example*
*In July 2018, George, a single man, gave his old friend Andrew £500,000 to help him out. Sadly, things continue to go from bad to worse for Andrew and, in 2020, he is declared bankrupt.*

*In March 2021, George dies and the earlier gift to Andrew becomes chargeable to IHT. George had also made earlier chargeable transfers in excess of his NRB during the seven years prior to July 2018, so the gift to Andrew is fully exposed to IHT (see Section 4.5).*

*As HMRC will be unable to collect the IHT due from Andrew, they will look to George's personal representatives to pay the tax out of the assets of the estate. Instead of the original £200,000 (at 40%), however, the IHT due on this gift will now be £333,333 (two-thirds: see Section 2.9).*

In short, HMRC doesn't really care who pays the tax, as long as it is collected. This is why it will often make sense to take out term assurance to cover IHT costs arising in the event of an early death and we will look at this further in Section 10.14.

## 2.11    LOANS AND OTHER LIABILITIES

A number of restrictions apply to the deduction of liabilities for IHT purposes. In this section, I will cover the general principles and look at how they apply in a few practical scenarios. As we progress through the guide, I will also look at how the restrictions affect various IHT planning techniques.

Note that, for the examples in this section, I am going to assume for the sake of illustration that neither the TNRB, nor the RNRB apply.

### Liabilities on Death

Subject to the restrictions discussed below, the general rule is that all the deceased's liabilities are deducted from the general assets of their estate. In particular, except as noted below, unsecured liabilities are not usually deducted from the value of assets eligible for payment of IHT by instalments (i.e. land and property: see Section 2.8).

However, some liabilities are, in the first instance, specifically allocated as follows:

- Secured loans (e.g. mortgages) are allocated against the assets on which they are secured
- Business liabilities (see Sections 7.9 and 7.12) are allocated against the value of the relevant business
- Foreign debts are allocated against foreign property

Where the liabilities exceed the value of the relevant assets, the excess will again generally be deducted from the general assets of the estate.

These allocations under general principles may be altered by the additional rules and restrictions discussed below.

### Restrictions

Liabilities may generally only be deducted from the value of the deceased's estate where the liability is actually discharged (i.e. paid) out of the assets of the estate. The only exception to this rule arises where:

i)      There is a commercial reason for the non-payment of the liability, and

ii)     The non-payment does not give rise to any tax advantage (or any such advantage that arises was not a main purpose behind the non-payment)

For there to be a valid commercial reason for the non-payment, it is necessary to show either that the liability was due to an unconnected party operating on an arms' length basis, or that an unconnected party operating on an arms' length basis would have accepted the non-payment.

As far as tax advantages arising out of the non-payment are concerned, this provision is very wide-ranging and generally covers any situation where any person enjoys any saving or deferral of any kind of tax. However, it only applies where the non-payment of the liability gives rise to a tax advantage: not simply because the liability itself creates a tax advantage.

### Example 1

*Leona dies and leaves her house to her daughter Alexandra. The house is subject to a mortgage. The lender allows Alexandra to take over the mortgage so that it does not need to be repaid immediately.*

*The lender is an unconnected party operating on an arms' length basis so, although the mortgage has not been repaid out of Leona's estate, it may still be deducted for IHT purposes.*

### Example 2

*Gareth lends £20,000 to his father, Simon, on condition it be repaid on the later of Simon and his wife's deaths. Simon dies first. The loan is not repaid at that time.*

*Allowing a loan to be repaid on the second of a couple's deaths is a normal commercial arrangement. Hence, although Gareth is a connected party, the non-payment of the loan at the time of Simon's death does not prevent the loan being deducted from the value of Simon's estate for IHT purposes.*

This example shows it is possible for a loan from a connected party to not be repaid immediately and still be deductible from the deceased borrower's estate: provided the non-payment is permitted on a normal commercial basis.

It is, however, vital that the loan documentation is drawn up correctly. If, for example, the loan agreement only stated that 'the lender may permit the loan to be repaid on the second death' then an unconnected party operating on an arms' length basis would generally call for the loan to be repaid on the first death – unless the loan were secured (on the borrower's home or other property) and subject to interest at a commercial rate. (Such interest would of course give rise to Income Tax liabilities for the lender.)

### Practical Implications

In other cases, a liability is only likely to be deductible if:

- It is a secured loan on full commercial terms and one or more of the deceased's beneficiaries takes over the liability together with the asset on which the loan is secured,
- It is an arms' length commercial arrangement, which one or more of the deceased's beneficiaries takes over (e.g. a business overdraft), or
- It is repaid out of the assets of the deceased's estate

## Paying Liabilities Out of the Estate

There are a number of ways in which liabilities may be paid out of the assets of the estate in order to qualify for deduction for IHT purposes.

Firstly, of course, the personal representatives can simply pay the liability out of cash held by the deceased or the proceeds of sale of the deceased's assets. There is no restriction where the cash or assets are themselves exempt (e.g. foreign bank accounts held by a non-UK domiciled individual).

Alternatively, the deceased's personal representatives could take out a new loan and use it to repay the liabilities. The new loan would need to be charged against the assets of the estate.

It would then either need to be repaid by selling some of the assets of the estate before they are passed to the deceased's beneficiaries or taken over by one or more of the beneficiaries inheriting those assets.

A new loan used to repay the deceased's liabilities could come from any source: including the deceased's beneficiaries.

### Wealth Warning
If a life insurance policy has been written in trust so that it falls outside the deceased's estate (see Section 10.13), it is vital that the proceeds are not used directly to settle the deceased's liabilities, as these would not have been paid out of the assets of the estate and would not be deductible.

### Tax Tip
Life insurance proceeds could, however, be paid out to one of the deceased's beneficiaries who could then lend those funds to the deceased's personal representatives to enable them to pay the deceased's liabilities.

### Example 3
*Sharon dies leaving a house worth £800,000. She had a life insurance policy written in trust which yields £250,000 and she owed her son Jack £200,000: the total of a number of loans he made to her in her latter years.*

*If Jack's loan is not repaid, it cannot be deducted from Sharon's estate and her IHT liability will be £190,000 (£800,000 - £325,000 = £475,000 x 40% = £190,000).*

*If the life insurance proceeds are paid directly to Jack to settle his loan then the loan will not have been settled out of the assets of Sharon's estate and her IHT liability will again be £190,000.*

*Instead, the life insurance proceeds are paid out to Sharon's sister, Kelly. Kelly then lends £200,000 to Sharon's estate. The loan is charged against Sharon's house. Sharon's personal representatives use the £200,000 borrowed from Kelly to repay Jack, meaning his loan can be deducted from Sharon's estate for IHT purposes. This reduces Sharon's IHT liability to £110,000 (£800,000 - £200,000 - £325,000 = £275,000 x 40% = £110,000).*

*Sharon's house is then passed to Kelly subject to the £200,000 charge against it. Since the charge is in Kelly's name, she can then have it removed.*

In theory, a similar strategy could be used where Jack was the sole beneficiary of both Sharon's estate and the life insurance policy. It would, however, be vital to ensure Jack's original loan was repaid by way of a new loan from him to the estate and not repaid directly out of the insurance proceeds. In such a case, a good lawyer who knew their way around all the necessary documentation would be essential!

## Liabilities Incurred to Acquire Relievable Property

Certain types of business property, agricultural property and woodlands are eligible for relief from IHT. We will look at these types of 'relievable property' and the relevant reliefs in detail in Chapter 7.

Prior to 2013, it was not necessary to match relievable property with the liabilities incurred to acquire it. Hence, it was often possible to acquire an asset that was exempt from IHT and still get a full deduction for any borrowings used to acquire that asset.

Since 2013, however, any liabilities incurred to finance the acquisition, enhancement or maintenance of relievable property, must now be taken to reduce the value attributed to that property (subject to the comments below regarding liabilities incurred before 6th April 2013).

A liability is deemed to have financed relievable property where it is used directly or indirectly for that purpose. Guidance issued by HMRC indicates they are taking a very broad view of what can be taken to have indirectly financed relievable property. An example of some of their thinking on this subject is included in Section 7.28 although, as ever, it must be emphasised that HMRC guidance is not the law and it is for the courts to decide whether such a case would actually be caught in practice.

## Liabilities Incurred Before April 2013

Liabilities incurred before 6th April 2013 are exempt from being attributed to relievable property and may generally be deducted from the general assets of the deceased's estate (subject to the other rules described in this section and the treatment of business liabilities discussed in Section 7.12).

However, where a liability incurred before 6th April 2013 is refinanced or varied on or after that date, it will be treated as a new liability and will then be caught by the rules discussed above.

> **Wealth Warning**
> Replacing or varying loans or other liabilities incurred before 6th April 2013 that have been used, directly or indirectly, to finance business property, agricultural property or woodlands, in any way, could lead to significant increases in your IHT liability.

I will look at the practical implications of the restriction on 'liabilities incurred to acquire relievable property' in more detail in Chapter 7.

## Liabilities Incurred to Acquire Excluded Property

A similar restriction operates where liabilities have been incurred to acquire 'excluded property'.

'Excluded property' means any assets that are exempt from UK IHT because they are non-UK assets and are owned by either:

- An individual who is non-UK domiciled and also not subject to deemed domicile (see Section 2.2 and Chapter 15), or
- An 'excluded property trust' (see Section 9.13)

Liabilities incurred to finance the acquisition, enhancement or maintenance of excluded property, must be taken to reduce the value attributed to that property. In effect, this means such liabilities are non-deductible for UK IHT purposes. This restriction applies to liabilities incurred at any time: there is no exemption for liabilities incurred prior to April 2013.

Once again, any liabilities which have indirectly financed the acquisition, enhancement or maintenance of excluded property are caught by this restriction and HMRC is taking a very broad view of the scope of this provision.

### *Example*
*Astrid is single and domiciled in Germany. She owns a house in Liverpool worth £600,000. She mortgages her UK house for £400,000 and uses the money to buy some shares on the London Stock Exchange. A year later, she sells her shares, realising an overall gain, and uses the proceeds to buy a house in Germany.*

*A short time later, Astrid dies. She is subject to UK IHT on the full value of her house in Liverpool (after deducting her NRB). Her mortgage cannot be deducted because it has been used indirectly to acquire excluded property (her German house).*

In this example, Astrid has realised an overall gain on her shares and hence the entire mortgage on her Liverpool house is deemed to have indirectly financed her German property. If she had made a loss on her shares, part of the mortgage would remain deductible from the value of her UK property.

For example, let's say Astrid sold her shares for £375,000 and used this sum to buy her German property. She would then be able to deduct £25,000 (her loss on the shares) from the value of her Liverpool property for UK IHT purposes.

### Date of Introduction and Scope

The restrictions described so far in this section apply to all transfers of value taking place from 17th July 2013 onwards.

### Interest-Free Loans

HMRC's IHT manual states: "The grant of an interest free loan repayable on demand is not a transfer of value (because the value of the loan is equal to the amount of it)." [IHTM 14317]

This opens up significant IHT planning opportunities and we will see several possible applications of this principle throughout this guide. The planning opportunities provided by interest free loans have, however, been severely curtailed since 2013 due to the restrictions discussed in this section.

In most cases, it will now be essential for the loan to be repaid out of the assets of the deceased's estate in order for the planning to work as intended. This may not always be possible. Nevertheless, we will look at the practical implications arising as we consider the relevant planning techniques throughout the remainder of this guide.

### Artificially Created Debts

No deduction is allowed for an artificially created debt where, in effect, the debtor themselves had originally provided the assets or funds which later gave rise to the debt. For example, if a father gifted some money to his son and then borrowed it back, there would be no deduction from the father's estate for this debt.

### 2.12   QUICK SUCCESSION RELIEF

Back in the 'bad old days' of Estate Duty, families were often financially crippled when two generations died in quick succession. Imagine it: just as the family was struggling to recover from one set of death duties, they were landed with another lot. This happened so much in the First World War that the 'Death on Active Service' exemption (see Section 3.8) was brought in.

Thankfully, we now have quick succession relief, which provides some relief from IHT when a transferee dies within five years of receiving an earlier transfer on which IHT was paid, or on which IHT later becomes payable (remembering that tax can arise up to seven years after the original transfer).

Having said that, the value of quick succession relief declines pretty quickly and hence the crippling effects of IHT are therefore unfortunately still with us.

The amount of relief is arrived at by way of the following formula:

QSR = 'Percentage' x Original Tax x Net Transfer/Gross Transfer

The 'Percentage' referred to above is as follows:

| Period between original transfer and transferee's death | Percentage |
| --- | --- |
| One year or less: | 100% |
| More than one year, but not more than two: | 80% |
| More than two years, but not more than three: | 60% |
| More than three years, but not more than four: | 40% |
| More than four years, but not more than five: | 20% |

### Example
*In May 2018, Ewan died leaving a legacy of £1.2m to his daughter, Kirsty; and the rest of his estate to his widow. Kirsty bore the IHT arising, which amounted to £350,000 (£1.2m – £325,000 = £875,000 x 40% = £350,000), leaving her with a net sum of £850,000.*

*Sadly, in December 2020, Kirsty dies in an accident and leaves her estate to her friend Shane. Kirsty's executors claim quick succession relief. The relevant amounts for the calculation are as follows:*

| | |
| --- | --- |
| *Percentage:* | *60% (death between two and three years after original transfer)* |
| *Original Tax:* | *£350,000* |
| *Net Transfer:* | *£850,000* |
| *Gross Transfer:* | *£1.2m* |

*The quick succession relief is therefore 60% x £350,000 x £850,000/£1.2m = £148,750.*

The reason for the 'Net Transfer/Gross Transfer' element of the formula is to ensure the relief applies only to the funds left in the transferee's estate after accounting for the IHT payable on the earlier transfer. If you think about it, Kirsty only received £850,000, so it would be illogical (though nice) for her to get relief for the tax on the entire £1.2m legacy.

Quick succession relief can also apply where either the first or second transfer (or both) was a lifetime transfer made within seven years of the transferor's death. It is not to be confused with taper relief (see Section 4.5), however, as the two reliefs operate independently of each other.

## 2.13 SIMULTANEOUS DEATHS

Where two or more individuals die simultaneously, or in circumstances where it is not possible to determine who died first then, for legal purposes, the oldest person is deemed to have died first (then the next oldest, etc).

For IHT purposes, however, they are deemed to have died at the same instant. The main effect of this is that, where the older person has left any funds or other assets to the younger person then, for IHT purposes, those funds or assets will be treated as passing directly from the older person to the younger person's beneficiaries.

When writing a Will, or undertaking any other IHT planning, it is worth bearing this in mind as, while it does prevent a double charge, there could still be some unwanted consequences, such as:

- Losing the ability to benefit from the TNRB (see Section 6.3)
- Assets passing to different beneficiaries to those the older deceased person would have intended
- The loss of the RNRB if the younger deceased person leaves a property passed to them by the older person to someone who does not qualify as a 'direct descendent' of that older person
- Difficulties in implementing a Deed of Variation (see Section 17.1) in respect of assets passing from the older deceased person to the younger deceased person's beneficiaries

For these reasons, many people introduce a clause in their Will to ensure their intended beneficiary is 'bypassed' if they do not survive them by a certain period. (Note that such a clause will not alter the way shares in some types of jointly held property pass: see Sections 10.5 and 10.7 for details.)

# Chapter 3

# The Main Exemptions

## 3.1    WHAT IS AN EXEMPTION?

IHT exemptions come in many different forms. Some are based on value, others on the relationship between the transferor and the transferee, still others on the nature of the transferee alone and some even on the circumstances of the transferor's demise.

Some exemptions have a general application, others apply only to lifetime transfers and others only to transfers made on death.

In Chapter 5, we will look at IHT exemptions that apply only to lifetime transfers. In this chapter, we will concentrate on exemptions that apply regardless of whether the gift or transfer is made during the transferor's lifetime or on death; or that apply only on death.

In each case, there are a number of exceptions designed to prevent the exemption being abused.

## 3.2    THE NIL RATE BAND

The NRB is probably the most important exemption for the vast majority of people. As the name suggests, an IHT rate of nil is applied to the first part of your estate, which falls within this band.

The amount of NRB available depends on the date of death (or the date of transfer in the case of chargeable lifetime transfers – see Section 4.2). The current NRB applying to deaths or chargeable lifetime transfers between 6th April 2009 and 5th April 2021 is £325,000.

Any part of the NRB that was not used on the earlier death of the deceased's spouse may additionally be claimed. This means up to double the normal amount of NRB may be available on the death of a widow or widower. This has enormous implications for IHT planning for married persons and we will look at this subject in detail in Chapter 6.

Despite this, it remains important to note that each individual has their own NRB. I will come back to this point, and explain its significance in IHT planning, later.

Until 2009, the NRB was generally increased on an annual basis in line with retail price inflation but, in 2010, Labour Chancellor, Alistair Darling, announced a five year freeze at its 2009/10 level of £325,000. This disgraceful departure from Gordon Brown's earlier promise to increase the band to £350,000 was later compounded by another despicable 'U-turn' from Chancellor George Osborne, who abandoned his party's plans to increase the NRB to £1m and extended Darling's five year freeze to twelve!

We are therefore stuck with a NRB of just £325,000 until *at least* 5th April 2021.

In 1997, the NRB stood at £215,000. In April 2021, it will still be just £325,000: a total increase over a twenty-four year period of just 51%. By contrast, in the period from May 1997 to January 2020, average UK house prices increased by *almost 275%!*

Hence, if the NRB had been increased, as seems appropriate, in line with house price inflation, it should have stood at over £800,000 by now.

This leaves many homeowners facing almost £200,000 in extra IHT simply because of the Government's failure to keep pace with property prices. Admittedly, this reduces to around £125,000 where the RNRB is available but, as we shall see in Section 3.4, this will not always be the case. How's that for stealth tax!

**The Future of the Nil Rate Band**

Among the many contradictory announcements made about the NRB by various Chancellors was a proposal that it would be increased in line with the Consumer Prices Index ('CPI') once the current freeze comes to an end.

The CPI takes absolutely no account of housing costs and has historically run at around 1% to 1.5% less than the Retail Prices Index. Using the lower index will severely slow the rate of increase in the NRB and lead to even greater shortfalls in future compared to house price inflation.

Given current circumstances, even these modest increases now seem far less likely and, as discussed in Section 18.5, there may be a strong possibility the freeze could be extended further. Hence, the NRB may remain at its current level for the foreseeable future. But they may surprise us yet!

This makes predicting the future (something one always has to do to some degree when engaged in long-term planning) very difficult. However, for the remainder of this guide, unless stated to the contrary, any predictions about the NRB beyond 2021 will be based on the following assumptions:

- A further three-year freeze to 5th April 2024
- Thereafter we will assume it is increased annually in line with the CPI and this lower inflation measure averages 2.5% per annum

However, I must emphasise, these assumptions are only my 'best guess', to be used purely for the sake of illustration. Frankly, at the moment, all bets are off, so what will actually happen is anybody's guess!

## 3.3 THE SPOUSE EXEMPTION

Except as noted below, transfers of property made directly to your spouse are completely exempt from IHT. This covers both lifetime transfers and transfers on death. The general exemption for transfers to a spouse opens up a wealth of planning opportunities, which we will return to in detail in Chapter 6.

### Transfers to a Non-Domiciled Spouse

The general exemption for transfers to a spouse usually operates without limit. However, in the case of transfers from a UK domiciled person to their non-UK domiciled spouse, the exemption is restricted.

It is possible to remove this restriction if the foreign domiciled spouse elects to 'opt in' and be treated as UK domiciled for IHT purposes. We will look at this election, its benefits and pitfalls, in more detail in Section 6.19.

In the absence of any such election covering the time at which a transfer is made from a UK domiciled person to their non-UK domiciled spouse, only the following maximum amounts may be covered by the spouse exemption:

- For transfers made before 6th April 2013: £55,000
- For transfers made after 5th April 2013: an amount equal to the amount of the NRB (currently £325,000)

These limits apply on a cumulative basis and, once exceeded, any further transfers, both during the transferor's lifetime and on death, will be treated just like any other transfer made to a person other than their spouse.

One single limit applies for the whole of the transferor's lifetime, even if they are divorced or widowed and later marry another foreign domiciled person.

### *Example*
*Donna is domiciled in the UK, but is married to Sean who is US domiciled. In 2012, Donna gave Sean £60,000 and, in 2020, she gave him a further £300,000.*

*£55,000 of Donna's first gift is covered by the spouse exemption, the remaining £5,000 is not. £270,000 of Donna's second gift is covered by the spouse exemption, the remaining £30,000 is not. The exempt amount is derived by deducting the previous exempt amount (£55,000) from the new limit (£325,000).*

*In 2023, Donna divorces Sean and marries Guy who is domiciled in France. In June 2026, when the NRB is £352,000, Donna gives Guy £50,000. £27,000 of this gift is covered by the spouse exemption; the remaining £23,000 is not. The exempt amount is derived by deducting Donna's previous cumulative total of exempt transfers (under the spouse exemption) from the current limit (which is equal to the current NRB in 2026/27). [£352,000 - £55,000 - £270,000 = £27,000]*

The amounts not covered by the spouse exemption remain eligible for other exemptions in the same way as transfers to any other person. As these are lifetime transfers, many of the exemptions covered in Chapter 5 would be available. Any amounts still not covered by any exemption would be potentially exempt transfers and would only become chargeable to IHT in the event of Donna's death within seven years (see Chapter 4).

Furthermore, it is important to note I have assumed each of the gifts in the example was a capital transfer of value. Many transfers between spouses will not be a capital transfer of value and would be exempted under the provisions covered in Sections 5.5, 5.7, 5.8, or sometimes even 5.9. Where these provisions apply, there is no capital transfer of value and any payments do not need to be counted towards the spouse exemption limit.

For transfers on death in excess of the limit, the NRB is available in the usual way, meaning a UK domiciled spouse will often be able to leave up to £650,000 to a foreign domiciled spouse free from IHT where they have not previously used any of their spouse exemption.

This does depend on whether they have any other beneficiaries and on whether they have made other chargeable transfers in the previous seven years. In other words, once the spouse exemption has been exhausted, the non-domiciled spouse is in the same position as any other beneficiary (unless they 'opt-in' – see Section 6.19).

Where either spouse is deemed to be UK domiciled (see Section 2.2), they will be treated as UK domiciled in applying the above rules. We will look at IHT planning for married couples with mixed domicile in Section 6.18.

### Transfers from a Non-Domiciled Spouse

There is no restriction on transfers in the opposite direction: from a foreign domiciled spouse to a UK domiciled spouse. Why would there be – such transfers may eventually increase the tax haul. Beware, however, these transfers may have foreign tax implications!

### Other Exceptions to the Spouse Exemption

The general exemption for transfers between spouses is also restricted in a few other circumstances. The exemption may be lost where:

i) The transfer only takes effect after the expiry of another third party's interest in the asset or after the expiry of some other period of time.

   **Tax Tip**
   It is, however, acceptable to have a condition in your Will that your spouse must survive you by a certain period before becoming absolutely entitled to the asset.

ii) The transfer is dependent on a condition that is not satisfied within twelve months after the date of transfer.

iii) The transfer is only made as consideration for the transfer of a reversionary interest in some other property.

## Transfers into Trust for the Benefit of a Spouse

The spouse exemption does not generally apply to a transfer into trust during the donor's lifetime.

Transfers on death that confer an 'Immediate Post-Death Interest' (see Section 8.12) on a surviving spouse continue to be eligible for the spouse exemption.

## What is a Spouse?

For IHT purposes, a spouse must be your legally married husband or wife or your legally registered civil partner.

A 'spouse' is not specifically defined in tax legislation but, for IHT purposes, HMRC takes the view that the exemption continues to apply to any transfer between persons who are still legally married at the time of that transfer. Unlike CGT, the IHT exemption for transfers between spouses continues to apply to separated couples right up until the granting of a decree absolute.

Transfers between spouses on separation or as part of divorce proceedings will be covered by the exemption if made before the granting of a decree absolute.

Generally speaking, a couple who are legally married under the laws of another country will similarly be recognised as legally married for tax purposes in the UK. This will even include polygamous marriages when they are legally valid in the taxpayer's country of origin. In such cases, the spouse exemption limit discussed above must be applied to the cumulative value of transfers made to all of the transferor's non-UK domiciled spouses.

> **Wealth Warning**
> The spouse exemption applies only to married couples. There is no exemption for transfers to common-law partners!

> **Tax Tip**
> If you intend leaving most of your estate to a common-law partner then try to get married before you die. Deathbed marriages have been known to save **millions** of pounds in IHT and it is one planning device that is almost impossible for HMRC to overturn.

## 3.4    THE RESIDENCE NIL RATE BAND (RNRB)

The RNRB provides an additional exemption on qualifying residential property. It operates in addition to the 'normal' NRB and is only available on death. Where the RNRB applies, it takes priority over the NRB (i.e. it is used first). The amount of RNRB available depends on the year of death, as follows:

| | |
|---|---|
| 2017/18: | £100,000 |
| 2018/19: | £125,000 |
| 2019/20: | £150,000 |
| 2020/21: | £175,000 |

Thereafter, we have been told the RNRB will increase in line with inflation, as measured by the slower-moving CPI. (Just as we were once told the NRB would increase in line with the same index from 2015/16 onwards!)

However, the same points made in Section 3.2 regarding the future of the NRB apply equally to the RNRB. Hence, again, and purely for the sake of illustration, for the remainder of this guide we will assume a three year freeze, with inflationary increases at an average annual rate of 2.5% from 2024/25 onwards.

## Qualifying Property

In order to qualify for the exemption, a property must have been the deceased's private residence at some point during their ownership. Generally, the property will also need to be in their estate at the time of their death (i.e. still owned by them); except that:

- Property included in their estate under the 'gifts with reservation' rules (see Section 4.9) may qualify
- The 'downsizing' provisions allow the exemption to be claimed where a more valuable qualifying residence has been sold in the past, or where the deceased no longer has a qualifying residence at the time of death. We will look at these provisions in more detail in Section 12.16.

If an individual dies still owning more than one qualifying property, their personal representatives may elect which property the exemption should apply to.

Where an individual resides in 'job-related accommodation', a property they had acquired with the intention of adopting it as their private residence may qualify for the exemption. See the Taxcafe.co.uk guide *'How to Save Property Tax'* for further details regarding 'job-related accommodation'.

## Closely Inherited

The RNRB exemption only applies where the property is passed, on death, to a direct descendant of the deceased. Step children, adopted children and foster children are all accorded the same status as natural children for this purpose. A child who was the deceased's step-child at any time is included. However, 'step-child', only includes children of a legally married spouse, and not children of an unmarried co-habitee, or other unmarried partner.

Generally, the property must pass directly to one or more direct descendants in order to qualify. However, the property may also qualify where it is passed to a trust for the benefit of one or more of the deceased's direct descendants. Only certain types of trust qualify for this purpose, as detailed in Section 8.6.

### Example

*Nicki divorced her husband many years before her death in June 2020. She leaves her estate, worth £600,000, to her daughter. Nicki's estate includes her former home, which is worth £250,000 at the time of her death. The RNRB for 2020/21 exempts £175,000 of the value of Nicki's former home. This reduces her taxable estate to £425,000 before deduction of her main NRB of £325,000, which reduces it to £100,000. The IHT payable on Nicki's estate at 40% is thus £40,000.*

## Tapering

The RNRB is withdrawn from estates worth in excess of £2m. This withdrawal is at the rate of £1 for every £2 by which the estate exceeds this threshold. We have been told the threshold itself will also be increased in line with the CPI from 2021/22 onwards (but, again, this needs to be considered in the context of earlier comments).

### Example

*Ollie has an estate valued at £2.1m at the time of his death in January 2021. This exceeds the threshold by £100,000, so his available RNRB is reduced by £50,000, from £175,000 to £125,000.*

The withdrawal of the RNRB means it may effectively be lost if the deceased's estate exceeds £2.35m. This effective threshold may be as high as £2.7m where the deceased is a widow or widower, for the reasons explained below.

The value of the deceased's estate for the purpose of tapering is as detailed in Section 2.6, including items (i) to (iii) listed in that section. The estate is valued before deducting any reliefs: so even qualifying business property and assets the deceased is leaving to their spouse will be counted.

Transfers of value prior to death are **not** included for the purpose of tapering, however. We will look at potential planning implications in Section 16.16.

> #### Tax Tip
> In practice, in many cases, the tapering rules could mean there is an effective marginal rate of IHT of **60%** on the value of the estate falling into the bracket from £2m to up to £2.35m; or even up to £2.7m in the case of many widows or widowers. This potentially makes any planning measures to reduce the amount of the estate within this bracket one and a half times as valuable (e.g. reducing the estate by £10,000 could save up to £6,000 in IHT).

## Unused Exemption Passing to Spouse

Like the main NRB, any unused proportion of the RNRB passes to the deceased's spouse. This is not automatic, however: the additional transferred RNRB must subsequently be **claimed** by the spouse's personal representatives when that spouse also dies.

Tapering applies to the amount that may be transferred. Hence, for example, in Ollie's case above, only 71.4% (£125,000/£175,000) of his RNRB would transfer to his spouse if he did not use it himself.

Where a married individual died before 6th April 2017, their entire RNRB is deemed to be unused and transfers to their widow or widower. This transfer also remains subject to tapering where the deceased spouse's estate was worth in excess of £2m.

It is important to remember it is the unused **proportion** which transfers, not the unused **amount**. We will look at this in further detail in Chapter 6.

Given that the RNRB is used first, in priority to the NRB, the amount of TNRB arising on deaths after 5th April 2017 may sometimes be enhanced (the consequences of having a TNRB are examined in Chapter 6).

However, for deaths prior to 6th April 2020, it is worth considering the fact that the RNRB was then increasing by £25,000 per year (and the NRB was frozen). Hence, it may be more beneficial to ensure the first spouse's RNRB was not used on their death, even if this means using more of their NRB instead.

For example, using £90,000 of the RNRB in 2019/20 would mean 60% of the band has been used and only 40% passes to the widow or widower. This means the surviving spouse could only claim £70,000 of transferred RNRB if they were to die in 2020/21 and a potential further £105,000 of relief would be lost. (The effect will be similar if the widow or widower dies in a later year, but the exact amounts may be different.)

Conversely, using £90,000 of the NRB in 2019/20 would mean the widow or widower loses out on 27.69% of a TNRB: and this will have the **same** value in 2020/21 (and a broadly similar value in later years).

In other words, using the RNRB on the death of a married person before 6th April 2020 will have a bigger impact (£15,000 more in our example) on their widow or widower than using their NRB.

Where a spouse has died within the previous two years then, as with a lot of IHT planning, the family can usually make the necessary adjustments via a deed of variation (see Section 17.1). Preserving the full RNRB on a death during 2018/19 could ultimately give the family up to £50,000 in additional relief compared with preserving the same amount of TNRB: a saving of up to £20,000 in IHT. (Further relief of up to £25,000 may be available for deaths during 2019/20.)

However, it is important to bear in mind that the RNRB has a quite restricted application whereas the TNRB is generally available against any assets in the widow or widower's estate. In some cases, preserving the RNRB may be of little or no benefit and maximising the TNRB may therefore be preferable. In particular, see Section 6.3 for advice on using the RNRB on the first spouse's death where the couple's combined estate exceeds £2m.

**Deaths after 5th April 2020**

Despite earlier comments about potential freezes to both bands, we would nonetheless expect the NRB and RNRB to increase at approximately the same rate in future years. Hence, for deaths after 5th April 2020, preserving either the TNRB or RNRB will have the same value. Since the TNRB is far more flexible, it will therefore generally make sense to reverse the stance outlined above and use the RNRB on the first spouse's death in preference to the NRB.

**Mortgages and Loans**

Any mortgages or other loans secured over a property may have to be taken into account when allocating the RNRB. This is due to the simple fact that the value being transferred to the direct descendant will be the equity value only unless the mortgage or loan is repaid from other sources.

For example, where a property worth £250,000 is passed to the deceased's son subject to the son assuming liability for the outstanding mortgage of £180,000, the exemption will be limited to just £70,000.

## 3.5    GIFTS TO CHARITIES & OTHER EXEMPT BODIES

Generally, all gifts to charity are exempt from IHT. This covers both outright gifts and transfers to a Charitable Trust. A charity is defined as 'any body of persons established for charitable purposes only'.

The exemption applies to UK-registered charities and similar organisations based anywhere in the European Union, Iceland, or Norway. For charitable organisations based outside the UK to qualify, they must meet the same criteria as would apply to an organisation wishing to register as a charity in England.

> **Wealth Warning**
> Foreign charities in countries not referred to above are excluded!

Gifts to certain other bodies are also exempt from IHT:

- **Gifts to Housing Associations**
  Transfers of value attributable to land in the UK and made to registered social landlords are exempt from IHT.
- **Gifts for National Purposes**
  Gifts to organisations such as the British Museum or any of the other bodies listed in section IHTM11224 of HMRC's manuals are exempt from IHT.
- **Gifts to Political Parties**
  Gifts to qualifying political parties are exempt from IHT. Funny that, isn't it? To qualify, the party must either have had at least two members elected to the House of Commons, or have received no fewer than 150,000 votes in total and had one member elected to the House of Commons, at the last General Election.

## 3.6    CHARITABLE LEGACIES

Charitable legacies are fully exempt from IHT: provided the charity meets the criteria we examined in Section 3.5. An additional relief also applies where the deceased leaves 10% or more of their 'net estate' to charity. The 'net estate' for this purpose is the deceased's remaining estate after deducting the NRB and other applicable IHT exemptions and reliefs.

Where the estate qualifies for the additional relief, a discount of 10% applies to the IHT rate. In other words, the IHT rate on the remaining estate is reduced from 40% to 36%.

### *Example*
*Carter, a divorced man, dies in May 2020 leaving an estate valued at £1m. He leaves £67,500 to the local dog and cat home (a registered charity) and everything else to his niece Yvonne.*

*Deducting the NRB of £325,000 from his estate leaves Carter with a 'net estate' chargeable to IHT of £675,000. He has given 10% of this amount to charity, so the IHT rate on Yvonne's inheritance is reduced to 36%.*

*After deducting the charitable legacy (which is exempt), and the NRB, the chargeable estate amounts to £607,500, so the IHT payable at 36% is £218,700. Yvonne will therefore inherit a net sum of £713,800 (£1m - £67,500 - £218,700).*

It is worth noting, if Carter had not left anything to charity, the IHT bill would have been £270,000 and Yvonne would have received a net sum of £730,000. The relief does not leave the non-charitable beneficiary better off than they would have been without the charitable legacy, so it is not worth contemplating such a legacy just to save IHT. But, if you are planning to leave a sizeable amount to charity, it is certainly worth checking whether you will meet the 10% threshold.

If, in our example above, Carter had left £60,000 to charity, his chargeable estate would have amounted to £615,000 (£1m – £60,000 – £325,000), giving rise to an IHT bill, at 40%, of £246,000.

Yvonne's net inheritance would then have been just £694,000 (£1m – £60,000 –£246,000). Hence, increasing the charitable legacy by £7,500 would actually leave her £19,800 better off overall!

### Planning Issues

For many years, it was thought it was not possible for charitable legacies to be 'topped up' to the required 10% threshold by way of a deed of variation (Section 17.1). Recent changes suggest HMRC may now allow this, although, being a cautious man, I would prefer not to rely on it. There are also a number of practical difficulties with deeds of variation, so my advice would generally be to make the appropriate provisions in your Will. As no-one can be sure exactly how much their 'net estate' will be, this requires a formula-based approach to ensure the correct result.

As we saw in our example, however, there is no point making charitable legacies just to save IHT: your main beneficiaries will still suffer an overall cost equal to at least 24% of the legacy, even after taking account of the relief.

But, as we also saw, where charitable legacies are already planned, there may be an overall saving for your main beneficiaries if you can 'top up' those legacies so they reach the 10% threshold. The question is: when does a 'top up' become worthwhile?

The answer is your main beneficiaries will generally be better off if you 'top up' your charitable legacies to the 10% threshold when you would otherwise have left charitable legacies equal to more than 4% of your 'net estate'.

For example, in Carter's case, he had a 'net estate' of £675,000, so Yvonne would benefit from an increase in his charitable legacies to the 10% threshold if he had already planned to give more than £27,000 to charity anyway.

## 3.7    NATIONAL HERITAGE PROPERTY

Have you ever wondered why so many stately homes are open to the public? Well, just like the bricked-up windows in Georgian houses and the roofless buildings we used to see back in the 1970s, it's all because of tax.

IHT arising on transfers of 'national heritage property' can be deferred when the owners give an undertaking to conserve and protect the property. They will also need to provide 'reasonable access to the public'.

The conditions to be satisfied to claim this exemption are somewhat complex, including, in most cases, the need for the property to be 'pre-eminent for its national, scientific, historic or artistic interest'. Simply allowing the punters to look at a couple of rusting chassis in your back garden will probably not qualify. But if your uncle leaves you his collection of classic cars, a claim under the 'national heritage property' provisions may be worth considering.

## 3.8    DEATH ON ACTIVE SERVICE

There is a complete exemption from IHT arising on the death of a person from wound, accident or disease contracted while on active military service. A certificate issued by the Ministry of Defence is required to support a claim. The exemption extends to emergency service personnel killed in the line of duty, or whose death is accelerated due to injuries sustained in the line of duty. The exemption has also been extended to aid workers dying under similar circumstances or due to a disease contracted while providing aid.

Serving and former police officers or service personnel who are targeted because of their status are also now covered by the exemption. Let us hope this exemption will be extended to NHS staff and other 'front line' workers in the near future. Let us also hope there will be very few claims.

The value of medals and certain other awards is exempt from IHT.

# Chapter 4

# Lifetime Transfers

## 4.1  INHERITANCE TAX ON LIFETIME TRANSFERS

In Section 2.1, we established what triggers IHT is not death, but a 'transfer of value'.

Despite this, however, very few transfers made during a person's lifetime actually give rise to any immediate IHT liability.

The reason for this seemingly contradictory position is the fact that any lifetime transfers to another individual are treated as 'Potentially Exempt Transfers' – free of IHT after seven years.

We will return to this concept in Section 4.3 because it remains important to realise 'potentially exempt' effectively also means 'potentially taxable' and most lifetime transfers are therefore still potentially subject to IHT.

## 4.2  CHARGEABLE LIFETIME TRANSFERS

As explained above, many lifetime transfers are 'potentially exempt'. However, lifetime transfers of value by an individual to:

- A company, or
- Any trust other than:
  - A disabled trust,
  - A bare trust, or
  - A charitable trust,

**will** be chargeable (i.e. taxable) lifetime transfers.

Before 2006, it was generally only transfers of value to a company or a discretionary trust that represented chargeable lifetime transfers. Some readers unfamiliar with the nature of trusts may not feel this change is particularly restrictive until I tell you many insurance premiums represent a transfer of value into trust (although most are exempt for other reasons, as we will see).

Chargeable lifetime transfers may be <u>immediately</u> chargeable to IHT, depending on the cumulative value of such transfers made by the transferor within the last seven years.

Transfers of value into companies are rare and the main incidence of chargeable lifetime transfers are therefore transfers into trust.

The amount of the chargeable transfer is arrived at by deducting any available exemptions (see Chapters 3 and 5) from the 'transfer of value'.

The amount on which IHT is actually chargeable is then the lower of the amount of the chargeable transfer, or the sum derived as follows:

| | |
|---|---|
| Other chargeable transfers within the last seven years | X |
| PLUS | |
| This chargeable transfer | X |
| LESS | |
| Nil rate band | (X) |

### Wealth Warning
Only one NRB may be deducted when calculating the IHT on a chargeable lifetime transfer. The TNRB available to widows or widowers, applies only on death.

IHT on lifetime transfers is charged at half death rates, i.e. 20%. Where other chargeable transfers made in the last seven years already equal or exceed the amount of the NRB, the tax due on the current chargeable transfer is simply a straight 20%.

### Example
*(In this example, I will ignore all exemptions and reliefs, other than the NRB)*

*Two years ago, Elvis gifted investments worth £50,000 into a discretionary trust, giving rise to a chargeable transfer. No IHT was payable at the time, however, as this was well within his NRB. Elvis now gifts his former home, Graceland, worth £375,000, into a discretionary trust (for the purposes of this example, it doesn't matter whether this is the same trust), on condition that the trust settles any IHT.*

*The trust's IHT liability is calculated as follows:*

| | |
|---|---|
| *Previous Chargeable Transfers within last seven years:* | *£50,000* |
| *ADD* | |
| *This Chargeable Transfer* | *£375,000* |
| *EQUALS:* | |
| *Cumulative Chargeable Transfers* | *£425,000* |
| *LESS:* | |
| *Nil rate band* | *£325,000* |
| *EQUALS:* | |
| *Amount chargeable* | *£100,000* |
| | |
| *IHT Payable at lifetime rate (20%)* | *£20,000* |

### Alternative Scenario – with 'Grossing Up'

*Note that, if Elvis had settled the IHT himself, it would have been subject to 'grossing up', as follows:*

| | |
|---|---|
| *Amount chargeable, as before* | *£100,000* |
| *Grossing up factor – one quarter* | *£25,000* |
| *Grossed up amount* | *£125,000* |
| *IHT Payable at lifetime rate (20%)* | *£25,000* |

**Wealth Warning**

In this example, Graceland was Elvis's <u>former</u> home. This is an important point since, as we will see later in the guide, it is difficult to make an IHT-effective transfer of your current home.

**Tax Tip**

If Elvis were married, he could have avoided any IHT on his gift of Graceland by first transferring it into joint names with his spouse before they both jointly gifted it to the discretionary trust. Each of them would have made a chargeable transfer of only £187,500. Even after taking his previous chargeable transfer into account, Elvis would then be covered by his NRB.

Elvis's spouse would also be covered by their NRB as long as they had not made other chargeable transfers within the last seven years in excess of £137,500. (As explained in Section 6.15, Elvis's spouse must be under no obligation to make the subsequent transfer to the ultimate intended recipient.)

## Avoiding 'Grossing Up'

In the above example, we have looked at the situation where the IHT is paid by the transferee (the Trust), as well as the situation where it is paid by the transferor (Elvis himself).

More tax is generally payable where the transferor is settling the liability. This is because the transferor is deemed to be making a gift not only of the original asset transferred, but also of the tax arising. This, in turn, is because the 'transfer of value' is once again calculated by reference to the reduction in value of the transferor's overall estate and the payment of the IHT arising naturally increases the amount of that reduction.

The bad news is, in the absence of any evidence to the contrary, the transferor is assumed to be liable for any IHT. Hence, if care is not exercised, you may find the value of any gifts you make turns out to be 25% more than you expected!

The way to avoid this is to draw up a memorandum which stipulates the transferee is to pay any IHT arising. See Memorandum 2 in Appendix C.

## 4.3    POTENTIALLY EXEMPT TRANSFERS

As explained in Section 4.1, many lifetime transfers are potentially exempt transfers, which fall out of the IHT net after seven years. Lifetime transfers made by an individual to one of the following are usually potentially exempt transfers:

i)   Another individual
ii)  A Bare Trust
iii) A Disabled Trust

46

Transfers made **by** a trust are subject to different rules and we will explore these in Chapter 8.

**Exceptions**

The following transfers will not be treated as potentially exempt transfers:

- Any transfers to your UK-Domiciled spouse (these are fully exempt, except as noted in Section 3.3)
- Transfers to your non-UK Domiciled spouse that are covered by the spouse exemption (see Section 3.3)
- Any other transfer covered by another general or lifetime exemption (see Chapters 3 and 5). This will be of no practical consequence unless the transferor dies within seven years of making the transfer
- Any transfer that does not result in an increase in the value of the transferee's estate (see further in Section 4.4)
- Transfers of value caused by alterations to share capital, loan capital, or other rights in most private companies
- A transfer of value to a disabled trust that does not consist of a transfer of property into the trust (see further in Section 4.4 below)

**So What Do We Mean By 'Potentially Exempt'?**

Put simply, these transfers are <u>potentially</u> exempt because all the transferor has to do is survive seven years after making the transfer for it to become fully exempt and completely free of any IHT liability (subject to the 'gifts with reservation' rules: see Section 4.9).

In the meantime, the transfer is treated as if it is exempt (i.e. no IHT is due) and only becomes chargeable if and when the transferor dies within seven years of the date the transfer was made. If the transferor is still alive at the beginning of the seventh anniversary of the transfer, full exemption will have been achieved.

*Example*
*On 4th August 2013, Chuck gave £1m to his little brother Richard. Sadly, on 11th August 2020, Chuck is electrocuted while playing his electric guitar in a rainstorm. The gift to Richard was a potentially exempt transfer and, since Chuck survived the requisite seven years (just!), this sum is exempt from IHT on Chuck's death.*

**Tax Tip**
If Chuck had died a week earlier, IHT would have been payable on his gift to Richard (see further in Section 4.5 below). Hence, it is essential to have the documentary evidence to prove the gift took place when it did. A memorandum along the lines shown in Appendix C should suffice for this purpose. See also Section 4.7 below regarding the timing of gifts made by cheque.

## 4.4  PROBLEMS WITH PETS

One little known, but potentially important, point about potentially exempt transfers is that there must be an increase in the value of the transferee's estate in order for the transfer to qualify.

Furthermore, where the transferee is a disabled trust, there must be an actual gift of property into the trust.

**Any transfers that do not qualify as potentially exempt transfers as a result of failing to meet these requirements will be chargeable lifetime transfers, unless some other exemption is available to cover them.**

Examples of transfers that do not increase the transferee's estate might include:

i) A grandparent paying their grandchild's school fees. The grandchild, while receiving an indirect benefit, does not enjoy any increase in the value of their estate.

ii) Paying an insurance premium on a policy held for someone else's benefit. The value of the policy remains the same before and after payment of the premium, so there is no increase in the value of the transferee's estate.

iii) A parent paying the maintenance costs for their adult child's house. The value of the house may not necessarily be increased through routine maintenance, so neither is the child's estate.

Each of these payments might, of course, be exempt under the 'normal expenditure out of income' exemption (see Section 5.7). It therefore only matters that they are not potentially exempt transfers when they are not already exempt under that exemption or one of the other exemptions for lifetime transfers that we will examine in Chapter 5.

Nevertheless, in IHT planning, it is important to understand the status of every transfer of value. Remember that chargeable lifetime transfers must effectively be accumulated over a seven-year period and IHT charges will result if the cumulative total exceeds the NRB.

Hence, a transfer made today, which turns out to be a chargeable lifetime transfer instead of a potentially exempt transfer, could cause additional IHT charges to arise at any time over the next seven years, even if the transferor survives throughout this period.

### Looking after your PETS

In the first situation outlined above, the grandparent could avoid the problem by giving the necessary funds to cover the school fees to the child's parent, who would then pay the school fees themselves.

Alternatively, the parent could contract to pay the school fees, with the result that the payment by the grandparent gives rise to an increase in the value of the parent's estate, thus meaning a potentially exempt transfer has taken place. The key point is that the grandparent should not contract directly with the school unless they can be certain the 'normal expenditure out of income' exemption will apply.

The second situation above is perhaps the one most likely to be covered by the 'normal expenditure out of income' exemption. In other cases, the position might be rectified by giving the money to pay the premium to the beneficiary, who then pays it themselves, although this does depend on who the policyholder is and whether the policy is held in trust. We will return to the subject of insurance premiums in Sections 10.12 and 10.13.

The position in the third situation above is perhaps arguable. In a case like this, there is a potentially exempt transfer to the extent that the value of the child's house is increased as a result of the work paid for by the parent. The remainder of the parent's expenditure, however, represents a chargeable lifetime transfer (unless it is covered by another exemption).

### Example
*Joe's daughter, Sam, would like to have her house completely redecorated. Joe offers to get the work done at his own expense. He contracts for a decorator to do the work, which is then carried out at a cost of £20,000. Joe has therefore made a transfer of value of £20,000.*

*Before the redecoration work, Sam's house was worth £300,000. Immediately after the work, it is worth £308,000. Joe has made a potentially exempt transfer of £8,000 (the increase in the value of Sam's house). The remaining spending of £12,000 will be a chargeable lifetime transfer (unless covered by other exemptions).*

Joe could have prevented any chargeable lifetime transfer very easily by simply giving all of the money for the work to Sam and leaving her to contract for the work and pay the bill herself. Alternatively, if Sam had contracted for the work herself and was therefore liable for the decorator's bill, Joe could settle that bill and this would also be a potentially exempt transfer as Sam's estate increases when her liability is settled. Either way, it is sensible for Sam to contract for the work!

### Wealth Warning
If Joe were contractually liable for the work on Sam's house, but he gave Sam the money to pay the bill and she settled it, this could result in further potentially exempt transfers of £20,000 both from Joe to Sam and from Sam to Joe, as well as the transfers already described in the example above.

If **either** of them died within seven years, this could result in additional IHT liabilities arising.

The requirements for a transfer to qualify as a potentially exempt transfer where the transferee is a trust are even more restrictive. If Sam's house was held by a disabled trust for her benefit, the only way for Joe to fund the redecoration work as a potentially exempt transfer would be for him to give the trust £20,000. The trustees could then contract and pay for the work.

If Joe settled the decorating bill, then this would be a chargeable transfer regardless of who had contracted for the work.

### Wealth Warning
Settling a debt on behalf of a disabled trust will not qualify as a potentially exempt transfer.

## 4.5    DEATH WITHIN SEVEN YEARS OF A LIFETIME TRANSFER

For CGT purposes, death is often a good tax-planning strategy. The same cannot be said of IHT.

Both chargeable lifetime transfers and potentially exempt transfers made in the seven-year period prior to death are effectively brought back into the deceased's estate for IHT purposes. This applies whether any IHT was payable at the time of the original transfer or not.

Subject to the tapering provisions set out below, IHT becomes payable at the death rate (40%) on transfers made within the seven years prior to the transferor's death. Any IHT paid on the original transfer may be deducted, so that just the excess arises on death.

The additional IHT liabilities arising are usually the responsibility of the transferees. In other words, the situation may be like this:

> "I'm very sorry to hear about your father, son, but do you remember that gift of £10,000 he gave you two years ago? Well, I'm afraid you're going to have to pay some tax on it now."

Now do you see why I call it an 'immoral and evil tax'?

The best way to avoid unwanted liabilities falling on transferees in the event of your death within seven years is to record your intention to bear any tax arising in a memorandum at the time of the gift (see Memorandum 3 in Appendix C). Alternatively, you can make a specific bequest in your Will in respect of the IHT falling on the transferee.

To avoid doubt, it is probably best to do both. There are two problems with both of these approaches, however:

i)    The payment of IHT arising at the time of your death from out of your estate will itself represent another transfer of value and hence 'grossing up' at full death rates may apply (see Section 2.9).

ii)   The primary responsibility for any IHT arising on death remains with the transferee. If there are insufficient funds remaining in your estate to cover the tax arising, the transferee will still have to foot the bill.

In practice, it often makes more sense for the transferee to take out term assurance on the life of the transferor in order to cover any potential IHT arising on the latter's death.

Conversely, the transferor will often be concerned to ensure any IHT arising on earlier gifts does not come out of his or her estate and thus reduce the value of the net estate passing to their primary beneficiaries.

In theory, of course, the IHT arising on transfers made in the last seven years of the transferor's life should be paid by the transferees. However, as we saw in Section 2.10, HMRC is more concerned with collecting the tax than with who gets hurt. To put matters (reasonably) beyond doubt, it is therefore wise to use a memorandum specifying the transferee's responsibility for any IHT arising (see Memorandum 2 in Appendix C). Sadly, however, even this will not help if the transferee simply does not have the ability to pay.

**Tapering**

Fortunately, there is some relief when death occurs more than three, but not more than seven, years after the lifetime transfer. In these cases, the rate of IHT arising on death is tapered as follows:

| No. of years after transfer before death occurs: | Proportion of 40% 'Death Rate' payable |
|---|---|
| Not more than 3 | 100% (=IHT @ 40%) |
| More than 3, not more than 4 | 80% (=IHT @ 32%) |
| More than 4, not more than 5 | 60% (=IHT @ 24%) |
| More than 5, not more than 6 | 40% (=IHT @ 16%) |
| More than 6, not more than 7 | 20% (=IHT @ 8%) |

> **Tax Tip**
> Thanks to the tapering provisions, IHT savings may start to arise once the transferor has survived three years. Hence, even if you don't think Great Aunt Maude stands any chance of lasting seven years, it may still be worth looking at getting her to make some gifts.
>
> Note that these savings only relate to the lifetime gifts made by the deceased. Tapering has no effect on the amount of IHT payable on the estate itself. Tapering can therefore only produce a saving where the deceased has made lifetime gifts in excess of the NRB.

The reductions in the amount of IHT payable occur on the day of the relevant anniversary.

In the case of chargeable lifetime transfers (see Section 4.2), the tapering provisions could result in the final IHT liability on death actually being less than the amount already paid. Unfortunately, this simply means no further IHT is due; it does not result in any repayment.

In calculating the IHT due on each transfer made within the seven years prior to death, any chargeable transfers in the seven years before <u>that</u> transfer must be taken into account. For this reason, chargeable lifetime transfers made up to fourteen years previously may continue to have an impact on the IHT arising on the transferor's death.

The calculation of the tax arising on transfers made within the seven years prior to death is almost a repeat of the calculation we saw in Section 4.2 for a chargeable lifetime transfer, except that:

- The full death rate (40%) is used
- Tapering relief (as set out above) is applied
- The NRB available at the date of death is used in the calculations, rather than the NRB applying at the time of the transfer
- Any unused NRB on the earlier death of the deceased's spouse is also available (see Section 6.3 for further details)
- Potentially exempt transfers made in the seven years prior to death must be brought into the calculation

### Example
*(As in previous examples, we will ignore any exemptions and reliefs, except the NRB)*

*Roy is a lifelong bachelor and a kind, generous, rich old man. Sadly, despite how much his nurses handle him with care, he dies on 3rd December 2020. Roy made no chargeable transfers prior to 2010 but, in the last decade of his life, he made the following gifts:*

- *On 10th December 2010, he gave £200,000 in cash to the Wilbury Discretionary Trust*
- *On 1st December 2013, he gave £50,000 in cash to his nephew George*
- *On 13th January 2014, he gave another £145,000 in cash to the Wilbury Discretionary Trust. He paid £5,000 in IHT at that time (grossing up applied)*
- *On 8th May 2016, he gave his friend Jeff some shares in the Electric Light Company Inc. At that time, these shares were worth £50,000*
- *On 4th December 2017, he gave his friend Tom some shares in Heartbreakers.com plc, which were worth £80,000 at that time*
- *On 24th August 2018, he gave his friend Bob £100,000 in cash*

*The IHT payable by each of these transferees on Roy's death is as follows:*

### The Wilbury Discretionary Trust – First Gift
*Roy's first gift to the Trust in December 2010 was made more than seven years prior to his death. This gift itself will therefore not be subject to IHT on his death. However, because gifts to discretionary trusts are chargeable transfers, it will continue to have an impact on gifts made in the following seven years.*

### George
*Roy's gift to George was a potentially exempt transfer made more than seven years prior to his death. On the seventh anniversary of that gift, 1st December 2020, it*

became fully exempt and hence can now be completely ignored for the purposes of calculating the IHT arising on Roy's death.

### The Wilbury Discretionary Trust – Second Gift

Due to the grossing up provisions, Roy's second gift to the Trust in January 2014 was deemed to have been £150,000. As this gift was within the last seven years of Roy's life, it is effectively pulled back into his estate for the purposes of his IHT calculation.

Furthermore, in calculating the IHT now due on this gift, we must also take account of his previous gift to the Trust, as that first gift was a chargeable transfer made within the seven-year period prior to the second gift.

The gift to George in December 2013 can be ignored, however, as this has become fully exempt.

The cumulative total of chargeable lifetime transfers made by Roy up to the time of the second gift to the Trust was therefore £350,000. After deducting the NRB of £325,000, there remains a chargeable sum of £25,000.

As the gift took place more than six, but less than seven, years before Roy's death, IHT is chargeable at 20% of the death rate, i.e. 8%. Hence the IHT charge arising on Roy's death is £2,000. As this is less than the IHT already paid by Roy at the time of the gift (£5,000), no further IHT is payable.

### Jeff

Roy's gift of shares to Jeff in May 2016 was a potentially exempt transfer. Unfortunately, as Roy has died within seven years of making that gift, it has now become a chargeable transfer.

Both of the gifts to the Wilbury Discretionary Trust took place within the seven-year period prior to the gift to Jeff, so the cumulative value of chargeable transfers at this point is £350,000, meaning the NRB has been fully exhausted and the gift to Jeff is fully chargeable to IHT.

However, since the gift took place more than four, but less than five, years before Roy's death, IHT is only chargeable at 60% of the death rate, i.e. 24%. Jeff therefore has an IHT liability of £12,000 (£50,000 x 24%).

### Tom

Tom really is going to be heartbroken. His gift took place just one day short of three years before Roy's death.

IHT is therefore payable at the full death rate, 40%. Furthermore, the cumulative value of total chargeable transfers within the previous seven years now amounts to £400,000, made up as follows:

|  | £ |
|---|---|
| First gift to Wilbury Discretionary Trust | 200,000 |
| Second gift to Wilbury Discretionary Trust | 150,000 |
| Gift to Jeff | 50,000 |
| Total | 400,000 |

*Both gifts to the Wilbury Discretionary Trust are included as they both took place within the seven-year period prior to the gift to Tom.*

*The gift to Jeff is also included, as it has now become a chargeable transfer due to Roy's death within seven years. The gift to George is not included, however, as it took place more than seven years before Roy's death and has therefore become exempt.*

*Tom therefore has an IHT liability of £32,000 (40% x £80,000).*

### Bob
*This gift took place within the last three years of Roy's life, so there is no tapering of the IHT liability.*

*The cumulative value of total chargeable transfers within the seven years prior to this gift amounts to £280,000, made up as follows:*

|  | £ |
|---|---|
| *Second gift to Wilbury Discretionary Trust* | *150,000* |
| *Gift to Jeff* | *50,000* |
| *Gift to Tom* | *80,000* |
| *Total* | *280,000* |

*The first gift to the Wilbury Discretionary Trust is not included as it took place more than seven years before the gift to Bob. Adding Bob's own gift to the above figure gives a total of £380,000. From this, we are able to deduct the NRB of £325,000, leaving Bob with a chargeable transfer of £55,000.*

*Bob's IHT liability is therefore £22,000 (40% x £55,000).*

### Points to Note

Firstly, we can see the total value of chargeable transfers in the last seven years of Roy's life amounts to £380,000. His NRB is therefore already exhausted before we even begin to look at his estate.

The next point to note is that the oldest gift in our example, made almost ten years before Roy's death, had a major impact on the recipients of his later gifts, despite the fact it was made well before the critical seven-year period.

It is also interesting to note that the oldest gift within the seven-year period did not give rise to any more IHT for the recipients of that gift. This will often be the case for chargeable lifetime transfers made more than five years prior to the transferor's death.

This position may be altered, however, where there are significant amounts of potentially exempt transfers made within seven years of the transferor's death but prior to the chargeable transfer in question.

As we saw in the example, these two earlier gifts used up all of Roy's NRB, which had a major impact on some of the later transferees.

This was particularly unfortunate for Tom since a mere seven days' delay to his gift would have meant the first gift to the Wilbury Discretionary Trust would have been made more than seven years previously. Tom's gift would then have been completely covered by the NRB.

> **Tax Tip**
> Where practical, it may make sense to leave a seven-year gap after making a large chargeable lifetime transfer before making further chargeable or potentially exempt transfers. Naturally, of course, delaying your gifts carries other conflicting risks, which you will need to weigh up.
>
> However, a delay of just seven days in order to bring the NRB back into play would surely make sense!

By the time of Bob's gift in 2018, part of the NRB was available once more, thus giving him a lower IHT bill on a larger value gift.

This ably demonstrates the fact that, with careful planning:

**The NRB is effectively available to each of us not just once a lifetime, but once every seven years!**

While none of us knows exactly when we have seven years left to go, it is also worth bearing in mind that gifts in the last seven years of your life will be dealt with chronologically when you die.

Although kind old Roy cannot really be blamed for the final outcome in the example, things might have turned out fairer if he had made some of the smaller gifts first.

**A Final Observation**

As discussed in Section 3.2, the NRB had originally been due to be increased to £350,000 in 2010 but was, instead, frozen at its 2009/10 level of £325,000.

By 2020/21, the NRB should perhaps be something like £480,000 (if increased in line with retail price inflation) – £155,000 more than it actually is.

At first glance, one might think this 'freeze' could only cost a maximum of £62,000 (£155,000 x 40%) in extra IHT on the occasion of one person's death. Think again!

In our example above, the freeze in the NRB has effectively cost Jeff £12,000, Tom £32,000, Bob £22,000, and will also cost Roy's estate an extra £40,000: a total of £106,000!

In fact, the freeze in the NRB could cost some bereaved families up to £248,000 in extra tax in 2020/21.

## 4.6     RELIEF FOR REDUCTION IN VALUE

Where IHT becomes payable on the transferor's death within seven years of making a lifetime transfer of property that has subsequently reduced in value, the transferee may claim relief from IHT in respect of that reduction in value.

To claim relief, the following conditions must be satisfied:

- i)   The property transferred must not be tangible moveable property with a predictable useful life not exceeding 50 years (e.g. a car, or any other plant and machinery), and
- ii)  Either:
  - a)   At the time of the transferor's death the property is still held by the transferee or their spouse, or
  - b)   The property has been sold by the transferee or their spouse by way of a sale at 'arm's length' to an unconnected person

When such a claim is made, the IHT on that particular transfer is calculated by substituting the property's market value at the 'relevant date' for the property's value at the date of the transfer. Where the property is still held by the transferee or their spouse at the date of the transferor's death, the 'relevant date' is the date of death. Where the property has been sold in an arm's length transaction with an unconnected party, the 'relevant date' is the date of the sale.

The IHT on any other transfers and on the deceased's estate is unaffected by this claim. This is because the value of the transferred property is reduced only for the purposes of this relief and not for the purposes of calculating cumulative chargeable transfers in any seven-year period.

### Example

*At the time of Roy's death, Jeff still holds the shares in the Electric Light Company Inc. that Roy gave to him when they were worth £50,000. Unfortunately, however, they are now worth only £30,000.*

*Nonetheless, Jeff is pleased to discover he can claim to reduce his IHT bill to just £7,200 (£30,000 x 24% - see Section 4.5 above for a full explanation).*

*Tom is also very excited at the prospect of a relief claim under these provisions as his shares in Heartbreakers.com plc fell rapidly in value after Roy gave them to him and Tom eventually sold them for just £1,000.*

*According to Tom's calculations, he should therefore be able to reduce his IHT bill to just £400 (£1,000 x 40%). However, it transpires that Tom sold the Heartbreakers.com plc shares to his son. This was not an 'arm's length' sale to an unconnected party and Tom's IHT bill remains £32,000 (see Section 4.5). Heartbroken again!*

**Points to Note**

The IHT liabilities for Roy's personal representatives and Bob are unaffected by Jeff's claim. (Nor would they be affected by Tom's claim if it had been valid.)

It does not matter whether Tom sold his shares to his son at market value. Because he and his son are connected, Tom loses his ability to claim relief for his shares' reduction in value. He therefore ends up with some shares that are virtually worthless and an IHT liability of £32,000.

Sometimes it **does** pay to look a gift horse in the mouth!

> **Tax Tip**
> A transferee holding property that was transferred to them less than seven years ago, and which has reduced in value since then, would be wise to avoid making any transfers of that property other than:
>
> - A sale at 'arm's length' to an unconnected person, or
> - A transfer to their spouse

## 4.7    TIMING OF LIFETIME GIFTS

A gift made by cheque is deemed to be made when the cheque is cleared by the transferor's bank. This will inevitably cause a slight delay to the date the gift is deemed to take place. While the delay may be slight, it could have disastrous consequences.

If the cheque clears after the transferor's death, for example, it will no longer be regarded as a lifetime gift and will form part of the transferor's estate on death. This will mean none of the lifetime exemptions can apply, including the annual exemption and the small gifts exemption.

For the sake of certainty, it may often be worth incurring the additional cost of putting the cheque through 'same day clearing'.

Alternatively, where the transferor has access to online or telephone banking facilities, it might be more efficient for them to make their gifts by way of electronic transfer.

While the point has not yet arisen in any suitable court case, it would seem logical to assume gifts made by way of electronic transfer will be treated as having been made when the funds are deducted from the transferor's bank account.

While this will undoubtedly speed up the process, it will remain vital to prepare suitable documentation to evidence the gift (see Section 4.8).

## 4.8    EVIDENCE

When making lifetime gifts, it is vital to have the evidence to back them up. HMRC will try very hard to get assets back into the deceased's estate in order to increase the amount of IHT payable.

"How do we know this money wasn't just a loan? Can you prove she didn't expect you to repay it?"

"Yes, we know your parents gave you the house, but what about the contents? There's nothing to prove they gave them to you."

To prevent these kinds of questions from arising, it is vital that gifts are evidenced. Furthermore, it is important that the documentary evidence of the gifts is specific about exactly what is being gifted.

Appendix C contains some brief examples of memoranda recording gifts. In practice, however, it will often make sense to record further detailed information; especially details of any household contents intended to be included in a gift of property.

## 4.9    GIFTS WITH RESERVATION

To give something away so that it is no longer part of your estate for IHT purposes, you really need to completely deprive yourself of that asset and any enjoyment of it. Any purported gifts where you retain a beneficial interest in the gifted asset are ineffective for IHT purposes and are effectively treated as still being part of your estate.

For example, if you 'give' a painting to your son but keep it in your house then you are still enjoying that asset and it remains part of your estate for IHT purposes.

These types of transfer are known as 'Gifts with Reservation'. This is a particular problem when looking at the family home and we will return to this subject in Chapter 12.

Broadly speaking, a 'Gift with Reservation' occurs whenever:

i)   The transferee does not obtain genuine possession and enjoyment of the gifted asset,
ii)  The transferor is not excluded from the enjoyment of the gifted asset, or
iii) The transferor has some form of contractual right over the gifted asset

We have already seen an example of (i): the gifted painting being kept in the transferor's house.

An example of (ii) would be to give a holiday cottage to your daughter, which you then use for a month each year.

An example of (iii) would be to grant yourself a lease over your own property and then transfer the freehold to your children.

Although you have to be excluded from the enjoyment of a gifted asset, there is a little leeway. If you give your son a painting, which he keeps in his house, there is no need to wear a blindfold every time you visit.

The strict rule is that the transferor must be 'virtually' excluded from the enjoyment of the asset. Mere incidental enjoyment of a gifted asset when making a short visit to the transferee is permitted.

Hence, if you give your daughter a house and visit her for dinner once every six months, you will not have a problem. If, on the other hand, you stay at the house every second weekend, there will be a gift with reservation.

Thankfully, one group of gifts that would otherwise almost always fall foul of the 'gift with reservation' rules are generally exempted from these provisions: gifts covered by the spouse exemption (see Section 3.3).

**Unforeseen Changes in Circumstances**

In the case of a property that a transferor has gifted to a relative, there will not be a gift with reservation if the transferor is forced to move back into that property due to an unforeseen change in circumstances whereby he or she is unable to care for themselves due to ill health, old age, or infirmity.

This, for example, may cover the situation where a person has transferred a property to their son or daughter and some years later has to move into the property so their family can care for them.

The move back into the property must be for the provision of 'reasonable care and maintenance' by the transferee who must also be a relative. You can't just move back in because you'd like to see a bit more of the grandchildren.

This change must also be unforeseen. If you are already ill when you make the gift, the gift with reservation rules will still apply.

**What's So Bad about Gifts with Reservation?**

Plenty! Firstly, although the gift is ineffective when it comes to excluding the gifted asset from your estate, it is nevertheless still a transfer of value and could give rise to an IHT charge if you die within seven years.

Some relief is given to prevent a double charge but it does not entirely eliminate the problem. In this situation, two IHT calculations must be prepared. Firstly, IHT is calculated as if the transfer had never taken place and you still owned the gifted asset at the date of your death. A second IHT calculation must then be prepared on the basis that the transfer did take place.

The bad news is the calculation that produces the greatest amount of IHT is then used. In other words, the tax payable is the greater of the amount payable on the transfer **or** the amount payable on the asset deemed to still be in your estate on death!

Generally, where the gifted asset is increasing in value, we would expect the greater tax to arise by including the asset in the estate on death. The overall effect of this is to render the gift ineffective for IHT purposes.

> **Wealth Warning**
> A gift with reservation where that reservation still applies at the time of the donor's death is at best ineffective and at worst may even increase the total IHT due.

Secondly, the gifted asset will also be included in the transferee's estate, thus giving rise to a possible double charge.

Thirdly, although the gift is ineffective for IHT purposes, it will still be a disposal for CGT purposes. This means CGT liabilities may still arise on the gift. Furthermore, the transferee may not be entitled to the same reliefs as the transferor would have been if they had retained the asset. We will look further at the potential impact of this in Chapter 11.

## What Happens When The 'Reservation' Ends?

If the 'reservation' ends during the transferor's lifetime, a new transfer is deemed to take place.

For example, if a mother gave a house to her two sons in 1999 but continued to live in it until 2020, there would be a deemed transfer of the house in 2020.

This time the transfer **is** effective for IHT purposes. It is treated as a potentially exempt transfer, so it will not cause any immediate IHT charges, but it does give rise to a few problems.

The main problem, of course, is that the transferor will have to survive at least seven years after the 'reservation' ends before the transferred asset is exempt from IHT.

Furthermore, the value of the deemed transfer will be the asset's value at the date the reservation ends, not the date of the original transfer.

Deemed transfers on the cessation of a 'reservation' are also ineligible for a number of reliefs, including the annual exemption.

If the transferor dies within seven years of the cessation of a 'reservation', the property subject to the 'reservation' will effectively fall into the deceased's estate. Hence, the mother in our example would need to live until 2027 for her transfer of the house in 1999 to be exempt from IHT. If she should pass away before then, the value of the house when she moved out in 2020 will effectively be brought back into her estate.

Where both the original transfer and the deemed transfer on cessation of the 'reservation' take place within the seven years prior to the transferor's death, it will again be necessary to prepare two IHT calculations: one including the original transfer and one including the deemed transfer. Once again, the calculation producing the greater amount of tax will be used.

## 4.10    WHY NOT JUST GIVE IT ALL AWAY?

After reading Section 4.3, you may have been thinking that avoiding IHT is simple. All you need to do is give everything away to your family and survive seven years. Well, yes, in theory, in the right circumstances, simply giving your property away during your lifetime can be an effective way to avoid IHT.

Certainly there is no problem with giving away whatever parts of your estate you can afford to. Just remember to make sure the gifts are potentially exempt transfers and then take good care of yourself for seven years. (Or take out some term insurance to cover the IHT risk – see Section 10.14.)

Unfortunately, however, in practice, there are a few 'catches'.

Firstly, as we have already seen, any gifts where you retain a beneficial interest are treated as still being part of your estate.

Secondly, even where a transfer appears to avoid the 'Gifts With Reservation' rules, there may be an Income Tax benefit-in-kind charge applying if the transferor continues to enjoy the use of the asset. This charge may also apply to any future use by the donor of an asset purchased with gifted funds (see Section 10.21).

Thirdly, when gifting assets other than cash, you may be exposed to CGT. Most lifetime gifts are treated like a sale at current market value for CGT purposes. (Here there is no problem with the family home, as it is generally exempt from CGT under principal private residence relief – this issue is fully explained in the Taxcafe.co.uk guide 'How to Save Property Tax'.)

Lastly, in practice, you cannot simply give all your assets away because you will need something to live off for the rest of your life!

It's fine if you're happy to spend the rest of your days in a monastery or nunnery, or live off your last £325,000 (for at least seven years) but, in reality, very few people would be happy to follow such a drastic course of action.

Hence, at this point, we need to start looking at what exemptions and reliefs are available and how you can plan to use them to best effect.

# Chapter 5

# Lifetime Exemptions

## 5.1 ABSOLUTE EXEMPTION

There are a number of exemptions available to cover lifetime transfers. These are absolute exemptions, not dependent on whether you survive for any particular period.

Transfers covered by these exemptions would be free from IHT even if you were to pass away the very next day, or even on the way home from the lawyer's office. (Don't laugh: I know of one sad, but true, case where the taxpayer was knocked down by a bus outside the lawyer's office!)

These exemptions therefore provide very useful IHT planning tools under the right circumstances. Sadly though, the monetary values of the exemptions covered in Sections 5.2, to 5.4 have remained the same since 1981, 1980 and 1975 respectively. These values are long overdue for an increase since retail price inflation alone would have almost quadrupled them by now!

## 5.2 THE ANNUAL EXEMPTION

The first £3,000 of any transfers of value, which are not otherwise exempt, that each individual makes in each tax year, are exempt from IHT. Married couples have an annual exemption of £3,000 each. If the annual exemption is not used one year, it may be carried forward and can be used in the next tax year if that following year's annual exemption is fully exhausted.

### *Example*
*Stevie makes the following gifts (having never made any before):*

| | |
|---|---|
| *2020/21:* | *£5,000 to his brother Marvin* |
| *2021/22:* | *£3,800 to his brother Smokey* |
| *2022/23:* | *£1,800 to his sister Dionne* |
| *2023/24:* | *£5,000 to his sister Aretha* |

*The first £3,000 of the gift to Marvin is covered by Stevie's annual exemption for 2020/21. His 2019/20 annual exemption is also still available, thus covering the remaining £2,000 of this gift. The gift to Marvin is therefore fully exempt from IHT.*

*The unused £1,000 of Stevie's 2019/20 annual exemption is simply lost, as it cannot be carried forward another year.*

*The first £3,000 of Stevie's gift to Smokey is covered by his 2021/22 annual exemption. The remaining £800 is a potentially exempt transfer.*

*The gift to Dionne is fully covered by Stevie's 2022/23 annual exemption. Furthermore, the unused £1,200 of this exemption may be carried forward to 2023/24.*

*The first £3,000 of Stevie's gift to Aretha is covered by his 2023/24 annual exemption. The next £1,200 is covered by the unused balance of his 2022/23 annual exemption. The remaining £800 is a potentially exempt transfer.*

### Tax Tip 1
If Stevie were married, he could have avoided the potentially exempt transfers to Smokey and Aretha by, in each case, first making a gift of £800 to his spouse who could then have gifted this sum to the ultimate recipient.

As explained in Section 6.15, however, such interim gifts to a spouse must be free of any conditions so that the spouse would be free to refuse to hand the gift on to the intended recipient if they so wished.

### Tax Tip 2
The annual exemption may not be very large, but it is important to bear it in mind when undertaking IHT planning. Making best use of the exemption is a matter of timing. The ability to carry it forward one year gives you a 'second chance', but the use of the annual exemption should nevertheless be reviewed at least every other year.

A couple who manage to make effective use of the annual exemption in the final few years of their lives will save around £20,000 in IHT.

## Who Benefits From The Exemption?

According to HMRC, the taxpayer's annual exemption must be applied on a strictly chronological basis. In their view, the exemption must be utilised against any potentially exempt transfers taking place before chargeable lifetime transfers made later in the same tax year. This could have some most unfortunate consequences.

### *Example*
*Brian gives £6,000 to his brother Carl on 6th April 2020. This (according to HMRC) uses up Brian's annual exemptions for 2019/20 and 2020/21, despite being a potentially exempt transfer.*

*On 10th April 2020, Brian gives £338,000 to the Wilson Phillips Discretionary Trust for the benefit of his many nephews and nieces. Unfortunately, this means he has made a chargeable lifetime transfer. After deducting the NRB of £325,000, the remaining £13,000 must be grossed up at the rate of one quarter, giving Brian an IHT bill of £3,250.*

*If, instead, Brian had made his gifts in the opposite order, his annual exemptions for 2019/20 and 2020/21 would have been deducted from his chargeable transfer, leaving just £332,000, or £7,000 after deducting the NRB. Brian's IHT bill would then have been reduced to just £1,750: a saving of £1,500.*

HMRC's interpretation on this point is based entirely on a flaw in the drafting of the IHT law. What Parliament actually intended was for the annual exemption to be used first against any chargeable lifetime transfers, with any excess remaining available to cover potentially exempt transfers if they subsequently became chargeable on the transferor's death.

This difference in interpretation will affect not only those making large chargeable lifetime transfers in excess of the NRB, like Brian in the example above, but also the transferees calculating their own IHT bill in the event of the transferor's death within seven years. In the latter case there will be winners and losers but, in the former, only HMRC can be the winner!

In practice, I would always advocate planning your affairs on the basis of HMRC's interpretation wherever possible.

> **Tax Tip**
> Chargeable lifetime transfers should be made earlier in the tax year than any potentially exempt transfers whenever possible.

But, if you find you are already in a position where their interpretation is putting you at a disadvantage, you should argue for the law to be applied as it was quite clearly intended by Parliament: an argument frequently used by HMRC, so why shouldn't the taxpayer argue the same!

Transfers made on the same day are treated as simultaneous. Any available annual exemption is divided between the 'same-day transfers' in proportion to their total value.

## 5.3   THE SMALL GIFTS EXEMPTION

There is also a general exemption for outright gifts of up to £250 to any one person each tax year. This exemption applies to any number of such 'small gifts' to separate persons each year. It can only apply to straightforward gifts to other individuals and cannot apply to transfers into trust.

A married couple may each use this exemption separately in their own right.

> **Wealth Warning**
> The small gifts exemption only covers gifts up to £250. Unlike the annual exemption, it does not cover the first part of a larger gift. Hence, a gift of £251 is not covered by this exemption at all.
>
> It should also be noted that the exemption has to cover all gifts to the same person in the whole tax year.
>
> This exemption cannot be used in conjunction with the annual exemption. In other words, it is not possible to exempt gifts totalling £3,250 to the same person by using both exemptions together.

## 5.4    GIFTS IN CONSIDERATION OF MARRIAGE

It's an expensive business when the kids get married, but it does provide an additional opportunity for some IHT planning. Gifts made in consideration of marriage are exempt from IHT up to the following limits:

- Parents:                                              £5,000
- Grandparents, Great-Grandparents, etc:   £2,500
- Bride to Groom or Groom to Bride:         £2,500
- Other Donors:                                      £1,000

All these limits apply on an individual basis and the relationships referred to must be to one of the parties to the marriage. Hence, for example, the groom could receive £5,000 from each of his parents, £2,500 from each of his grandparents, and £1,000 from each of his aunts and uncles; while the bride could receive the same from her family.

Alternatively, the bride's family could make their gifts to the groom or the groom's family could make their gifts to the bride.

Additionally, within the same exemption (and within the same overriding limits set out above), gifts could be made to a trust for the benefit of:

i)    The bride and/or groom
ii)   Children of either or both parties to the marriage
iii)  Future spouses of children of either or both parties to the marriage
iv)   A future spouse of either party to the marriage
v)    Children of any subsequent spouse of either party to this marriage and future spouses of those children

This all sounds terribly complicated, but it means the marriage provides an opportunity to put some money into trust for both living and unborn children of either or both parties without giving rise to a chargeable lifetime transfer.

To fall within the exemption, gifts must be made on or shortly before the marriage and must be fully effective when the marriage takes place. For example, 'I give you my property at Valotte on condition you marry my daughter.'

Where the gifts exceed the limits shown above, the excess may be covered by the annual exemption, if available. Otherwise, the excess will be treated like any other lifetime transfer, as explained in Chapter 4.

For the purpose of this exemption, a 'parent' includes the parent of an illegitimate child, adopted child, or legally recognised step-child (see Section 3.4: the same principles apply here) and, as explained in Section 1.3, all of the above applies equally to same sex marriages and registered civil partnerships.

## 5.5    MAINTENANCE OF FAMILY

Anything you do for the maintenance of your 'family' is exempted from being a transfer of value for IHT purposes. Just as well since otherwise, every time you bought the weekly groceries you would be at risk of causing an IHT liability! This covers expenditure for the maintenance of your spouse, plus any expenditure for the maintenance, education or training of the following:

- A child of either you or your spouse who is either under 18 or still in full-time education or training on the last 5th April prior to the time of the relevant expenditure.
- Any other child who is not in the care of a parent and is under 18 on the last 5th April prior to the time of the relevant expenditure.
- Any other child who has been in your care for a substantial period and was still in full time education or training on the last 5th April prior to the time of the relevant expenditure.

Your 'child' for the purposes of this exemption includes a stepchild, adopted child or illegitimate child.

One major absentee from this list, however, is your unmarried partner and hence, technically, any expenditure for the maintenance of a common-law co-habiting partner could be a transfer of value.

Thankfully, however, such expenditure will often be covered by:

- The 'Normal Expenditure Out Of Income' exemption (Section 5.7), or
- The exemption for 'transfers not intended to confer a gratuitous benefit' (Section 5.8): since most 'transfers of value' in an unmarried couple are simply domestic cost-sharing arrangements.

Even so, this might still present a significant problem, as a large part of a co-habiting partner's expenditure in the last seven years before their death could potentially be subject to IHT. Furthermore, since much of this 'maintenance' expenditure will not increase the value of the transferee's estate, it might even be considered a chargeable lifetime transfer!


## 5.6    DEPENDENT RELATIVES

This same exemption extends to expenditure that represents a reasonable provision for the care or maintenance of a dependent relative. A 'dependent relative' for this purpose is:

i)    Your widowed, separated or divorced mother or mother-in-law (by concession, an unmarried mother may also be included, as long as she is genuinely financially dependent on the donor)
ii)   Any other relative of yours or your spouse's who is incapacitated by old age or infirmity, as a consequence of which they are unable to maintain themselves

*It can be seen that sexism is alive and well and living in the UK tax legislation. I wonder when we will see a case taken to court demanding equal treatment for a widowed, separated, or divorced father?*

HMRC should, for example, accept that renting a property for your elderly and financially dependent relative to live in represents reasonable provision for their maintenance. They will not, however, accept buying a property for them and transferring it into their name to give them added security, as 'reasonable care or maintenance'.

This exemption is useful when a person pre-deceases one of their parents or where a person is providing 'care or maintenance' for a disabled relative, such as a sibling or adult child.

### 5.7    NORMAL EXPENDITURE OUT OF INCOME

Lifetime transfers are exempt to the extent that:

i)   They are part of the normal, habitual, or typical, expenditure of the transferor,

ii)  Taking one year with another, they are made out of income (i.e. not out of capital), and

iii) The transferor is left with sufficient net income to maintain his or her usual standard of living

This is an extremely useful exemption, since, unlike the annual exemption, there is no financial limit to the amount that can be covered if the transferor can afford it.

The amount of gifts or other expenditure involved does not need to be exactly the same every year, as long as it is part of a regular pattern. All of the following might potentially be covered as long as they meet the three tests set out above:

- Giving your son £10,000 every year
- Giving your granddaughter all your dividend income every year
- Paying your nephew's school fees
- Buying your brother a new car every three years
- Passing all of the income you receive from a trust each year over to your elderly father
- Paying a monthly life assurance premium on a policy in favour of your daughter

### Maintaining Your Usual Standard of Living

It is generally accepted that this test is met if the transferor is left with sufficient income to maintain his or her usual standard of living **on average**.

It has also been suggested that the Capital Taxes Office (the HMRC department responsible for policing IHT) does not generally question the validity of gifts out of income if they do not, in total, exceed one third of the transferor's net annual after-tax income. Nevertheless, I imagine they would still scrutinise any case where they had reason to think otherwise!

In some circumstances, the transferor might reasonably gift a greater proportion of his or her income and still maintain their usual standard of living, e.g. a very wealthy person with a very frugal lifestyle.

I have, however, met the 'chicken and egg' situation where HMRC has argued that the transferor's modest standard of living arose **because** of the expenditure in question. To avoid this argument, there will clearly need to be some surplus income remaining.

## What Is Income?

The first point to note is that HMRC regards 'income' for the purposes of this exemption as net after-tax income.

Furthermore, not everything that is treated as 'income' for Income Tax purposes will be regarded as 'income' for the purposes of the exemption. (Yet another example of HMRC having their cake and eating it!) There are, for example, cases where the proceeds of sale of company shares may be treated as income for Income Tax purposes. This often occurs as a result of specific statutory provisions relating to employee shares.

The underlying nature of this 'income', however, would remain capital and hence this would not be 'income' which could be relied upon for the purposes of the 'normal expenditure out of income' exemption.

For a self-employed transferor, 'income' for the purposes of the exemption would generally be based on the results shown in their business accounts.

Hence, 'income' will be arrived at after deducting items such as depreciation and business entertaining, even though these are not allowed for Income Tax purposes. As stated above, however, the full Income Tax charge will need to be deducted from the accounts income in order to arrive at the net after-tax income available for the purposes of the exemption.

Tax exempt income such as dividends and interest within an ISA, or winter fuel payments and attendance allowance, may be included as income for this purpose. However, items that form an effective 'income stream', but which are actually capital in nature, cannot generally be counted. This includes the annual tax-free 5% withdrawal from an investment bond; loan repayments received from family investment companies (see Chapter 13) or loan trusts (Section 9.12); payments from a discounted gift trust (Section 9.11); and other director's loan account repayments (Section 7.22).

## Habitual Gifts

Establishing a gift as being part of your normal, habitual expenditure is a question of fact. The matter will be determined by looking at the particular facts of each individual case and considering the behaviour of the transferor over a number of years.

HMRC will usually consider expenditure to have become normal, or habitual, when it has been made three times, with the intention of continuing to make further similar payments.

It is, however, possible to establish a gift has become part of your normal, habitual expenditure even if you should die after only one such gift. This is because the exemption will still apply if it can be shown it was the transferor's intention to make the gift regularly on a habitual basis.

A contractual commitment to make regular payments will usually be accepted as evidence of an intention to make the expenditure part of the transferor's normal pattern of expenditure. In the absence of such a commitment, some other documentary evidence of the transferor's intentions is advisable.

### Tax Tip
Establishing an intention to make a gift on a habitual basis will require some evidence to prove it. For example, if you intend paying your niece's school fees on a regular basis, it would be wise to write a letter to the school confirming this.

If you should then unfortunately pass away soon after paying the first set of fees, the letter will confirm this payment was intended to be normal habitual expenditure and thus exempt from IHT (as long as the other requirements set out above are also met).

### Wealth Warning
To be covered by this exemption, the relevant gifts or expenditure must be maintained on a regular basis. Hence, you must be sure to keep making your 'habitual' gifts every year (or such other period as is your habit). Unlike the annual exemption, there is no scope for carrying this exemption forward!

## The Danger of Irrelevance

Where the gifts concerned are made directly to another individual, this all only becomes relevant when the transferor has died within seven years since, otherwise, the gifts will be potentially exempt transfers in any case (see Section 4.3).

Unfortunately, what this means in practice is that the true status of these transfers is generally never established until after the transferor's death, leaving a great deal of uncertainty for their beneficiaries. It is vital, therefore, to maintain appropriate records of your normal expenditure out of income throughout your lifetime, to assist your executors in establishing the correct position when dealing with your estate after your death.

## 5.8 TRANSFERS NOT INTENDED TO CONFER GRATUITOUS BENEFIT

There is a general exemption for a transfer of value that is not intended to confer a gratuitous benefit on the transferee.

An important example of such a transfer is one made as part of a divorce settlement (when made in circumstances where the spouse exemption does not apply).

### Tax Tip
This provides the opportunity to put property into trust as part of a divorce settlement without creating a chargeable lifetime transfer. Not only is this probably preferable from a practical perspective (e.g. the ex-spouse's interest can be terminated in the event of their re-marrying), it also means the property will not fall into the ex-spouse's estate and can later pass to the children without a 40% charge on the ex-spouse's death.

Note that, while the property can pass into the trust free from IHT under this exemption, anniversary and exit charges will still apply (see Chapter 8). Nevertheless, on balance, the technique will often be beneficial overall.

Settlements between common-law partners might also be covered under this exemption, as well as simple transactions, such as friends sharing the cost of a holiday or restaurant bill (when we can all do such things again).

## 5.9 TRANSFERS ALLOWABLE FOR INCOME TAX OR CONFERRING RETIREMENT BENEFITS

'Transfers of value' that are made for the purposes of a trade, and are thus allowable for Income Tax, are exempt from IHT. This covers paying your employees' wages, for example; including employees who are also family members, provided they genuinely earn those wages through the effort they put into your business.

There is also an exemption for payments securing pension or other retirement benefits for:
- i) any employee of the transferor, who is not otherwise connected with the transferor, or
- ii) the widow, widower or dependants of a person within (i) above

Payments securing pension benefits for family members are not covered by this exemption (but could be covered by other exemptions).

# Chapter 6

# IHT Planning for Married Persons

## 6.1 SCOPE OF THIS CHAPTER

In this chapter, we are going to take a detailed look at the IHT planning opportunities available as a consequence of marriage. We will cover people who are married now; widows and widowers; and those contemplating marriage in the future.

Everything that applies to married people applies equally to civil partners and everything that applies to a widow or widower applies equally to a surviving civil partner.

Unless expressly stated to the contrary, it is assumed throughout this chapter that both spouses are (or were) UK domiciled, deemed UK domiciled (see Section 2.2), or have (or had) elected to be treated as UK domiciled at the relevant time (see Section 6.19).

## 6.2 A BRAVE NEW WORLD?

On your death, your personal representatives may claim any unused part of an earlier deceased spouse's NRB. In simple terms, this means all widows and widowers are potentially entitled to a double NRB. Furthermore, since we all have the potential to become a widow or widower one day, this actually means we all have the potential to double our NRB. This has turned a great deal of IHT planning on its head!

Before 2007, a great deal of IHT planning centred around ensuring the first member of a married couple to die fully utilised their NRB since it would otherwise go to waste. Now we often find it is better to ensure none of the first spouse's NRB is used on their death.

Many of the planning techniques that were used to ensure the first spouse's NRB was fully utilised would now appear to be highly disadvantageous in many cases. We will look at when to undo such planning in Section 6.13.

Many people are also now entitled to any unused part of an earlier deceased spouse's RNRB. Further details on the amount available are included in Sections 3.4 and 12.16.

## 6.3 THE TRANSFERABLE NIL RATE BAND & RESIDENCE NIL RATE BAND

Any part of the NRB that is unused on a married person's death is transferable to their spouse.

The TNRB must be claimed by the widow or widower's personal representatives within two years of the widow or widower's death. No claim is necessary on the first spouse's death and it does not matter how long ago the first spouse died.

Furthermore, it does not matter whether the first spouse actually had any assets at the time of their death. Even if they died penniless, their widow or widower can still claim a TNRB.

It is the **proportion** of the NRB unused on the first death that transfers, not the amount. This means the widow or widower benefits from any increase in the NRB since their spouse's death.

In the simplest case where none of the NRB was used on the first spouse's death the widow or widower will be entitled to a double NRB. For widows or widowers dying between 6th April 2009 and 5th April 2021, this amounts to £650,000 (regardless of when the first spouse died).

Where some of the first spouse's NRB was used, the amount transferred to the survivor will be reduced.

### Example
*Lee died on 1st September 2002 when the NRB was £250,000. Lee left a legacy of £100,000 to her son Peter and her remaining estate to her husband Lenny. 60% of Lee's NRB was unused (£150,000/£250,000) and transfers to Lenny.*

*Lenny dies in May 2020 and is entitled to his own NRB plus a further 60% transferred from Lee. His total NRB is thus as follows:*

| | |
|---|---|
| *Own NRB:* | *£325,000* |
| *Nil rate band transferred from Lee (£325,000 x 60%):* | *£195,000* |
| *Total NRB available* | *£520,000* |

### The Transferable Residence Nil Rate Band

Similar principles apply to the transfer of a spouse's RNRB, although this is subject to the tapering provisions explained in Section 3.4.

### Example Continued
*As Lee died in 2002, she would not have used any of her RNRB. If her estate was worth no more than £2m at the time of her death, her entire RNRB will therefore transfer to Lenny, giving him a total RNRB at the time of his death in May 2020 of £350,000: made up of his own RNRB of £175,000 and Lee's unused RNRB of £175,000.*

*Combining his RNRB of £350,000 with his enhanced NRB of £520,000 (see above) gives Lenny a total potential exemption of £870,000. He will, however, have to meet the rules outlined in Section 3.4 in order to benefit from the RNRB element of this exemption.*

## Using the Residence Nil Rate Band on First Death

As explained in Section 3.4, tapering provisions apply to reduce the amount of RNRB available on the death of an individual with an estate worth in excess of £2m.

Where a married couple's **combined** net assets exceed £2m, it may be worth ensuring the RNRB is utilised on the first spouse's death. Otherwise, it will be reduced or eliminated through the tapering that applies on the second death.

Where a married couple's combined net assets exceed £4m, there are also potential savings to be made by keeping one spouse's estate to no more than £2m. In that way, the 'poorer' spouse will retain their full RNRB entitlement.

To use that entitlement, it may also be necessary to leave some property qualifying for the RNRB directly to a 'direct descendant' on the 'poorer' spouse's death. For this reason, it would generally be preferable for the 'poorer' spouse to be the one with the shorter life expectancy, although this may require a little 'negotiation' among the family!

See Section 3.4 for advice on whether it is wise to use the RNRB on the first spouse's death in the case of smaller combined estates worth less than £2m.


### 6.4    NIL RATE BAND TRANSFERS IN PRACTICE

Applying the TNRB system in practice is fraught with problems. The first spouse may have died many years ago with a total estate that was clearly nowhere near the amount of the NRB. No-one will have given much thought to IHT at that time since it was clearly irrelevant.

Now, many years later, we will be faced with the prospect of attempting to ascertain how much of the NRB was used at that time.

The first question is 'how much was the NRB?' Here, at least, HMRC has been helpful and has published the NRBs going back to 1914. These can be found at: https://tinyurl.com/ihtnrbs

Where the first spouse died before 1986, they will have been subject to a different death tax regime but the previous equivalent of the NRB is used for the purposes of calculating the TNRB.

There is a particularly nasty problem for widows and widowers whose spouse died before 13th March 1975 under the Estate Duty regime. Under Estate Duty, there was no general exemption for transfers to spouses. For deaths occurring between 21st March 1972 and 12th March 1975 there was a limited exemption of £15,000. Prior to that, there was no spouse exemption at all.

Hence, where the first spouse died before 13th March 1975, there may be little or no TNRB available even if the first spouse's entire estate passed to their widow or widower.

The families of those who have been widows or widowers for a long time could be badly affected by this.

### Example
*Vera has been a widow since her husband Glen went missing during a fishing trip in 1945. Glen left his entire estate, worth just £30, to Vera. Despite the tiny size of Glen's estate, this nevertheless used up 30% of his NRB which was then just £100.*

*Only 70% of Glen's NRB will be available to Vera. At today's rates this means she has lost £97,500 of TNRB, resulting in a potential additional IHT burden for her family of £39,000, or 1,300 times the value of Glen's estate!*

There will of course be some straightforward cases where the first spouse did not use any of their NRB. This will include cases where the first spouse:

- Died after 12th March 1975 and left their entire estate to their widow or widower,
- Left everything to charity,
- Had nothing of any financial value, or
- Died on active service (see Section 3.8)

Remember, the first spouse may have used some of their NRB if they:

a) Made transfers of value in the last seven years of their life (see Section 4.5),
b) Made any gifts with reservation (see Section 4.9), or
c) Elected to include an asset in their estate in order to prevent an Income Tax charge (see Section 10.21)

### Example
*When Pete died in March 2006, he left everything to his civil partner Roger. However, Pete had also given £100,000 to his friend Keith in 2002. The gift to Keith in 2002 became chargeable on Pete's death. This was not important at the time as Pete left his entire estate to his civil partner but it meant Pete used £100,000, or 36.36% (£100,000/£275,000), of his NRB. Only 63.64% of Pete's NRB therefore transfers to Roger, or £206,818 at current rates.*

## Practical Problems

As we have already seen, the impact of even small gifts and legacies made by the first spouse could be quite significant. In practice, we may therefore see some extensive queries from HMRC whenever a TNRB is claimed.

In other words, whenever a widow or widower dies with an estate worth more than the NRB, we can expect to face detailed enquiries regarding the first spouse's estate and any transfers they may have made in the last seven years of their life.

For married couples who are both still alive, it will therefore be vital to keep accurate records of all transfers that take place.

## 6.5    REMARRIAGE

It is, of course, not unusual for a widow or widower to remarry. Furthermore, some people (particularly widows) go on to outlive two or more spouses.

Sadly, however, a widow or widower can only be entitled to a maximum of one TNRB regardless of how many spouses they bury.

### *Example*
*In 1987, Liz married Eddie. He died in 1995 leaving Liz his entire estate. She remarried in 1998, to Richard, who died in 2001 and also left her his entire estate. Although Liz has survived two husbands, neither of whom used any of their NRB, she is only entitled to one TNRB. Liz herself dies in March 2021. Her personal representatives may therefore claim a NRB of £650,000, comprising her own NRB plus one TNRB.*

A widow or widower whose spouse used part of their NRB may, however, continue to accumulate further TNRB through remarriage until such point as they have accumulated a total of one additional NRB.

### *Example*
*Kurt died in 1991 when the NRB was £140,000, leaving a legacy of £70,000 to his cousin Dave and the remainder of his estate to his wife, Courtney. Courtney is thus entitled to a TNRB of 50% from Kurt.*

*In 1998, Courtney remarried to Michael. Sadly, in May 2020, Michael died, leaving a house worth £260,000 to his sister Kylie and the rest of his estate to Courtney. Kylie's legacy used up 80% of Michael's NRB so, this time, Courtney is only entitled to a TNRB of 20%.*

*Courtney can, however, add her two TNRBs together to give her a total 70% of TNRB. If she should die before 6th April 2021, her personal representatives could therefore claim an additional TNRB of £227,500 (£325,000 x 70%) in addition to her own NRB of £325,000.*

*If Courtney were to remarry again and subsequently be widowed for a third time, she would be entitled to claim any unused NRB on the death of her third husband up to a maximum of 30% (a further 30% would bring her up to a total of one TNRB).*

The key point is many widows and widowers will already have the maximum amount of TNRB when they remarry. We will look at the IHT planning consequences of this in Section 6.8.

### Taking the Residence Nil Rate Band into Account

Similar principles apply to ensure a widow or widower who remarries can only ever be entitled to a maximum of one additional RNRB. Those who outlive more than one spouse will again be able to accumulate additional proportionate amounts of RNRB until they reach an additional 100%.

At first glance, one might expect someone like Courtney, in our example above, to already be entitled to a full additional RNRB, since her first husband died before the exemption became available. However, it is important to remember, if his estate was worth in excess of £2m at the time of his death, tapering would apply and the proportion of RNRB passing to Courtney would be reduced (see Section 3.4 for more details).

## 6.6    SEPARATION & DIVORCE

As we saw in Section 3.3, for the purposes of the spouse exemption a couple continue to be regarded as married for IHT purposes throughout any period of separation and right up until the granting of a decree absolute.

As far as we know, it is reasonable to assume the same definition of marriage can be used in applying the TNRB system.

In other words, even if the couple were separated at the time of the first spouse's death, it appears the surviving spouse will still be entitled to claim any part of the first spouse's NRB or RNRB that is unused.

### Example
*Mick and Marianne met in the late 1960s and led a wild life together for a few weeks. One drunken night in Las Vegas they got married. Shortly afterwards they drifted apart. They never got divorced. Marianne continued to lead a wild life and died penniless in the 1990s.*

*Mick got his act together and eventually went on to become very rich. Despite the fact that it has been over 50 years since their brief marriage, Mick would appear to be entitled to claim Marianne's unused NRB and RNRB. That drunken night in Las Vegas could therefore save his family up to £200,000!*

*(Based on the NRB and RNRB applying in 2020/21: £325,000 + £175,000 = £500,000 x 40% = £200,000)*

There is a major practical problem with this situation. An estranged spouse like Mick may find it very difficult to ascertain how much of Marianne's NRB is available for him to claim. This will make any tax planning more difficult. Mick's personal representatives will also face difficulties when the time comes to claim the unused proportion of Marianne's NRB.

In an extreme case like Mick and Marianne's, the survivor may not even know their spouse has died!

There is also the danger of more detailed legislation designed to restrict the use of TNRBs. It is possible the CGT definition of 'married' may be applied to IHT. This would mean a couple would cease to be treated as married when they separated. If the IHT rules were changed in this way, a separated spouse would not benefit from the TNRBs.

We can only speculate about the precise nature of any future detailed rules. In the meantime, there remains a fair possibility the TNRB and RNRB will have the wide application suggested by the example above. We will return to some other implications of this in Section 6.17.

**Divorce**

Divorce was always a costly business! Now, there is a further cost: the loss of the TNRBs.

If the IHT definition of 'married' continues to apply as set out in Section 3.3 a separated couple will both continue to have the potential to claim any part of their estranged spouse's NRB or RNRB that is unused on the spouse's death.

If the couple divorce the TNRBs will no longer be available to either of them. Hence, for IHT purposes, it makes sense for separated couples to stay married. If your ex is not that well off when they die, you may benefit!

In many cases, it is the couple's children who will ultimately benefit from any TNRB or RNRB, which provides even more incentive to stay married.

## 6.7    INHERITANCE TAX PLANNING FOR MARRIED COUPLES

The TNRB has completely changed the IHT planning landscape for married couples. Before 2007, the first step was always to ensure the first spouse to die would use their NRB effectively. Now, in most cases, this is no longer necessary, as any unused NRB will transfer to the surviving spouse.

In fact, there is a case for saying the best planning now is to ensure none of the NRB is used on the first spouse's death.

'But surely it doesn't make any difference,' I hear you say. This is the impression Alistair Darling tried to give when announcing the TNRB, suggesting those who had taken steps to use their NRB would be 'unaffected'.

I suppose this was true in a strict literal sense, but a more accurate statement would have been to say, 'those who have already taken steps to utilise their NRB will not benefit.'

Am I just splitting hairs? No!

The important point is the surviving spouse is able to claim whatever **proportion** of the NRB is unused on the first spouse's death. The **amount** of that claim will depend on the amount of the NRB at the time of the widow or widower's death. This means some former IHT planning techniques may sometimes now have a disadvantageous effect.

### *Example*
*John and Dee were a married couple. Some years ago, they took professional advice on their IHT position. Following this advice, they amended their Wills to implement a 'Widow's Loan Scheme' (see Section 6.12) when the first of them died.*

*The effect of the scheme was to ensure the first of them to die would utilise their NRB. The survivor would then be able to deduct an amount equal to that NRB from their estate. This was good planning at the time since, as things stood, this was likely to save John and Dee's family over £100,000 in IHT.*

77

*John died in May 2020 and the 'Widow's Loan Scheme' was put into action. A sum of £325,000 was left to a discretionary trust. Dee inherited the remainder of John's estate and, following one of the mechanisms explained in Section 6.12, was left owing a sum of £325,000 to the discretionary trust.*

*At this point everything seems fine. Dee still has her own NRB and will also be able to deduct her debt of £325,000 from her estate (provided the debt is repaid out of the assets of her estate – see Section 2.11). This provides a total effective exemption of £650,000 and, if Dee herself were to die while the NRB still stands at the same level of £325,000, the effect would be the same as under the TNRB system.*

*Let us suppose, however, that Dee lives on for many years, through many changes of Government and much political manoeuvring and eventually dies when the NRB is £1.5m. On her death, Dee's NRB and her debt to the discretionary trust add up to a total of £1.825m of effective exemption from IHT.*

*If John and Dee had not implemented the 'Widow's Loan Scheme', however, John's NRB would have been unused and would have transferred to Dee. On Dee's death, her personal representatives would have been able to claim a TNRB of £1.5m in addition to her own NRB, giving her estate a total effective IHT exemption of £3m.*

In this example, the earlier planning has resulted in the loss of £1.175m worth of IHT exemption for Dee's family. This would cost the family up to £470,000 in extra IHT at today's rates. The reason for this is the fact that the NRB increased by £1.175m during the period between John and Dee's deaths.

This gives us the general principle that a married couple's family will lose out to the extent of:

- The proportion of the NRB used on the first spouse's death TIMES
- The increase in the NRB between the first spouse's death and the second spouse's death TIMES
- The rate of IHT at the time of the second spouse's death

**What Does This Mean for IHT Planning for Married Couples?**

Any use of any part of the NRB on the first spouse's death may potentially have a detrimental effect on the second spouse's death. The first spouse may use part of their NRB through any of the following:

- Legacies to anyone other than their spouse or one of the exempt bodies set out in Section 3.5
- Chargeable lifetime transfers in the last seven years of their life
- Potentially exempt transfers in the last seven years of their life
- Gifts with reservation of benefit (Section 4.9)
- An election to include an asset in their estate in order to prevent an Income Tax charge (Section 10.21)

Any of the above now put some or all of any married person's NRB in jeopardy and may have a detrimental effect on their spouse's IHT position.

This means any transfer of value by a married person that does not enjoy immediate complete exemption carries an element of risk. This is particularly relevant to potentially exempt transfers, as well as chargeable lifetime transfers covered by the transferor's NRB (see Chapter 4 for further details).

Before 2007, it was fair to say such lifetime transfers could be made with an attitude of 'there's nothing to lose'. If you survived seven years, there was no problem, if you survived three, there might be some benefit and, if you died sooner, the position was probably no worse than it would have been anyway.

But now every lifetime transfer by a married person not covered by one of the absolute exemptions set out in Chapter 5 puts their spouse's TNRB at risk.

### Example
*In January 2015, Richard gave his son Zak a gift of £65,000. This was a potentially exempt transfer as Richard had already used up any other available exemptions. Sadly, Richard dies in March 2021 and leaves his entire estate to his wife Barbara. The earlier gift to Zak becomes chargeable and uses up 20% of Richard's NRB. This means Barbara receives a TNRB of only 80%.*

*Whatever the NRB may be when Barbara dies, she will lose out on 20% of it because of Richard's gift to Zak.*

### Lifetime Transfers by Married People

At this point, it is tempting to suggest all married people should avoid making any lifetime transfers that are not covered by an immediate exemption. This is not the case; it only means many such transfers now carry a degree of risk that they might actually make the position worse.

Lifetime transfers by married people will often be beneficial, such as when:

- The transferor survives at least seven years
- The transferor's spouse already has a TNRB from a previous marriage (see Section 6.5)
- The assets grow in value faster than the increase in the NRB

### Example Revisited
*Let us suppose the gift from Richard to Zak in our previous example comprised quoted shares worth £65,000. Let's also suppose these shares increase in value at an average compound rate of 5% per year until Barbara's death in early 2035. This means Zak's shares will be worth £172,500 at the time of Barbara's death.*

*If the shares had not been transferred to Zak, they would still have been in Barbara's estate and would thus increase her IHT liability. Instead, the gift to Zak means the shares are not in Barbara's estate. However, the same gift also means Barbara loses 20% of the TNRB.*

*Hence, if the NRB for 2034/35 is less than £862,500 (£862,500 x 20% = £172,500), the family will be better off overall because of Richard's original gift to Zak.*

**It may still be worthwhile for a married person to use part of their NRB on the transfer of funds or assets that will grow in value faster than the rate at which the NRB increases.**

Following this principle in practice may be difficult, as it involves a good deal of 'crystal ball gazing'. Will a future Government increase the NRB significantly at some stage? Will the current freeze be extended as forecasted in this guide, or for even longer? Will we be stuck with simple inflationary increases for many years to come? At present, no-one can say.

For a lifetime transfer, there is the added bonus that any growth in the value of the transferred asset up to the point of the transferor's death is effectively free of any IHT cost. In our example, for instance, it was the value of the shares when they were transferred in 2015 that was used to calculate the restriction in Barbara's TNRB, not their value at the date of Richard's death (which may have been around £87,000, although this assumes current reductions in value will have reversed by the time of his death).

### Planning On the First Death

At this point, it seems reasonable to say most married couples will be better off if they **do not** use any of the planning schemes previously designed to utilise the first spouse's NRB without actually passing any wealth to other beneficiaries at that time.

We saw an example of the detrimental effect such planning could now have in John and Dee's case above. The planning techniques set out in Sections 6.9 to 6.12 are therefore no longer beneficial for most married couples. (We will look at when and how such planning carried out in the past can be undone in Section 6.13.)

The position may differ where one or both of the couple have remarried following the death of a previous spouse. We will look at planning for these couples in Section 6.8. It is mainly for the benefit of these couples that the techniques set out in Sections 6.9 to 6.12 are still included in this guide.

Those couples aside, any other married couple should now generally avoid using any scheme that simply uses up the first spouse's NRB without actually passing any assets or funds to other family members.

What is less certain is whether it's worth using the first spouse's NRB on genuine legacies to other family members. Here we must go back to the principle set out above, i.e. such legacies may be worthwhile if they consist of funds or assets that will grow faster than the rate at which the NRB increases.

In the case of a legacy, however, the proportion of TNRB lost will be based on the value of the relevant asset at the date of the first spouse's death. This means the growth rate must be greater than in the case of a lifetime transfer before the legacy is worthwhile for IHT purposes.

Remember also that the reduction in the surviving spouse's TNRB caused by a legacy to another beneficiary is permanent. A gift of the same asset from the surviving spouse to another person would instead be a potentially exempt transfer and would be exempt if that spouse survives another seven years.

In many cases, therefore, and especially where the survivor still has a long life expectancy, it may be preferable to avoid legacies to other beneficiaries. Subject to the comments below, the family will often achieve a better overall result if the surviving spouse makes lifetime transfers instead.

## Passing on Wealth Tax Efficiently

Of course, it's all very well me telling you not to give your children (or other beneficiaries) anything unless they are going to invest it at better rates of growth than the NRB, but what if they need money now, or you simply want to help them out?

In most cases, you will probably give them money during your lifetime and this will be a potentially exempt transfer. As we know, this will lead to a reduction in the TNRB if the person making the potentially exempt transfer dies within seven years.

You will therefore reduce the risk of a reduction in the TNRB if the spouse with the longer life expectancy makes the potentially exempt transfer. This is not foolproof, but it improves your chances.

Remember, you can pass wealth to your spouse first free from any IHT risk (subject to the points below) and they can then make the potentially exempt transfer if they choose to do so.

### Wealth Warnings
You cannot make it a pre-condition of a gift to your spouse that they will pass that gift on to another person. If any such condition existed, the first gift is ignored and you will be treated as having made the gift directly to the ultimate recipient, meaning you will have made the potentially exempt transfer.

There is no problem if your spouse chooses to pass the gift on of their own free will.

The transfer to your spouse may itself be a potentially exempt transfer if they are non-UK domiciled (see Section 3.3).

Alternatively, you may wish to pass some wealth to someone other than your spouse when you die. As we have already discussed, a direct legacy has the drawback of causing a permanent reduction in the amount of TNRB that can ultimately be claimed against your spouse's estate.

You may therefore wish to consider passing the wealth to your spouse and leaving it in their hands to decide what to do.

This would enable the surviving spouse to make appropriate gifts as potentially exempt transfers. If the survivor lives another seven years, these will be exempt from IHT and the full TNRB will be available against the rest of their estate.

As with a lifetime transfer, it is imperative there is no prior agreement that your spouse will pass the assets or funds to another person. You **must** leave the decision entirely in their hands. This point is crucial, and is explored in Section 6.15, where we will also see it is often wise for the surviving spouse to wait at least two years and a day after the first spouse's death before making any transfers of assets or funds inherited from their late spouse.

## 6.8 THE SECOND TIME AROUND

Where one or both of a married couple have remarried following the death of an earlier spouse, the position may be different to that outlined in the previous section. This is because one or both of them may already have an entitlement to claim all or part of a TNRB unused on the death of their previous spouse.

If, however, the whole of the previous spouse's NRB was used on their death (and this cannot be undone – see Section 6.13), then the current married couple will still be in the same position as a 'first time' couple and should go back to Section 6.7 for advice on their IHT planning position.

This leaves us with those who already have some entitlement to a TNRB. As explained in Section 6.5, a widow or widower cannot claim more than one additional NRB. This, in turn, means we are back in the position where some or all of the NRB of the first spouse in the current couple to die will effectively go to waste unless we undertake some appropriate planning. Let me explain this further with an example.

### *Example*
*When George died a few years ago, he left a sum equal to half the NRB to his son Ravi and the rest of his estate to his wife Patti. Patti is therefore already entitled to claim an additional 50% TNRB, or £162,500 at current rates. Patti is now married to Eric (who has never married before). At the moment, Eric and Patti's Wills both leave everything to each other.*

*If Patti dies first, her NRB will go unused and will transfer to Eric. The additional half NRB that transferred from George to Patti will go to waste.*

*If Eric dies first, his NRB will go unused and will be available to transfer to Patti. However, as Patti already has half a TNRB, she will only be able to claim half of Eric's unused NRB and the other half will go to waste.*

*Either way, whether Eric or Patti dies first, half a NRB will go to waste!*

As we can see, where one of a couple already has an entitlement to part of a previous spouse's unused NRB, that entitlement will go to waste if the couple do not plan effectively.

Where the previous spouse's NRB was completely unused, we are back into familiar territory, as that whole NRB may potentially go to waste. At current rates, that amounts to £130,000 worth of wasted tax relief.

Whatever amount of TNRB is already available, the current couple will achieve the best result by ensuring the same proportion of NRB is used on the first of their deaths. We will look at how this is done in the next few sections.

## Double Second-Timers

Where both of the current couple already have some entitlement to a TNRB, the amount potentially going to waste on the first death will be the sum of their existing entitlements.

Preserving both existing entitlements in this case will necessitate the first spouse to die using all their existing TNRB plus all or part of their own NRB.

### Example
*Buddy died some years ago and used 25% of his NRB. His widow, Holly, later remarried to Waylon, who was a widower himself. Waylon's previous wife Jenny had used 60% of her NRB when she died.*

*As things stand, Holly is entitled to a 75% TNRB and Waylon is entitled to a 40% TNRB. The couple's existing entitlements total 115% and this is how much will go to waste without effective planning.*

*Holly and Waylon therefore both draw up Wills to put a 'Widow's Loan Scheme' into effect on their death that will utilise 115% of the value of the NRB at that time. (I am assuming each of them has enough wealth to do this.)*

*If Holly dies first, the 'Widow's Loan Scheme' will use up all her existing TNRB entitlement, plus 40% of her own NRB, leaving a further 60% TNRB entitlement to transfer to Waylon.*

*If Waylon dies first, the 'Widow's Loan Scheme' will use up all of his existing TNRB entitlement, plus 75% of his own NRB, leaving a further 25% TNRB entitlement to transfer to Holly.*

*Either way, the survivor will end up with a full TNRB entitlement and none of the couple's existing entitlement will have gone to waste.*

In the case of a couple who both have an existing entitlement to a full TNRB, the amount of additional relief that can be preserved in this way will be equal to double the amount of the NRB. At current rates, this amounts to £260,000 worth of tax relief.

## Is It Worth It?

Before we look at how to use an existing TNRB entitlement effectively, it is worth pausing to consider whether we think it is worth the effort.

Before October 2007, a married couple had a potential exposure to IHT whenever their combined total wealth exceeded £300,000. The purpose of any planning designed to utilise the NRB on the first death was to double the point at which that IHT exposure began, to an effective £600,000, and thus save the couple's family up to £120,000 (at 2007/8 rates).

Now we have a starting position where most married couples only have a potential exposure to IHT when their combined total wealth exceeds £650,000. In some cases, where there is a suitable qualifying property and the couple intend to leave it, or its eventual sale proceeds, to their children, the potential exposure will only be on wealth in excess of £1m (due to the RNRB – see Section 3.4 for details).

The planning we are now considering is designed to increase the point at which the couple's IHT exposure begins to an even greater level, often as much as £975,000 or even £1.3m: PLUS whatever further exemption they can achieve with the RNRB.

Whether this is worthwhile really depends on how large an estate you anticipate the second spouse having at the time of their death. I can only leave you to judge that, but I will give you an example to think about first.

### Example
*Aaliyah and Marsha are a married couple who have both been married before and both already have an existing entitlement to a full TNRB.*

*When Marsha dies in December 2020, Aaliyah is advised there is no need to carry out any IHT planning since the property she has just inherited is worth £650,000 and is therefore covered by her NRB plus her existing TNRB entitlement.*

*However, between 2020 and Aaliyah's death in March 2031, house prices triple. [This is the same as the increase that occurred during the period of equal length, from June 1997 to September 2007, so this is entirely possible!]*

*Following a fifteen year freeze to 5th April 2024, the NRB is increased by just 2.5% each year thereafter (as per our forecasts: see Section 3.2). We will also assume the RNRB is increased at the same rate.*

*When Aaliyah dies, her property is worth £1.95m, but the NRB is just £391,000 and the RNRB is £211,000. Even after claiming her two TNRBs, this leaves £746,000 (£1.95m – 2 x £391,000 – 2 x £211,000) of Aaliyah's estate exposed to IHT, costing her family £298,400.*

*Worse still, if Aaliyah has no direct descendants who she wishes to pass her property to (not everyone does Mr Osborne!), then £1.168m (£1.95m – 2 x £391,000) of her estate will be exposed to IHT, robbing her beneficiaries of £467,200 of their rightful inheritance.*

*If only they had done some planning when Marsha died!*

Why a nephew, niece, lifelong friend, or step-child from an unmarried partnership should suffer an extra £168,800 in IHT defies all understanding!

## 6.9    USING THE TRANSFERABLE NIL RATE BAND

As explained in the previous section, many 'second time around' couples will benefit from using all or part of the first spouse's NRB plus, in some cases, their existing entitlement to a TNRB. The amount of additional relief generated in this way may be up to double the amount of the NRB, producing savings of up to £260,000 at current rates.

### *Example*
*Thomas died in March 2021, leaving his net estate worth £3m to his son Arthur (who is also Thomas's executor). Thomas was a widower who had survived two wives: Alice who died in 1985, without using any of her NRB, and Doris, who died in November 2020.*

*After claiming the TNRB to which Thomas was entitled, as well as Thomas's own NRB, Arthur is left to bear IHT at 40% on £2.35m (£3m – 2 x £325,000), i.e. £940,000.*

*However, within Thomas's estate there was a property worth £650,000 that he had inherited from his second wife Doris. Doris herself had been entitled to a TNRB as a result of a previous marriage to Tony, who had died some years ago without using any of his NRB.*

*Since Doris left the property to her husband and it was exempt anyway, both her NRB and her TNRB (from Tony) were never used. What Doris should have done was leave her property to Arthur. No IHT would have been payable on her death, as her property was covered by the sum of her NRB and her TNRB entitlement.*

*But when Thomas died later, his estate would have been worth £650,000 less, i.e. £2.35m. After deducting Thomas's NRB and TNRB entitlement, Arthur would have had to pay IHT at 40% on just £1.7m. Arthur's IHT bill would thus have been £680,000, giving him a saving of £260,000.*

*In effect, Arthur would have benefited from four NRBs instead of just two!*

### Non-Spousal Legacies

The non-spousal legacy (e.g. the one from Doris to Arthur in the above example) does not need to be one specific property. It could be a whole group of assets, or simply worded as a legacy equal to the appropriate multiple of the NRB to be paid out of the general assets of the estate.

### But What if You're Not That Well Off?

The non-spousal legacy strategy is pretty simple to follow when, like Thomas and Doris above, there are plenty of assets around. The problem for some 'second time around' married couples is they can't afford to simply give their children, or other beneficiaries, up to £650,000 when one of them dies.

The surviving spouse will need to retain sufficient assets to support them for the rest of their life including, in most cases, the family home. As we shall see, there are some planning strategies available to deal with this dilemma.

### Too Much of a Good Thing?

When including a non-spousal legacy or any other technique designed to use all or part of your NRB, in your Will, it is usually best not to word the legacy as a specific sum.

What you may wish to do instead is draft your Will so it includes a legacy equal to the appropriate proportion of whatever the NRB happens to be at the time of your death. That way, the amount of the legacy will automatically adjust in line with the NRB (when the happy day does *finally* come at last that the NRB starts to increase again!)

This may have some practical drawbacks, however. If a future Government were to drastically increase the value of the NRB, this strategy could cause some practical problems for your family.

'What's the problem,' you say: after all, you can just amend your Will if that happens. Probably, yes, and if you keep the situation under review you will be able to do this. But what happens if you no longer have legal capacity (see Section 16.15) at that time?

To guard against this possibility, you may also wish to place a 'cap' on the maximum value of the legacy.

### What About the Residence Nil Rate Band?

You will also need to factor the RNRB into your planning. It is likely that anyone with an existing TNRB entitlement will also have an entitlement to their former spouse's RNRB: although this will not always be the case, for the reasons we explored in Section 3.4. Nonetheless, where one or both of the current spouses have an existing entitlement to a previous deceased spouse's unused RNRB, this may provide scope for some further savings.

### *Example Revisited*

*Let's take the same facts as before, except we will say the property Doris left to Arthur was worth £1m and was a qualifying property for RNRB purposes. Let us also say the former spouses, Alice and Tony, each died with estates worth less than £2m.*

*None of this would alter Arthur's IHT bill of £940,000 if Doris had left her entire estate to Thomas. However, if Doris had left her property worth £1m to Arthur (instead of Thomas), it would have been fully exempted by her own NRB, her TNRB (from Tony), her RNRB and the RNRB transferred from Tony (£325,000 x 2 + £175,000 x 2 = £1m).*

*Thomas's estate would now be worth £2m, meaning he would be entitled to his own RNRB and the one transferred to him from his first wife, Alice. If his estate included a qualifying property worth at least £350,000, or the sale proceeds from such a property (see Sections 3.4 and 12.16), this would provide a further exemption of £350,000, leaving him exposed to IHT on just £1m (£2m – £325,000 x 2 – £350,000) and giving Arthur an IHT liability of just £400,000.*

In conclusion, a non-spousal legacy on the first death in a 'second time around' couple could produce savings of up to £540,000!

**If Only We'd Known About This Before!**

Don't despair if you think you've left it too late. Any of the methods described in this guide that are available to utilise a TNRB or a former spouse's RNRB can be put in place through a Deed of Variation made within two years of the relevant spouse's death. See Section 17.1 for further details.

## 6.10    ESTATE EQUALISATION

One thing you cannot do, even with a Deed of Variation, is put money into the hands of the deceased!

For a 'second time around' married couple with some existing TNRB entitlement, it is therefore vital to ensure both spouses have sufficient net assets in their own right to utilise the appropriate proportion of the NRB on their death (plus the RNRB where appropriate). As you do not know which of you will die first, nor even when this will be, it is usually advisable to share your assets equally throughout your marriage, or at least until you each have net personal assets well in excess of the required amount.

This strategy is known as 'estate equalisation' and makes perfect sense as long as you are happy your marriage will last 'Until Death Do Us Part'!

For a number of reasons, it is generally preferable for the couple to equalise their estates throughout their married life rather than rely on large transfers between them as they get older. Such transfers may render some IHT planning techniques void, although in Section 16.16 we will look at situations where they can still be effective.

As explained in Section 6.3, however, there may now be an exception to all this in cases where a married couple's combined net assets exceed £4m.

## 6.11    WILL TRUSTS

One method for using an existing TNRB is to set up a discretionary trust through your Will (see Chapter 8 for an explanation of discretionary trusts).

Assets with a value equal to the appropriate proportion of the NRB (which will otherwise go to waste – see Section 6.8), are left to the trust. The surviving spouse will be one of the beneficiaries of the trust and, in practice, can retain all the benefits of ownership of the assets within the trust. This can be achieved by ensuring the trustees exercise their 'discretion' in such a way that the surviving spouse receives the income from, and enjoyment of, the assets.

There is, however, a danger HMRC may attack this type of discretionary trust on the basis it is really a 'de facto' interest in possession trust. This would mean the trust constituted an 'Immediate Post-Death Interest' (see Section 8.12). This, in turn, would mean the assets of the trust remain in the surviving spouse's estate for IHT purposes, thus rendering this planning void.

Nevertheless, this type of Will trust should still work where the trust is genuinely discretionary in nature. This would necessitate avoiding the usual 'Letter of Instruction' to the trustees stating the surviving spouse is to receive all income from the trust. It would also be wise to ensure that other beneficiaries did, indeed, receive some trust income.

This method cannot be used to utilise a transferred RNRB. It is also generally unsuitable for IHT planning with the family home, although we will see some variations that may be suitable in Chapter 12.

> **Wealth Warning**
> Some standard 'off the shelf' Will trusts will give rise to an interest in possession and are thus of no use for this type of planning. This can even apply to standard Will trusts provided by some quite reputable organisations. As usual, this just goes to show there is no substitute for taking proper professional advice.

## 6.12   THE WIDOW'S LOAN SCHEME

Another method for utilising an existing TNRB is to leave a specific legacy of a sum equal to the appropriate proportion of the NRB (see Section 6.8) to a discretionary trust in your Will and the remainder of your estate (or most of it) to your spouse. Your spouse would be a beneficiary of the trust, together with other family members (usually).

There are a number of variations to this method but, in essence, the basic principle is that all (or most) of the deceased's assets are passed to the surviving spouse who therefore ends up owing a sum equal to the appropriate proportion of the NRB to the trust.

The 'charge scheme' is one such variation and, unlike the simple Will Trust (see Section 6.11), it is well suited to IHT planning with the family home. Under this scheme, the trust initially takes possession of the deceased's share of the family home and then takes a charge over it for a sum equal to the required proportion of the NRB. The deceased's share of the property is then passed to the surviving spouse subject to the charge.

When the surviving spouse subsequently dies, the amount of this charge is deductible from their estate (subject to the points below regarding payment of the debt), thus effectively providing relief for the TNRB that would otherwise have gone to waste (see Section 6.8).

Some experts suggest that where the 'charge scheme' is being used, the surviving spouse should not be an executor of the deceased's estate. It is not absolutely clear if this would actually be a problem, but it is certainly wise to 'play it safe' in these matters.

The so-called 'debt scheme' is a simpler variation of the 'Widow's Loan Scheme', but has some technical problems that can lead to difficulties if the main 'bread-winner' turns out to be the survivor.

Another variation that appears to avoid such technical problems is to leave the appropriate proportion of the NRB to a discretionary trust and leave the remainder of your estate to an interest in possession trust for the benefit of your spouse, rather than to your spouse directly.

As explained in Section 8.12, the interest in possession trust is entitled to the spouse exemption, but will be left owing the appropriate sum (which you need in order to utilise the existing TNRB) to the discretionary trust.

Once again, the debt due to the discretionary trust will be deductible from the surviving spouse's estate on their subsequent death (subject to the points below regarding payment of the debt).

### Wealth Warning
There is a school of thought that it may be necessary for the discretionary trust to charge interest on the loan to make the 'Widow's Loan Scheme' effective. Although some interest charged could be passed back to the surviving spouse (as a trust beneficiary), this would still lead to an Income Tax cost (see Section 8.21).

## Payment of the Debt

In most cases, it will be essential that the debt due to the discretionary trust is actually repaid out of the assets of the surviving spouse's estate (see Section 2.11). Where an interest in possession trust is used (as described above) the debt will need to be repaid from the assets of that trust.

In many cases, this will be easy to achieve by simply selling some or all of the assets of the estate (or the interest in possession trust, as the case may be) and making a suitable cash payment to the discretionary trust. In other cases, one of the alternative techniques outlined in Section 2.11 may be used instead.

As discussed in Section 2.11, there may also be some cases where the debt is structured on a sufficiently commercial basis that it can be left outstanding. This would generally require, as a bare minimum, that:

- The loan is subject to interest at a commercial rate
- The interest is actually paid to the discretionary trust (see Section 8.21 regarding the Income Tax consequences of this)
- The loan is secured
- The loan is taken over by a person or persons who do not pose a greater risk than an arms' length lender would generally be willing to accept

**Final Points**

Whichever variation is followed, the 'Widow's Loan Scheme' cannot be used to utilise a transferred RNRB.

It is a complex scheme, so professional advice is essential. Despite its name though, it does work equally well in principle for a widower.

## 6.13   WHEN AND HOW TO UNDO OBSOLETE PLANNING

For a long time before 2007, the first priority in IHT planning for married couples was to ensure the NRB was fully utilised on the first death. As discussed in Section 6.7, however, this is now the very last thing most married couples should do. (Although there are exceptions to this, as we have already seen in Section 6.8.)

Some people are therefore in the position where they have implemented some form of IHT planning that now looks to be disadvantageous. What should these people do now?

### Married Couples

Where both members of the couple are still alive and have undertaken some IHT planning through their Wills, the answer is simple: rewrite your Wills to revise your planning along the lines set out in Section 6.7.

If, however, you have undertaken some planning that involved making lifetime transfers to use up your NRB, you will be unable to reverse this and will need to wait seven years before your NRB is available again. Hopefully, there are very few people in this position as it is now over twelve years since the TNRB was introduced.

### Widows and Widowers

If you have outlived two or more previous spouses, you may find you already have the maximum TNRB entitlement even if one of your previous spouses undertook some planning to utilise their NRB. The planning carried out remains effective and should probably be left in place.

Similarly, if you were a widow or widower but have remarried since the earlier IHT planning was implemented by your previous spouse, you still have the potential to acquire a TNRB from your current spouse and the earlier planning again probably remains effective. As far as any further planning is concerned, you will be in the same position as a 'first time' couple that we examined in Section 6.7.

The same can be said if you are expecting to remarry again in the near future.

In other cases, previous steps put in place to utilise your late spouse's NRB may now be disadvantageous to your position.

If, however, your estate will clearly never exceed the NRB this will probably never be of any consequence unless, perhaps, you should win the lottery (see Section 10.16 for important advice if you play the lottery).

If earlier planning has put you at a disadvantage, you may be able to undo it if your spouse died within the last two years. A widow or widower whose spouse died within the last two years may be able to enter into a Deed of Variation (see Section 17.1) to alter the terms of their spouse's Will to benefit from the TNRB regime. This will only help if the deceased spouse utilised their NRB on death; it will not be possible to alter any lifetime transfers.

## 6.14    THE DAUGHTER-IN-LAW PLAN

I am not sure how many people would be prepared to follow this plan in practice but, in theory, it should work.

### *Example*
*Frank, a widower, is almost 90 years old. He has a huge estate, which he wishes to leave to his son, Frank Junior. Unfortunately, Frank has done no IHT planning and now realises that relying on surviving seven years may not be good enough.*

*Frank Junior is engaged to Mia, a 30-year-old, UK-domiciled, actress. However, what the family decides is that, instead of marrying Frank Junior, Mia should marry 90-year-old Frank. Shortly after the marriage, Frank gives everything he owns to Mia. This transfer is exempt under the spouse exemption.*

*A little while later, Mia divorces Frank and marries Frank Junior. She can now (if she wishes) transfer everything to Frank Junior and it will again be exempt from IHT under the spouse exemption.*

As I said, this works in theory. Like any other tax-planning strategy, this probably depends on how well it is done. To date, HMRC has not had any success challenging the validity of a marriage.

But the real problem with this plan lies in the phrase 'if she wishes'. What is there to stop Mia from running off with all of the family's money?

The above strategy can easily be adapted to pass wealth from a mother to her daughter, from father to daughter, or from mother to son.

## 6.15    THE SPOUSE BRIDGE

A spouse with a longer life expectancy can be used as a 'bridge' to transfer assets to children or other beneficiaries.

Assets are transferred to the spouse either during lifetime or on death and this transfer is tax free (subject to the points set out in Section 3.3). The spouse can then transfer the assets to the children as a potentially exempt transfer (see Section 4.3) and, as long as the spouse survives for seven years after that transfer, IHT is avoided.

In theory, any spouse will do for this strategy, including an estranged spouse who the transferor has not yet divorced, or a spouse who is not actually a parent of the children who are ultimately supposed to benefit.

### *Example*
*Tremela divorced her ex-husband many years ago and has single-handedly managed to raise her daughter Alisha, as well as building up a large portfolio of investment properties. Tragically, Tremela has found out she has only a short time to live and wishes to leave everything she owns to Alisha, who is now a young adult.*

*Tremela has been friends with Brian for many years and now decides to marry him. When Tremela dies a short time later, she leaves £325,000 to Alisha but leaves the rest of her estate to Brian. No IHT is due as everything is covered by either the NRB or the spouse exemption.*

*Brian can then give Alisha all the property received from Tremela and, as long as he survives seven years, IHT will be avoided.*

Unfortunately, there are a few possible problems with this strategy. Firstly, potentially exempt transfers of anything other than cash may give rise to CGT liabilities. However, transfers of recently inherited assets should not usually give rise to significant CGT liabilities due to the 'uplift on death' (see Section 11.2).

Secondly, where there is an informal request asking the beneficiary under a Will to transfer inherited property to another person and the beneficiary does indeed make the transfer within two years of the deceased's death, the transfer is treated as a direct transfer from the deceased to that other person.

This particular provision can be side-stepped by either making a lifetime transfer to the spouse (but see further below) or by the spouse waiting two years and a day after the deceased's death before passing the assets to the ultimate recipient. While the latter approach may mean suffering some CGT on the capital growth in the assets' values, this cost is likely to be considerably less than the IHT at risk.

Thirdly, and perhaps more importantly, there is the question of whether the transferee spouse will behave as the transferor hopes. They cannot be forced to pass the assets to the children, or the initial transfer will be ignored.

Preliminary transfers to a spouse are a perfectly good way to avoid or reduce IHT liabilities, as long as there is no obligation on the transferee spouse to make the subsequent transfer to the ultimate recipient. If, however, the arrangement for the second transfer is already in place, the initial transfer to the spouse would be disregarded and the position would revert to that given by a single transfer direct from the transferor spouse to the ultimate recipient.

This is why in the previous section we had to leave Mia to transfer assets to Frank Junior 'if she wishes'.

As explained in Section 6.14, HMRC has not yet had any success in challenging the validity of a marriage itself. A similar method that might be used to pass assets to a minor child is set out in Section 9.10.

**Further Hazards for Lifetime Transfers to Spouses**

Where the initial transfer to the spouse is a lifetime transfer then, even with no fixed arrangements for the assets to be passed to the children, there is still some risk HMRC might invoke the associated operations rules (see Section 10.19). That initial transfer would then again be ignored, resulting in the loss of the spouse exemption. How anyone could do this in the face of such a terrible tragedy as Tremela's premature death escapes me, but that is the nature of IHT!

In the more usual case of a married couple still living together at the time of the initial transfer, this risk is greatly reduced, as HMRC does not usually attack arrangements between married couples still living together.

In the case of a separated couple, or a 'marriage of convenience' like Tremela and Brian, the risk of such an attack is greater, but may possibly be avoided if the transferee retains the assets for a few years before passing them to the ultimate recipient.

Finally, it is important to remember a lifetime transfer to a spouse means foregoing the 'uplift on death' for CGT purposes (see Section 11.2), so it will often be inappropriate for investment property and other appreciating assets.

## 6.16    THE FAMILY DEBT SCHEME

A sale of an investment asset to your spouse can be used as a means to reduce the value of your estate for IHT purposes without increasing the value of theirs to the same extent.

The asset, such as an investment property for example, is sold to the spouse for any price up to its full market value. Although the transfer is not a gift, the sale still represents a transfer between spouses and is therefore exempt from both IHT and CGT.

Some form of Stamp Duty will be payable in most cases, however, and the rates involved can be quite prohibitive where residential property is used (see the Taxcafe.co.uk guide *'How to Save Property Tax'* for details). Nonetheless, SDLT can be avoided if the property is a non-residential property and is sold for a consideration not exceeding £150,000.

If you sell shares to your spouse, Stamp Duty will be payable on the sale consideration at the rate of 0.5%.

The sale consideration is left outstanding as a loan; or an 'IOU' if you like. The vendor spouse then gives the 'IOU' to their children or other intended beneficiaries. This is a potentially exempt transfer, meaning the value of the 'IOU' will be exempt from IHT if the vendor spouse survives seven years.

This provides the reduction in the vendor spouse's estate since they no longer hold either the original asset or the 'IOU'.

On the purchasing spouse's death, the value of the 'IOU' will be deducted from their estate: ***provided*** the sum due under the 'IOU' is actually paid out of the assets of their estate (see Section 2.11). This will cancel out some or all of the value of the transferred property.

This method is generally used for investment assets not qualifying for business property relief (see Chapter 7), including rental property. The debt does not fall foul of the 'artificially created debt' rules (see Section 2.11) since there is an actual sale of property from one spouse to the other and the debt is owed by the purchaser.

## 6.17    GRAB A GRANNY (OR GRANDAD)

As explained in Section 6.6, it is possible we may in future see more detailed provisions designed to restrict the TNRB and perhaps, in particular, to prevent separated couples from benefitting. This would reduce the attractiveness of some potential planning. In the meantime, however, there are some interesting planning ideas for people who are currently single.

As things stand, a surviving spouse will benefit from any unused NRB on the death of a spouse at any time, even many years before their own death. Once a person has a TNRB, they can remarry and preserve the benefit of their TNRB by following the planning strategies set out in Sections 6.9 to 6.12. Hence, a potential IHT planning measure is to marry someone with a much shorter life expectancy and very few assets, wait for them to die, and benefit from a TNRB that could ultimately save your family up to £130,000.

## 6.18    MARRIED COUPLES WITH MIXED DOMICILE

In Section 2.2, we saw that a non-UK domiciled person acquires deemed UK domicile when they have been resident in the UK for 15 or more of the previous 20 UK tax years. However, they lose their deemed UK domicile once they commence a fourth consecutive tax year of non-UK residence.

In Section 3.3, we also saw the limit on exempt transfers to a non-UK domiciled spouse would cease to apply if that spouse acquired deemed UK domicile.

This opens up some interesting planning ideas for married couples with mixed domicile.

### *Example*
*Jim is UK domiciled but has significant foreign assets. His husband Farrokh is domiciled in Zanzibar but has lived in the UK for over 20 years and therefore has deemed UK domicile for tax purposes.*

*Jim can transfer all his foreign assets to Farrokh and this transfer will be fully exempt from IHT. Farrokh could then leave the UK and would automatically lose his deemed UK domicile at the beginning of his fourth tax year of non-UK residence. All of Jim's foreign assets, now held by Farrokh, would then be free from UK IHT.*

"Couldn't Jim achieve the same result by emigrating himself?" you may ask. Yes, he could, but, as we shall see in Chapter 15, it would be much harder for him to shed his UK domicile whereas, for Farrokh, it will be automatic.

### Wealth Warning

This strategy is effective for IHT purposes, but may not be for CGT. If Farrokh is still UK resident at the time of the transfer, Jim will continue to be subject to UK CGT on the transferred assets for as long as he remains UK resident himself.

### Tax Tip

One way around this might be to make the transfer after Farrokh has ceased to be UK resident but before the end of the period he continues to have deemed UK domicile.

## 6.19   THE OPT-IN ELECTION

A non-UK domiciled person with a UK domiciled spouse may elect to 'opt-in' and be treated as UK domiciled for IHT purposes. A non-UK domiciled widow or widower who had a recently deceased UK domiciled spouse may also make an election.

Where the UK domiciled spouse is still alive, the election may be backdated by up to seven years; but can never apply to dates earlier than 6th April 2013.

Where the UK domiciled spouse is deceased, the election must be made within two years of their death and may be backdated by up to seven years prior to that date. Once again, however, the election cannot apply to a date earlier than 6th April 2013.

The person making the election must be non-UK domiciled under general principles but they are not barred from making it if they have deemed UK domicile (see Section 2.2).

Where both spouses are deceased, the personal representatives of the non-UK domiciled spouse may make the election on their behalf (subject to the time limits described above).

### Impact of Election

The effect of the 'opt-in' election is that the non-UK domiciled spouse is treated as UK domiciled for IHT purposes with effect from whichever date the election is specified to apply from (subject to the limits described above).

The election is irrevocable and hence will apply for the remainder of the electing spouse's lifetime and on their death – unless they become non-UK resident for a period of four consecutive tax years, in which case the election automatically ceases to apply.

While the election generally means the non-UK domiciled spouse is treated as UK domiciled for most UK IHT purposes, there are a few exceptions:

- Certain Government securities and similar assets with 'excluded property' status (see Section 2.2), will retain that status
- The provisions of any applicable Double Tax Treaty (see Section 2.2) are unaffected
- Double tax relief will continue to be available where the person is also subject to IHT (or a similar tax) in another country

The election does not alter the non-UK domiciled spouse's status for the purposes of Income Tax or CGT.

**Advantages of Making the Election**

- Complete exemption from IHT on all transfers from the UK domiciled spouse to the non-UK domiciled spouse during lifetime (from date on which the election becomes effective) and on death

- The ability to use an unlimited spouse exemption to transfer assets into an immediate post-death interest trust free from IHT (Section 8.12)

- The ability to obtain a full TNRB on the UK domiciled spouse's death (where the entire estate is left to the non-UK domiciled spouse)

- Other exemptions, such as the annual exemption (see Section 5.2) will not be used up by lifetime transfers to the non-UK domiciled spouse after the election becomes effective

- The ability to carry out planning mechanisms available to UK domiciled spouses (e.g. the 'spouse bridge' in Section 6.15)

- Unlimited exemption from the 'gifts with reservation of benefit' rules (see Section 4.9) on transfers between spouses after the election becomes effective

**Disadvantages of Making the Election**

- The non-UK domiciled spouse's entire worldwide estate will be subject to UK IHT (subject to the terms of any Double Tax Treaty)

- Transfers of assets, including foreign assets, by the non-UK domiciled spouse to anyone other than the UK domiciled spouse may potentially use part of the non-UK domiciled spouse's NRB and reduce the TNRB available

- The non-UK domiciled spouse would be unable to use an excluded property trust (see Section 9.13) to shelter assets they held on or after the date the election becomes effective

**Tax Tip**
The non-UK domiciled spouse could set up an excluded property trust before the election becomes effective. It is vital to ensure the election is not backdated prior to the date assets are transferred into the trust.

- The pre-owned assets charge (see Section 10.21) may apply to foreign assets enjoyed by the non-UK domiciled spouse (unless held within an excluded property trust before the election becomes effective)

- Lifetime transfers of foreign assets by the non-UK domiciled spouse may be chargeable lifetime transfers or may become chargeable lifetime transfers in the event of their death within seven years

**Tax Tip**
It is important to consider the impact of backdating any 'opt-in' election where the non-UK domiciled spouse has made transfers of foreign assets, or funds held abroad, to any person other than their spouse. It may also be worth considering such transfers before making an 'opt-in' election, although the CGT implications should also be considered where the non-UK domiciled spouse is UK resident.

## In Summary

While the decision whether to make an 'opt-in' election is something that requires professional advice, it seems fair to say, in general terms, that an 'opt-in' election is likely to be beneficial where the UK domiciled spouse has the majority of the couple's assets.

On the other hand, the election is likely to be disadvantageous where the non-UK domiciled spouse has substantial foreign assets, or may acquire them in the future (e.g. by way of their own inheritance).

## Planning Revisited

In some cases, it may be possible to adapt the planning set out in Section 6.18 so it works where the non-UK domiciled spouse has previously made an 'opt-in' election.

### *Example*
*Whitney is UK domiciled but has significant foreign assets. Her husband Bobby had a 'domicile of origin' (see Section 15.2) in Massachusetts but elected to 'opt-in' and be treated as UK domiciled with effect from 6th April 2013. Some years later, Whitney transferred all her foreign assets to Bobby.*

*In March 2021, Bobby moves to Jamaica and ceases to be UK resident. On 6th April 2025, after four consecutive years as a non-UK resident, Bobby's 'opt-in' election automatically ceases to apply. As a result, the foreign assets formerly held by Whitney are now exempt from UK IHT.*

### Wealth Warning 1
See Section 6.18 regarding the potential CGT drawbacks of this strategy, which apply equally here.

### Wealth Warning 2
Following the introduction of the statutory residence test in 2013, it is now generally more difficult to achieve non-UK residence: especially if you still have a UK resident spouse!

Having said that, it probably remains easier for Bobby to achieve non-UK residence for four years than for Whitney to achieve non-UK domicile!

### Wealth Warning 3
The strategy outlined in the example is appropriate for those who have made an 'opt-in' election some time earlier: well before leaving the UK.

If the election were made only a short time before the non-UK domiciled spouse left the UK, it is likely HMRC would seek to block this planning strategy.

# Chapter 7

# The Tax Benefits of Business Property

## 7.1 INTRODUCTION

Where the appropriate conditions are satisfied, relief is available on the transfer of relevant business or agricultural property. The two reliefs are known, quite appropriately as 'business property relief' and 'agricultural property relief'. For the rest of this guide, to save a little space, we will refer to them as 'BPR' and 'APR' respectively.

As a result of BPR and APR, it is possible to pass on many family businesses free from IHT. Care must be exercised, however, as there are a great many pitfalls awaiting the unwary. In particular, property rental businesses will very rarely qualify for relief and other businesses where the use of land or buildings by customers is one of the main elements are also at high risk. We will look at this issue further in Sections 7.5 and 7.6 and some ways to potentially resolve the problem in Sections 7.7 and 7.23.

Another major problem is caused by the rules relating to deduction of liabilities (see Section 2.11). These rules create a whole extra set of problems for business owners looking to pass their business to the next generation. In some cases, these rules may effectively wipe out the benefit of the relief. We will see an example of this in Section 7.11.

The reliefs for business and agricultural property apply, in principle, to both lifetime transfers and transfers on death, although, as we shall see in Section 7.19, there are other conditions to be met in the case of lifetime transfers.

In many cases, where available, relief is given at 100%, meaning the transfer of the business or agricultural property may potentially escape IHT altogether.

Where relief is given at less than 100%, the relief is given before applying other exemptions (such as the annual exemption or the NRB). Where relief is available at 50%, this effectively doubles the value of these exemptions.

### Example
*Cliff has an industrial building worth £662,000 on which BPR is available at the rate of 50%. He wishes to transfer the building to the Marvin-Welch Discretionary Trust. This will be Cliff's first chargeable lifetime transfer. After BPR at 50%, the chargeable transfer is reduced to £331,000. Cliff's annual exemptions for the current and previous years are still available. Deducting these (at £3,000 each) leaves a chargeable transfer of £325,000, which is covered by Cliff's NRB.*

Note that, in the above example, there is a risk IHT liabilities will arise if Cliff dies within seven years of making this transfer. We will return to the subject of BPR on lifetime transfers in Section 7.19.

Technically, no actual 'claim' is required, as these reliefs apply automatically when the relevant conditions are met. In practice, one still has to 'claim' the conditions have been met though.

**Trusts**

These reliefs also apply to the anniversary and exit charges for trusts (see Chapter 8). Naturally, the trust will need to meet all the necessary conditions, including the minimum ownership period (see Section 7.17). In practice, the trust will generally need to hold any business or agricultural property for at least two years before passing it to a beneficiary in order to obtain the relief.

## 7.2    WHEN IS BUSINESS PROPERTY RELIEF AVAILABLE?

BPR is available on transfers of business property that meet each of the following three conditions:

i)    The business concerned is a qualifying business (see Sections 7.4 to 7.7),
ii)   The asset itself is relevant business property (see Section 7.8), and
iii)  The asset has been owned by the transferor for at least the relevant minimum period (see Section 7.17)

There is no requirement for the business to be located in the UK (but see Section 7.29 regarding agricultural property).

## 7.3    JUST HOW USEFUL IS BUSINESS PROPERTY RELIEF?

There is absolutely no limit to the amount of BPR a taxpayer may claim where the qualifying conditions are met. The relief could potentially be used to completely exempt an estate worth **billions** of pounds from IHT!

An obvious piece of IHT planning is therefore to maximise the value of assets qualifying for BPR within your estate. We will return to this in Section 7.21.

But BPR isn't just for those with an existing business. The relief provides a useful mechanism to give IHT-exempt funds to family and friends, as we shall see in Section 7.26. There are even some types of investment that may qualify, as we shall see in Section 7.27.

Furthermore, it generally takes just two years for assets to achieve exemption through BPR, which is much better than the seven-year waiting period for potentially exempt transfers.

Sadly, however, it is all too easy to lose BPR by failing to meet the qualifying conditions at the appropriate time. There are some particularly nasty pitfalls to watch out for with BPR. In fact, not only is the relief very easy to lose, but this also has a tendency to happen at the point in life when IHT planning is becoming most important.

There is also the problem that some quite normal commercial structures will leave the business owner with BPR at just 50% on their most valuable asset when they could so easily have had 100%.

Furthermore, the rules on liabilities incurred to finance relievable property (see Section 7.11) mean some business owners will enjoy little or no benefit from BPR. Worst of all, refinancing an existing loan could lead to the loss of relief in some cases (see Section 7.15).

Given the importance of this relief and the ease with which it can be lost, we will now take a long, detailed look at the relevant qualifying conditions. Some of this gets quite technical but it is important for anyone wanting to benefit from what is arguably the most powerful way to save IHT.

## 7.4    QUALIFYING BUSINESSES – BASIC PRINCIPLES

For this purpose, any business is a 'qualifying business' as long as it is being carried on with a view to profit and does not consist wholly or mainly of dealing in securities, stocks or shares, or land and buildings, nor of making or holding investments (except for the holding company of a trading group).

This may not initially sound too restrictive but, as we shall see, the definition of what constitutes 'making or holding investments' can be a great deal broader than what one might normally think, especially in the case of land and buildings.

Despite this, Lloyd's underwriters generally qualify for at least some BPR and the businesses of 'market makers' or 'discount houses' on the Stock Exchange also generally qualify. As in many fields of taxation, special rules apply.

### What is a Business?

Case law suggests a business exists where at least some of the following six tests apply. Namely, the activity being undertaken:

i)   Is a 'serious undertaking earnestly pursued' or a 'serious occupation'
ii)  Is 'an occupation or function actively pursued with reasonable or recognisable continuity'
iii) Has 'a certain measure of substance as measured by the value of supplies made'
iv)  Is 'conducted in a regular manner and on sound and recognised business principles'
v)   Is 'predominantly concerned with the making of supplies to consumers'
vi)  Involves the supply of goods or services 'of a kind which, subject to differences in detail, are commonly made by those who seek to profit by them'

Where some or all of the above tests are satisfied, the activity will constitute a business and will generally qualify for BPR unless it falls under one of the exclusions outlined above.

## The Importance of the Profit Motive

Even though it may be accepted that a business exists, the intention to make a profit remains essential. The profit motive requirement means businesses like stud farms or the business activities of artists or authors may sometimes be ineligible for the relief.

> ### Tax Tip
> Preparing a credible business plan would provide valuable supporting evidence that you had a reasonable expectation of making a profit from your business. A documented annual review of the plan will also be useful, as the 'profit expectation' test must be met at the time of the eventual transfer. However, a business plan will not help if it clearly bears no resemblance to your actual behaviour.

## 7.5    PROPERTY INVESTMENT OR LETTING BUSINESSES

Unfortunately, as so often seems to be the case in UK taxation, property investment or letting businesses are generally not accepted by HMRC as qualifying businesses for the purpose of BPR.

The HMRC view is that holding investment property and collecting rent does not constitute a business for BPR purposes (although this does not seem to stop them collecting tax on income generated by this 'non-business' activity!)

Sadly, HMRC's view is supported by the fact that it was specifically stated the letting of land would not qualify for BPR during the parliamentary debates when the relevant rules were first enacted.

Doubtless, those of you with property letting businesses will think this is unfair. This is certainly what the executor of a certain Mrs Burkinyoung thought in 1995 when he made a claim for BPR on the furnished flats Mrs Burkinyoung had been letting.

Unfortunately, when the case got to court, the judge decided otherwise, holding that Mrs Burkinyoung's properties were only investments and did not constitute a 'business' for IHT purposes.

It also turns out it would not have helped the Burkinyoung family if the late Mrs Burkinyoung had instead been letting out commercial property. In another case, BPR was denied where the deceased's business consisted of letting out small industrial units. Once again, the judge held that the lettings amounted to the mere holding of investments.

### Ancillary Services

That same judge went on to say the provision of security services, heating, or cleaning as part of the terms of the lease would still not be sufficient, in his opinion, to create a qualifying business. The judge felt these services would be merely incidental to the holding of investments, even though he acknowledged such services would constitute a qualifying business if provided independently of the letting business.

### Tax Tip
Separating out ancillary services into a separate business may provide landlords with scope to get BPR on at least part of their business.

In a later case, property maintenance services were added to the list of ancillary services that would be regarded as merely incidental to the holding of investments. Again, therefore, it might be helpful to separate these out into a separate business.

## Does Size Matter?

You may think, perhaps, that the reason the cases referred to above were lost could be that the letting businesses concerned were too small. Sadly, this is not the case since, in yet another case a company letting out more than a hundred properties was still not regarded as having a qualifying business.

## Furnished Holiday Letting

I don't know where they get these judges from, or why they persist in regarding property letting as an easy and passive way to make a living. Nevertheless, as the law stands, it appears the only type of rental properties that might occasionally attract BPR are furnished holiday lettings.

The rules for BPR on furnished holiday lettings are very restrictive and far from clear. They are dependent on case law rather than any statutory definition and, just because a property qualifies as a furnished holiday let for Income Tax and CGT purposes (as explained in the Taxcafe.co.uk guide 'How to Save Property Tax'), doesn't mean it will qualify for BPR.

Historically, the view generally taken was that furnished holiday lets might be accepted as a 'business' for BPR purposes when the lettings were predominantly short-term (e.g. a week or fortnight) and the owner was substantially involved with the holidaymakers' activities.

However, following a recent spate of cases that have gone against the taxpayer, it now seems the courts are willing to support HMRC's view that furnished holiday lets will not generally qualify for BPR, even when significant services are provided to tenants.

Nonetheless, there is room for some hope as the taxpayer was successful in one recent case: although it seems the bar has been set very high when it comes to what constitutes being 'substantially involved with holidaymakers' activities'.

The successful case concerned the late Louise Graham who provided guests at her self-catering holiday flats with use of the following:

- Solar-heated outdoor pool
- Extensive well-maintained gardens
- Sauna
- Games room
- Laundry
- Barbecue area
- Guest lounge with books

All these facilities were regularly maintained. A golf buggy and bicycles could also be hired and each flat was supplied with:

- Fresh flowers
- Homemade food and drink
- Bed linen and towels
- Toiletries and cleaning materials

Furthermore, guests were provided with a welcome pack and refreshments on arrival and the property owners were on hand to help take in shopping, organise birthday and other celebrations and advise on local activities.

There was no doubt that this was a business (even HMRC accepted that), but the question in court was whether it was a business of 'making or holding investments' or whether this was outweighed by other components such as the services provided and the onsite facilities.

The taxpayer won in this case but, like me, you are probably shocked there was ever any doubt over the issue. You will be even more shocked to hear that, when the judge gave his decision, he stated this "was an exceptional case which does, *just*, fall on the non-investment side of the line."

*"Just!"* It beggars belief, but there it is. The courts seem to think you need to lavish the level of personal care given by Louise Graham before a furnished holiday let can qualify for BPR.

### Wealth Warning
Even this astonishing case is not yet settled beyond doubt as HMRC has appealed against the decision.

## Furnished Holiday Letting Summary

There is no doubt that a very high level of involvement with holidaymakers is required before a furnished holiday let might qualify for BPR. Services provided to tenants will need to be far beyond the 'normal' level where landlords merely provide maintenance and cleaning services. Significant additional facilities will need to be provided. In the vast majority of cases you simply have to accept the relief will not be available and plan accordingly.

In the rare cases where you are able to turn the property into something more like a holiday park (as Louise Graham did), you might succeed but it will be far from certain. (See Section 7.31 for a good way of testing the position)

**In Conclusion**

Investment property is highly unlikely to qualify for BPR. You will usually need to be using property in a qualifying trading business. A few furnished holiday letting properties may qualify, but this will be quite rare.

## 7.6    BUSINESSES EXPLOITING LAND (AND BUILDINGS)

A great many businesses involve the 'exploitation of land'. This is a legal term to cover any situation where the use, by customers, of land or buildings is a vital component of the business.

Before everyone panics, let me first reassure you I am not talking about businesses where the customer merely enters the land or buildings in order to be provided with goods or services. Hence, retail businesses, restaurants, cafes, health professionals, and most other trading businesses are unaffected. The problem only arises where the customer has some form of right to use the land or buildings themselves. In these cases, HMRC will often attempt to argue the business consists merely of the 'holding of an investment'.

The best defence against this argument is to show the provision of services or sale of goods is essential to the business. The customer must want the goods or services provided rather than the use of land or buildings alone. Many taxpayers have failed in BPR claims where the services provided were merely ancillary to the use of land or buildings rather than being core to the customers' needs.

There is a key distinction between land or buildings held as an investment that will generate income in its own right, as opposed to land or buildings that are an essential component integral to some other business activity. HMRC has a tendency to regard all businesses that involve the use of land or buildings by customers as being investment businesses, but this is not always the case.

Let's take a look at how the 'exploitation of land' argument has been interpreted in some specific types of business.

### Hotels
Hotels do not usually fall foul of the 'making or holding investments' rule and hence generally qualify for BPR. There may, however, be problems for hostels, guest-houses or hotels with long-term residents.

### Serviced Offices
Generally speaking, serviced offices do not qualify for BPR as the services provided are regarded as merely ancillary to the rental of the offices. In one case, the office tenants were provided with meeting rooms, receptionist, restaurant, gallery area, gym, hair salon, and social events: and yet the court *still* denied BPR on the basis that what the tenants really wanted was office space and the additional services supplied were merely incidental.

Note that, as explained in Section 7.5, if ancillary services were provided by a separate business then *that* business might qualify for BPR.

## Property Development
While dealing in land and buildings does not qualify for BPR, a property development business will qualify and both the business's own trading premises (and other assets) and the land and buildings held as trading stock will be covered by the relief.

## Livery Businesses
In a recent case, HMRC tried to deny BPR for a livery business, arguing that, if similar accommodation and services were provided to humans rather than horses, the business would be regarded as akin to a furnished holiday let and thus merely the 'holding of an investment' (see Section 7.5 regarding BPR for furnished holiday lets).

Luckily this rather peculiar analogy did not convince the judge: perhaps partly because it is difficult to envisage the owner of a furnished holiday let worming their guests, or checking them for lameness and bloating.

The late owner's son (also her executor) argued that a livery business was more akin to a children's nursery than a furnished holiday let, since the owner was responsible for the animals' health and wellbeing.

In the end, the judge accepted the business offered significantly more than the right to occupy a parcel of land and hence BPR was allowed.

## Stately Homes
Stately homes open to the public may be covered by BPR. In one case, a claim for BPR was upheld by the court when just 78% of the property was open to the public. Despite the fact that 22% of the property was closed to the public, the whole property qualified as it had to be viewed as a single asset and, furthermore, the entire exterior was important to the paying public's enjoyment of the property.

The implication is that any building, of which more than 50% is used for the public's enjoyment, as part of a commercial enterprise, might qualify for BPR.

This would surely also extend to private museums and other similar enterprises, as long as the 'profit motive' (see Section 7.4) is present.

(All is not lost where less than 50% of the property is used for business purposes, as we shall see in Section 7.9.)

## Caravan Parks
Caravan parks have occupied a lot of the courts' attention when it comes to BPR and, to date, there have been five major cases on the subject. So far, the score is HMRC 3 – Taxpayers 2.

In essence, the taxpayers lost the cases where the majority of income came from site fees or pitch fees (which are basically a form of rent) but won the cases where the majority of income came from the provision of other services or sale of caravans.

Most recently, the long and tortuous case of *George & Loochin (Stedman's Executors)* was eventually decided in favour of the deceased's executors when it reached the Court of Appeal. This case concerned a caravan park where a major proportion of the business income comprised site fees for the storage of caravans and mobile homes. However, the saving grace for this caravan park was the fact that 72% of those fees were absorbed by overheads, mainly the upkeep of common parts of the park.

Nevertheless, HMRC still argued the site fees represented income from the 'exploitation of land' and the caravan park business was thus tantamount to the mere 'holding of an investment'.

Thankfully, the judge in the Court of Appeal stated the holding of property as an investment was only one component of the business and did not prevent it from qualifying for BPR. He found it difficult to see why an active family business of this kind should be excluded from BPR just because a necessary component of the business was the holding of land.

This last judgement tells us a few things:

- An 'active' business should qualify for BPR
- Caravan parks are very much a 'borderline' case, as they are partly concerned with the exploitation of land
- You get a better quality of judge in the Court of Appeal

But seriously, any business that involves some element of 'exploitation of land' runs a risk of not qualifying for BPR.

### General Guidelines
The key to obtaining BPR in any case where the 'exploitation of land' is present is to ensure the majority of the business income comes from the provision of services and not from the mere 'exploitation of land'.

We will look further at the question of what constitutes the majority of the business income in the next section.

### Life Interests in Land
The cases where difficulty arises due to the 'exploitation of land' argument involve taxpayers who actually own that land. Naturally, this means their estate is extremely valuable, which is why the BPR claim is so important.

It has been established, however, that a taxpayer who only held a 'life interest' in land could not be held to have a business that consisted of 'making or holding investments'. That taxpayer's business therefore qualified for BPR, which was very useful since, as we shall see in Chapter 8, there are some cases where the full value of the underlying assets in which the deceased had a life interest has to be included in their estate.

This provides a possible method for ensuring that a business that could potentially fall foul of the 'exploitation of land' problem will qualify for BPR.

The drawback, however, is that BPR is only given at the rate of 50% where the transferor had a life interest in the property rather than absolute ownership (see Section 7.8).

Nevertheless, in some cases, BPR may be maximised by splitting the ownership of the business from the ownership of the underlying land and placing the land in a life interest trust. This should enable the owner to claim 100% relief on the business and 50% relief on the land when there may have been no relief at all if they had owned both the business and the underlying land outright.

### Example

*Tom owns a caravan park in South Wales. On his death, he leaves the park business to his wife Joan and the land on which the park is set to a life interest trust with Joan as the beneficiary. Tom's NRB is unused and therefore transfers to Joan (see Section 6.3).*

*On Joan's subsequent death in March 2021, her executors claim 100% BPR on the park business, worth £750,000, and 50% BPR on the park land, worth £1.3m.*

*After BPR, the chargeable value of the caravan park is thus reduced to £650,000 and this is covered by Joan's NRB plus the TNRB received from Tom: leaving no IHT to pay on the park.*

*If Joan owned both the park business and park land outright, she might not have been eligible for any BPR. The IHT arising on the park would then have been at least £560,000 (£750,000 + £1.3m - £650,000 = £1.4m x 40%).*

The drawback to this technique is it may mean 50% relief on the value of the underlying land has been sacrificed if, in fact, the business would have qualified for BPR anyway. A better approach may therefore be to only put the structure described above into place via a Deed of Variation after a BPR claim on the first spouse's death has already failed. (See Section 7.31 for further details on how to safely test the position on the first spouse's death.)

### Wealth Warning
The method described above is based on an old case that was only won in the Court of Appeal on a 2-1 majority. It is therefore possible this decision could be overturned in a later case!

## 7.7 WHAT DOES 'WHOLLY OR MAINLY' MEAN IN PRACTICE?

As stated in Section 7.4, a business will not qualify for BPR if it consists 'wholly or mainly' of 'dealing in securities, stocks or shares, or land and buildings, or making or holding investments'.

Naturally, however, it follows that while it cannot consist 'wholly or mainly' of these activities, it can still consist 'partly' of them.

**But How Much?**

Quite simply, 'wholly or mainly' means 'at least 50%'. "50% of what?" I hear you ask. Case law has sometimes, though not exclusively, interpreted the 50% test as relating to net profits. To be on the safe side, however, I would suggest trying to ensure the business consists of qualifying activities to the extent that these account for over 50% of each of the following:

- Turnover (i.e. sales)
- Gross profit
- Net profit
- Proprietor's time
- Employees' time
- Assets employed in the business (although, as we have seen already, land employed in the business may be regarded in a number of ways)

**Hybrid Businesses**

It is important to remember what is required for BPR purposes is that the business consists 'wholly or mainly' of qualifying business activities. If the 'wholly or mainly' test is met then the whole business will qualify, including those parts that are not themselves qualifying activities.

This has important IHT planning implications as it means BPR may be available in respect of an investment business component that represents a minority element of a qualifying business.

***Example***
*Ray and Dave run a property business, Kink Properties, in partnership together. Kink Properties derives around 75% of its income from property development and the remainder from property letting. While HMRC would argue that part of the business amounts to the non-qualifying activity of holding investments, the main part, property development, represents a qualifying activity. Kink Properties therefore qualifies for BPR. Furthermore, the whole business qualifies, including the investment properties.*

To get relief on the whole value of the business, it is important to ensure all the assets held by the business are actually used in the business. A completely unrelated quoted shareholding, for example, might be regarded as a non-business asset and would thus be ineligible for relief.

There is an important distinction between business assets used in a non-qualifying part of the business (like Ray and Dave's investment properties), which do attract relief, and assets that are not business assets at all (like those unrelated quoted shares), which are excluded from relief.

Assets excluded from relief are known as 'excepted assets' and we will return to this concept again in Section 7.9.

## 7.8   RELEVANT BUSINESS PROPERTY

The following types of property may qualify for BPR:

**Relief at 100%:**

i) An interest in a qualifying unincorporated business (i.e. a sole trade or profession, or a share in a partnership)
ii) Unquoted shares in a company carrying on a qualifying business
iii) Unquoted securities (e.g. loan stock) in a company carrying on a qualifying business that, either alone, or with other unquoted shares or securities, give the transferor control of the company

**Relief at 50%:**

iv) Quoted shares or securities in a company carrying on a qualifying business that, either alone, or together with other quoted shares or securities, give the transferor control of that company
v) Assets held personally by the transferor but used wholly or mainly for the purposes of a qualifying business carried on by a company under the transferor's control, or a partnership in which the transferor is a partner (or was prior to death in the case of transfers on death)
vi) Assets held in an interest in possession trust on behalf of the transferor and used wholly or mainly for the purpose of a business under the transferor's control or a business carried on by a partnership in which the transferor was a partner. (This applies only to 'interests in possession' that are deemed to form part of the transferor's estate for IHT purposes – see Chapter 8)

**Partnership**
A partnership includes a Limited Liability Partnership (LLP).

> **Wealth Warning**
> Members' capital accounts in a Limited Liability Partnership carrying on a qualifying business will qualify for BPR but members' loan accounts do not!

**Unquoted**
'Unquoted' means not listed on a recognised Stock Exchange. Shares that are only traded on the Alternative Investment Market ('AIM') are not 'listed' and thus qualify as unquoted for BPR purposes.

Shares traded on either tier of the American Nasdaq are regarded as quoted. In general, any stock market recognised by the laws of the country in which it is situated will usually be regarded as a 'recognised stock exchange' and shares traded there will therefore be treated as quoted.

The legislation refers only to whether the shares or securities themselves are quoted. HMRC's notes, however, refer to a 'quoted company'. This will seldom make any difference, but there remains the question of how to treat unquoted classes of shares or securities issued by a company that has a stock market quotation for another class of shares or securities. On a strict interpretation of the legislation, I would argue these continue to be 'unquoted', but it's not a point I would like to rely on.

## Control

An important point to note about headings (iii) and (iv) above is that it is only shares or securities that actually contribute to the transferor's control of the company that qualify for BPR. For example, a shareholder who controls a quoted company by means of voting Ordinary Shares will not be entitled to BPR on non-voting Preference Shares held in the same company. It also follows that very few securities (e.g. loan stock, etc.) will qualify for BPR.

'Control' is generally taken to mean the transferor is able to control over 50% of the voting powers on all questions affecting the company as a whole. A transferor holding 50% of the voting shares plus the right to a casting vote will also have 'control'. In deciding whether the transferor can control the requisite proportion of voting power, we can include:

- Shares held by their spouse
- Shares transferred by them or their spouse to a charity, or other exempt body, after 15th April 1976 and still held by the transferee body at any time within the last five years
- Shares treated as part of their estate or their spouse's estate (e.g. some types of 'interest in possession' – see Chapter 8)

Control need only exist immediately before the relevant transfer. The availability of BPR is unaffected by whether control is lost as a result of the transfer in question (although, of course, subsequent transfers may be affected).

### Tax Tip

When planning a transfer of shares that may result in a loss of control of the company, it may make sense to make other transfers first, such as other small share transfers or transfers of property used in the company's business falling under headings (v) or (vi) above.

### Wealth Warning

A company that is held 50/50 by two individuals is not under the control of either individual. Hence, unless those individuals are a married couple, this means there can be no relief for any property under headings (v) or (vi) above. Subject to commercial requirements, it may therefore make sense to make a slight change to the company shareholdings so that one of the individuals has control and will therefore be eligible for relief.

## 7.9 WHAT IS THE VALUE OF A BUSINESS?

For BPR purposes, the value of an unincorporated business is made up of the total value of all the assets of the business, including goodwill, less any business liabilities.

The assets and liabilities of the business are all those items a purchaser would take into account in order to ascertain a value for the whole business.

Business liabilities (like trade creditors, for example) need to be deducted in arriving at the value of the business. Loans and other liabilities are not generally deducted in arriving at the value of the business but may need to be deducted from that value for the purposes of the BPR claim. We will look at the distinction between these two types of liabilities in more detail in Section 7.12.

Money owed to a transferor by their own business cannot be included as an additional asset in a BPR claim.

Non-business property on which business loans are secured cannot be included as part of the value of the business. However, loans and other liabilities incurred to purchase or finance the business may need to be deducted from the value of the business for the purposes of the BPR claim. Again, we will look at these in more detail in Section 7.12.

**Excepted Assets**

The general rule is that BPR is not available on the value of an asset which neither:

a)   Has been used wholly or mainly for business purposes for the period of two years prior to the transfer, or the period since acquisition, if less; nor
b)   Is required for the future use of the business.

In the case of property falling under heading (v) in Section 7.8, however, the above rule is revised so that, in order to qualify for BPR, the asset in question must have either:

a)   Been used for the purpose of the business of the partnership or company throughout the two years prior to the transfer, or
b)   Replaced a similar previous asset (see Section 7.18) and the two assets taken together were used in the relevant business for a combined total period of at least two years within the five-year period prior to the transfer.

Remember, however, as discussed in Section 7.7, the asset only needs to be used in the business. In the case of a 'hybrid business' qualifying under the 'wholly or mainly' rule, the asset might be used in a non-qualifying component of the business and could still qualify for BPR.

**Buildings – Partial Business Use**

In Section 7.6, we saw that a building used at least 50% for business purposes would qualify for BPR as a result of the 'wholly or mainly' rule. In many cases, however, a smaller proportion of a building may be used for business purposes. Examples might include a dentist, doctor or vet using part of their home for an office, waiting room and surgery; or a shopkeeper using the ground floor of their three-storey house as shop premises.

In cases like this, HMRC permits a BPR claim in respect of the business portion of the property, provided that this portion is used exclusively for business purposes. This applies to claims under headings (i), (v) or (vi) in Section 7.8.

## 7.10    BUSINESS PROPERTY RELIEF FOR SHARES AND SECURITIES

In Section 7.8, we examined the conditions that need to be satisfied before shares or securities may qualify for BPR.

Just because the shares or securities do, in principle, qualify for BPR, does not necessarily mean the whole value of those shares or securities qualifies.

In order to calculate the available BPR, it will be necessary to take into account any 'excepted assets' held by the relevant company.

The definition of 'excepted assets' for this purpose is the same as the general definition given in the previous section (not the revised one for transfers under heading (v)).

### Example
*Tommy owns 60% of the share capital in Pinball Ltd, a trading company operating amusement arcades. The company has total assets valued at £1m, net of business liabilities. However, this includes £300,000 in cash held in a deposit account, which is surplus to the company's business requirements and not used in its trade.*

*The total value of Tommy's shares is £600,000. However, 30% of the company's value is attributable to a non-business asset (the surplus cash). Hence, Tommy's BPR must be restricted to £420,000, leaving £180,000 (or 30%) chargeable to IHT.*

### Goodwill

In the above example, we ignored the value of goodwill. Any goodwill in the company's business would be a trading asset and would increase the proportion of the shares eligible for BPR.

### Example Revisited
*If Pinball Ltd had trading goodwill worth £200,000, the total value of its assets would be £1.2m. The £300,000 of surplus cash would represent just 25% of the company's assets and Tommy's BPR would be increased accordingly.*

### Valuing Shares

Valuing company shares is a highly complex subject worthy of an entire book in its own right.

When valuing company shares it is necessary to take account of goodwill and all the company's liabilities. There is no distinction here between business liabilities and other liabilities such as loans. All the company's tax liabilities will also need to be taken into account (this may sometimes include the potential tax arising if it were to sell its assets at current market value: although this depends on the valuation method used).

To establish what proportion of a company's value is based on excepted assets, however, we continue to follow the principles outlined in the previous section regarding the valuation of a business.

### Example Part 3
*Let's suppose that Pinball Ltd has a £100,000 Corporation Tax liability and also owes Roger, the company's founder, £500,000: a long-term loan he gave to the company many years ago. These liabilities reduce the value of the company (including goodwill) to £600,000, but the £300,000 of surplus cash still represents just 25% of the total value of its net business assets (£1.2m).*

*Tommy's shares are now worth just £360,000 (£600,000 x 60%), but he may still claim BPR of £270,000 (£360,000 less 25%).*

## Cash On Deposit

Just because a company has cash on deposit, this does not necessarily make that cash an excepted asset. The question is whether that cash is surplus to the company's business requirements.

In a case like Pinball Ltd, it will often be possible to argue at least some of the cash is required for working capital. Exactly how much will depend on the circumstances of each case.

Cash held by a company for a specific identifiable business purpose may be included as a business asset.

### Example
*Johnny owns San Quentin Ltd, a company he originally formed to own and operate a nightclub, 'Ring Of Fire'. In August 2020, San Quentin Ltd sells Ring Of Fire for £1m. The company keeps the money on deposit because Johnny is actively looking for a new nightclub San Quentin Ltd can buy. Sadly, however, Johnny dies before the company can buy the new nightclub.*

*Johnny leaves his San Quentin Ltd shares to his son, Sue. Thankfully, full BPR is available on the shares because the cash held on deposit was earmarked for a specific business purpose.*

This example is based on a real case (but with different names – especially the boy named Sue), which the taxpayer's executors won.

In another case, however, a similar claim was denied when the executors claimed surplus funds were being held pending a suitable business opportunity. The court felt this was too vague and cash on deposit could only be counted as a business asset when it was required for a palpable business purpose. Hence, in Johnny's case, if he had decided he'd had enough of the nightclub business and was looking for another investment opportunity, BPR would have been denied.

**Tax Tip**
The key to maintaining full BPR on shares in a company holding surplus cash is to have an identifiable business requirement for that cash. This should be documented in business plans, cashflow projections, directors' board minutes, etc.

It is also worth noting the same surplus cash would not generally qualify for BPR when held personally. Hence, it may often make sense to retain business sale proceeds within a company when intending to reinvest them.

## Other Investments

Other short-term investments held by the company might be eligible for inclusion as business assets if the same rationale as set out above regarding surplus cash can be established.

Alternatively, as we saw in Section 7.7, the company may have a 'hybrid business', and the investments might therefore be business assets in their own right.

HMRC accepts the holding of investments by a company may often be part of its normal business activities, although they will still attack cases where they perceive the company is simply being used as a repository for non-business assets in order to artificially increase the amount of BPR available.

## Financing the Company

Loans and other liabilities incurred by a shareholder in order to purchase company shares, or to finance the company in some other way, may need to be deducted from the value of the borrower's shares when claiming BPR. We will look at this issue in more detail in Section 7.13; as well as the position where a shareholder lends funds to their own company.


## 7.11 FINANCING A BUSINESS

As explained in Section 2.11, liabilities incurred by the transferor to finance the acquisition, enhancement or maintenance of qualifying business property, must be deducted from the value of that property for BPR purposes.

Liabilities incurred before 6th April 2013 are exempt from this rule, but this exemption can easily be lost. We will return to this point in Section 7.15.

These rules apply equally to all forms of qualifying business property (as listed in Section 7.8). Their most frequent application will be to unincorporated businesses (sole traders and partnerships), which we'll look at in this section and the next, and company shares, which we'll look at in Section 7.13.

Nonetheless, the principles explored in this section (and in Sections 7.15 and 7.16) apply equally to all forms of qualifying business property.

### *Example*
*In 2016, Amy (who is single) borrowed £600,000 by remortgaging her house and used the money to buy a trading business, 'The Wine House'.*

*In March 2021, Amy dies. She leaves her house to her sister Adele and she leaves The Wine House to her brother Pete. By this point, her house is worth £1m and The Wine House is worth £800,000. Amy's Will specifies both beneficiaries are to bear the tax arising on their legacies.*

*The Wine House is eligible for BPR, so it can be passed to Pete without any IHT liability. However, the deemed value of The Wine House for BPR purposes is only £200,000, as Amy's mortgage must be deducted from its actual value of £800,000.*

*Amy's executors arrange for her house to be transferred to Adele subject to the existing mortgage (this satisfies the requirement for a commercial reason for non-repayment: see Section 2.11). Adele therefore acquires a house with equity of just £400,000 (£1m – £600,000). However, she will be liable for IHT on the full £1m value of the house (less Amy's NRB) because the mortgage has been set against the value of The Wine House.*

*This gives Adele an IHT liability of £270,000 (£1m – £325,000 = £675,000 x 40% = £270,000), which amounts to 67.5% of the value of her inheritance!*

These rules create an incredibly unfair result. The IHT due on Amy's house falls on Adele, but she is denied any relief for the mortgage she has taken over. She ends up facing liabilities totalling £870,000 as a result of inheriting a house worth only £1m. Meanwhile, Pete obtains a business worth £800,000 free from any liabilities at all! It seems unlikely this is what Amy would have intended.

### Practical Pointer
Business owners who have borrowed to finance their business may wish to consider adjustments to the legacies they bequeath to different beneficiaries in order to prevent such unfair results. For example, Amy could have left an additional sum of £240,000 to Adele and specified this was to be charged against the assets of The Wine House. This would have compensated Adele for being denied relief for the mortgage on Amy's house.

In addition to the unfairness seen above, these rules could also lead to the collapse of many businesses.

### *Example*
*In 2015, Dusty borrowed £1m by mortgaging her house and invested it in her business. Over the next few years, she borrowed further sums by way of personal loans, credit cards, etc, in order to fund her business.*

116

*In 2020, Dusty, who has never married, dies and leaves her entire estate to her brother Tom. At this point, her house is worth £1.2m and the other debts she incurred to fund her business total £300,000.*

*Tom will be denied any relief for the mortgage over Dusty's house or the other debts she has incurred to fund her business, so he will be left with an IHT bill of £350,000 (£1.2m – £325,000 = £875,000 x 40% = £350,000).*

*Leaving the business to one side for the moment, Tom has inherited a house worth £1.2m but faces total debts of £1.65m, made up of:*

| | |
|---|---|
| *Mortgage* | *£1,000,000* |
| *IHT* | *£350,000* |
| *Other debts* | *£300,000* |
| *Total:* | *£1,650,000* |

*Hence, even if Tom were to sell Dusty's house, he would still face liabilities of £450,000 (more after taking sale costs into account). If Tom had no significant assets of his own, this would have to be funded from Dusty's business meaning that, in all likelihood, Tom would be unable to continue trading.*

It is worth noting the amount of BPR Dusty receives is drastically reduced. If her business had been worth, say, £1.5m, she would have received BPR of just £200,000 (£1.5m less £1m mortgage less £300,000 of other liabilities).

## Business Property with a Lower Value than the Liabilities

In the last example, I assumed Dusty's business had a value in excess of the liabilities she incurred to fund it (£1.3m). Where the value of the business property is less than the outstanding liabilities incurred to finance it, the excess liabilities may be deducted from the remainder of the owner's estate.

### *Example Revisited*
*Let's take the same facts as above, but assume Dusty's business is worth just £800,000 at the time of her death.*

*The liabilities incurred to finance her business total £1.3m, but it will now only be necessary to set £800,000 of these against the value of the business. This leaves £500,000 that can be set against the remainder of her estate.*

*This reduces Tom's IHT bill on Dusty's house to £150,000 (£1.2m – £500,000 – £325,000 = £375,000 x 40% = £150,000).*

In this revised example, Dusty receives no BPR at all: since the value of her business for this purpose is reduced to nil.

I assumed throughout both versions of the example that Dusty's liabilities are eligible to be deducted from her estate (see Section 2.11).

## Inherited or Transferred Liabilities

Where a beneficiary takes over a liability secured on an inherited or transferred asset, the treatment of the liability in their estate, or on any lifetime transfers **they** make, is unaffected by the treatment applied to the transferor.

Hence, in the examples in this section, the mortgages taken over by Adele and Tom would be fully deductible from their estates if they were to die while these liabilities were still outstanding.

## 7.12 DEDUCTION OF LIABILITIES FOR UNINCORPORATED BUSINESS OWNERS

As explained in Section 7.9, business liabilities must always be deducted in arriving at the value of an unincorporated business for BPR purposes. Loans and other liabilities incurred to finance the business will only need to be deducted from the amount of BPR available when the liability was incurred after 5th April 2013 (but see Section 7.15 for further details). To see what this means in practice, let's look at a typical business.

### Example Part 1
*Duffy has her own business with qualifying business assets worth a total of £2m. She also has the following liabilities:*

| | |
|---|---|
| *Trade creditors* | *£200,000* |
| *Business overdraft* | *£20,000* |
| *Long-term business loan* | *£300,000* |
| *Hire purchase liability on own car* | *£10,000* |
| *Hire purchase liability on employees' cars* | *£25,000* |
| *Income Tax on business profits* | *£30,000* |
| *Mortgage on her home* | *£500,000* |
| *Loan from her brother Warwick* | *£250,000* |

*The trade creditors are a business liability and must therefore be deducted from the value of the business.*

*In most cases, a business overdraft is an integral part of the business, meaning it would usually need to be taken into account in order to ascertain a value for the business and is therefore a business liability. There will be some cases where this does not apply, but we will assume the overdraft is a business liability in this case.*

*The long-term business loan is not classed as a business liability for BPR purposes. This is because a purchaser looking to buy the business would not usually take over the loan. The loan therefore only needs to be deducted from the value of the business if it was taken out after 5th April 2013. In this case, we will assume the loan was taken out in 2012.*

*It is questionable whether Duffy's own car is an asset of the business. While she may use it for business purposes, a purchaser looking to buy the business is unlikely to want to buy the car. Hence, as the car is not a business asset, the hire purchase liability on it does not need to be deducted from the value of the business.*

*The employees' cars are assets of the business: they will (most likely) transfer with the employees who are, in turn, an integral part of the business. Hence, the hire purchase liabilities on these cars are business liabilities and must be deducted from the value of the business.*

*Duffy's Income Tax bill is a personal liability. It does not matter that it has arisen on business profits; it will not need to be deducted from the value of her business.*

*Duffy's mortgage will only need to be deducted from the value of her business if it was taken out after 5th April 2013 and has been used in any way, directly or indirectly, to finance her business. In this case, we will assume the mortgage was taken out in 2008, has not been varied in any way since then, and has been used to finance Duffy's business.*

*Duffy borrowed the money from her brother in 2014 and used it to purchase some business assets and reduce her business overdraft. This loan will therefore need to be deducted from the value of Duffy's business for BPR purposes.*

Having established the status of each of Duffy's liabilities, we will now look at the position on a transfer of value before 17th July 2013. (This will still be relevant in some cases, such as where Duffy made a lifetime transfer before 17th July 2013.)

### Example Part 2
*Let us assume Duffy transferred her business into trust in June 2013. As the transfer took place before 17th July 2013, the liabilities that need to be deducted are limited to business liabilities only, as follows:*

| | |
|---|---|
| *Trade creditors* | *£200,000* |
| *Business overdraft* | *£20,000* |
| *Hire purchase liability on employees' cars* | *£25,000* |
| *Total:* | *£245,000* |

Duffy will therefore be entitled to BPR of £1.755m (£2m - £245,000). The other liabilities listed above are excluded and can be deducted from the general assets of her estate on her subsequent death.

We will now compare this with the position arising on a transfer of value after 16th July 2013.

### Example Part 3
*Let us now assume Duffy did not make the transfer described under Part 2 above, and subsequently dies in December 2020. The facts in Part 1 remain unaltered.*

*In addition to the business liabilities described above, any further liabilities incurred after 5th April 2013 that have been used, directly or indirectly, to finance the business must also now be deducted for BPR purposes. This leads to the following deductions:*

| | |
|---|---|
| Trade creditors | £200,000 |
| Business overdraft | £20,000 |
| Hire purchase liability on employees' cars | £25,000 |
| Loan from Warwick | £250,000 |
| Total: | £495,000 |

*While they were incurred to finance her business, the long-term business loan and mortgage on Duffy's home do not need to be deducted because they were taken out prior to 6th April 2013.*

*The loan from Warwick will have to be deducted, however, as this liability was incurred after 5th April 2013.*

*Duffy's BPR will be reduced to £1.505m (£2m – £495,000). Her family's IHT bill will be increased by £100,000 because the loan from Warwick can no longer be deducted from the general assets of her estate (£250,000 x 40% = £100,000).*

The position will get even worse if Duffy subsequently refinances either her long-term business loan or her mortgage. Let's return to the example one last time to see the effect of this.

### Example Part 4
*In 2018, Duffy remortgaged her house for £800,000 and used the new loan to pay off both her old mortgage and her long-term business loan. All other facts outlined in Part 1 above remain the same at the time of her death in 2020. The liabilities to be deducted from the value of her business for BPR purposes are now as follows:*

| | |
|---|---|
| Trade creditors | £200,000 |
| Business overdraft | £20,000 |
| Hire purchase liability on employees' cars | £25,000 |
| Mortgage | £800,000 |
| Loan from Warwick | £250,000 |
| Total: | £1,295,000 |

*Duffy's BPR is reduced to just £705,000 (£2m – £1.295m). None of the liabilities listed above can be deducted from the general assets of her estate. Compared with the position before July 2013 (Part 2), this will cost her family an extra £420,000 in IHT.*

See Section 7.15 for further details on the perils of varying a loan taken out before 6th April 2013.

### 7.13    DEDUCTION OF LIABILITIES FOR COMPANY OWNERS

As explained in Section 7.10, when calculating the value of shares that qualify for BPR, all of the issuing company's liabilities need to be taken into account. The owner of the shares will also need to deduct liabilities incurred after 5th April 2013 that they have used to directly or indirectly finance their shareholding or maintain or enhance its value.

To demonstrate these principles in practice, let's look at a similar example to the one we used in Section 7.12 but, this time, the qualifying business property is company shares.

### Example Part 1

*Robbie owns all the shares in a trading company, Old Swinger Ltd. We will assume the value of the company before taking account of any liabilities is £2m (in practice, valuing company shares is a more complex process than this). The company also has the following liabilities:*

| | |
|---|---|
| *Trade creditors* | *£200,000* |
| *Business overdraft* | *£20,000* |
| *Long-term business loan* | *£300,000* |
| *Hire purchase liability on Robbie's car* | *£10,000* |
| *Hire purchase liability on employees' cars* | *£25,000* |
| *Corporation Tax due* | *£30,000* |
| *Loan from Robbie's brother Mark* | *£250,000* |
| *Total:* | *£835,000* |

*All these items are company liabilities and must therefore be taken into account in establishing the value of the company and Robbie's shares. In this case, we will assume it is appropriate to simply deduct them from the value described above, leaving a net value for Robbie's shares of £1.165m (£2m – £835,000).*

*(I am assuming Robbie's car is a company asset: i.e. a company car. If it was his own private car then neither the car nor the hire purchase liability on it would be taken into account)*

*In 2008, Robbie mortgaged his house for £500,000 in order to buy his shares in Old Swinger Ltd. As this liability was incurred before 6th April 2013, it does not need to be taken into account for BPR purposes.*

*Hence, as things stand, the value of Robbie's shares for BPR purposes is the same (£1.165m) in the case of a transfer of value either before or after 16th July 2013.*

It can readily be seen that the rules applying to transfers of value after 16th July 2013 will generally have less impact on company owners than other business owners.

However, company owners still remain vulnerable to the perils of varying existing loans taken out before 6th April 2013 (see Section 7.15).

### Example Part 2

*In 2018, Robbie remortgaged his house for £800,000 and used the new loan to both pay off his old mortgage and lend £300,000 to Old Swinger Ltd to enable the company to repay its long-term business loan. All other facts, as outlined in Part 1 above, remain the same at the time of his death in December 2020.*

*The value of Robbie's shares remains unaltered (£1.165m). The company has paid off its long-term loan but has simply replaced this liability with another: the debt due to Robbie. However, Robbie's estate now includes the £300,000 debt due from*

*Old Swinger Ltd as an additional asset. This asset is not eligible for BPR (see below).*

*Robbie's new mortgage was taken out after 5th April 2013, so any part used, directly or indirectly, to finance the purchase of his shares, or enhance their value, must be deducted for BPR purposes and cannot be deducted from the general assets of his estate.*

*The £500,000 used to repay the original mortgage has been used indirectly to finance Robbie's shares and is thus caught by these rules. This sum must therefore be deducted from the value of Robbie's shares, reducing his BPR to £665,000 (£1.165m – £500,000).*

*As explained above, the £300,000 Robbie loaned to the company did not enhance the value of his shares, which was the same before and after he made the loan. Hence this part of his new mortgage can still be deducted from the general assets of his estate.*

*On the other hand, the loan has become an additional chargeable asset in its own right, so there is no overall IHT saving.*

*The change in Robbie's position caused by the remortgaging can be illustrated as follows:*

|  | *Before* | *After* |
|---|---|---|
| ***Chargeable Assets:*** | | |
| *Shares in Old Swinger Ltd* | *£1,165,000* | *£665,000* |
| *Loan to Old Swinger Ltd* | *-* | *£300,000* |
| | *£1,165,000* | *£965,000* |
| ***Less Deductions:*** | | |
| *Business property relief* | *£1,165,000* | *£665,000* |
| *Mortgage* | *£500,000* | *£300,000* |
| ***Net\**** | *(£500,000)* | *Nil* |

*\* - the net sum available to be deducted from the general assets of Robbie's estate*

*As we can see, the remortgaging will cost Robbie's family an additional £200,000 (£500,000 x 40%) in IHT.*

## Loans to Your Own Company

In Part 2 of the example, we saw the impact of lending money to your own company. From the company's perspective, the borrowed funds will enhance its value but this will be matched by the liability due to you. Hence, there is no overall impact on the company's value.

You will have a new asset: the debt due to you from the company. This will need to be included in your estate. A debt due to you from your own company, often known as a 'director's loan account', is a separate asset in its own right and is highly unlikely to attract BPR. The treatment of director's loan accounts is examined further in Section 7.22.

In summary, lending money to your own company will not generally provide you with any additional BPR and will not immediately save any IHT. Naturally, however, there are many other good reasons why you might lend money to your company and we will revisit this topic in Section 7.14.

**Rights Issues**

In Section 7.21, we will look at the potential benefits of rights issues for increasing the amount of BPR available to a company owner. In that section, it is assumed the company owner has substantial private wealth available to fund the rights issue.

Funding the rights issue by way of borrowings taken out after 5th April 2013 will not work so well, however.

*Example Part 3*
*The facts are the same as in Part 2 above except that, instead of lending £300,000 to the company, Robbie subscribes for additional shares by way of a rights issue.*

*The value of the company has now increased to £1.465m (£1.165m + £300,000) because there is no debt due to Robbie to match the liability that has been paid off.*

*Robbie will not have acquired any additional asset: he will only have enhanced the value of his existing shareholding. As a result of this, however, the entire £800,000 of Robbie's new mortgage must now be deducted from the value of his shares for BPR purposes because it has all been used, directly or indirectly, to finance the purchase of his shares, or enhance their value. The end result is thus as follows:*

**Chargeable Assets:**
*Shares in Old Swinger Ltd*      *£665,000 (£1,465,000 – £800,000)*

**Less Deductions:**
*Business property relief*      *£665,000*
*Mortgage*      *Nil*
**Net**      *Nil*

*The overall position remains the same as in Part 2 and, once again, the remortgaging will have cost Robbie's family an additional £200,000 in IHT.*

## 7.14 BORROWING TO INVEST IN YOUR BUSINESS

The examples in Sections 7.11 to 7.13 demonstrate the fact that new borrowings used to finance your business, by any means, will not give rise to any immediate IHT savings.

Refinancing or varying earlier borrowings used to finance your business will often lead to additional IHT costs and should be avoided wherever possible.

Naturally, however, financing your business will usually have other benefits and it is hoped the value of your business will increase as a result. This may lead to some indirect IHT savings as future growth in your business's value will be sheltered by BPR whereas future growth in funds or investments held privately outside the business would be fully exposed to IHT.

In other words, the real benefit lies in making sensible commercial investments through the medium of a qualifying trading business and thus increasing your BPR as you grow your business (provided such investments do not endanger the business's trading status – see Section 7.7).

## 7.15    LIABILITIES INCURRED BEFORE APRIL 2013

As explained in Sections 2.11 and 7.11, liabilities incurred before 6th April 2013 are exempt from the rules we have been looking at over the last few sections. However, any variation in the terms of such a liability will make it a new liability for these purposes and will mean it must be deducted from the value of the relevant qualifying business property.

We have seen the disastrous consequences in several examples already, but it is vital to understand, in addition to a complete refinancing of those existing liabilities, those same consequences may arise in the event of other, less significant, variations in the terms of the liability, such as:

- Changes to the term (period) of a loan
- Changes in the security for a loan
- A change from fixed interest to variable interest, or vice versa (unless such a change is already part of the existing terms)
- Additional advances on the same loan account

The last point is not entirely certain but it is far safer to arrange for additional advances to be treated as a separate loan account. While the additional advances would still be subject to the new rules, the exempt status of the existing balance should be protected.

Simple changes in the interest rate on a loan should not cause any problems: provided such changes are within the original terms of the loan.

An important issue, as yet unresolved, is whether a change in the lender that is beyond the borrower's control (e.g. where one bank takes over another's mortgage book) will lead to the loan being treated as a 'new liability'. I would argue strongly that this does not create any 'new liability' as it must surely have been within the terms of the original contract (since it does not require the borrower's consent), but only time will tell.

## 7.16    MULTIPLE TRANSFERS

Over the past few sections, we have seen how liabilities incurred after 5th April 2013 to finance qualifying business property must be deducted from the value of that property on a transfer of value. This applies to any chargeable transfer, including:

- Transfers on death
- Chargeable lifetime transfers (see Section 4.2)
- Potentially exempt transfers becoming chargeable on the transferor's death within seven years (see Section 4.5)
- Trust anniversary and exit charges (see Sections 8.18 and 8.19)

Once a liability has been taken into account on one chargeable transfer, it cannot be taken into account again on another transfer made by the same transferor (except where the earlier 'transfer' was a trust anniversary charge). Remember, however, that a potentially exempt transfer only becomes a chargeable transfer if the transferor dies within seven years.

### Example
*In 2014, Woody mortgaged his house for £1m and used the money to purchase shares in a trading company, Movenelo Ltd. In 2020, Woody gives his shares in Movenelo Ltd to his elder daughter, Bev. This is a potentially exempt transfer.*

*In 2027, Woody dies, leaving his remaining estate to his younger daughter, Kelly.*

*If Woody died within seven years of his gift to Bev, that gift will have become a chargeable transfer and his mortgage will have to be taken into account for BPR purposes. Kelly will then be denied any relief for the mortgage.*

*If, on the other hand, Woody was still alive on the seventh anniversary of his gift to Bev, that gift will have become fully exempt. Kelly will then be entitled to claim a deduction in respect of Woody's mortgage, saving her £400,000 (£1m x 40%) IHT.*

I have assumed in this example that Woody's mortgage will meet the necessary conditions for a deduction, as explained in Section 2.11.

### Tax Tip
Where liabilities have been incurred to purchase, enhance, or maintain qualifying business property, full relief for those liabilities can be restored by making a potentially exempt transfer of the relevant business property and then surviving seven years.

## 7.17 THE MINIMUM HOLDING PERIOD

To qualify for BPR, the relevant property must have been owned by the transferor for a minimum of two years prior to the transfer.

There is an exception to this requirement where the property replaced other qualifying property (see Section 7.18) and both assets taken together had been owned by the transferor for at least two years out of the five-year period preceding the transfer. This effectively provides a form of rollover relief for business assets for IHT purposes.

When a widow or widower inherits business property, the ownership period for this purpose includes the ownership period of their deceased spouse.

**Wealth Warning**

A transferor spouse's previous ownership period is **not** included in the case of a lifetime transfer of business assets.

Additionally, the minimum ownership period requirement is ignored when two successive transfers of the same property take place within two years and:

i)   the earlier transfer qualified for BPR,
ii)  the second transfer would otherwise qualify for BPR, and
iii) at least one of the two transfers occurred on death

## 7.18   REPLACEMENT BUSINESS PROPERTY

The replacement of relevant business property by other relevant business property has been referred to a few times in the preceding sections. Broadly, this means on a disposal of the original business property, the same value was reinvested in new qualifying business property.

The replacement business property does not need to be in the same kind of business as the original business property, nor does it need to be the same type of property. For example, an individual could sell an unquoted manufacturing company and reinvest the proceeds in a partnership share in a hotel business.

Provided all the other necessary rules are met, BPR may still be available even when more than one replacement has taken place. Hence, in the preceding sections, where I refer to 'the two assets taken together', this could also apply to three or more assets, each of which replaced their predecessor.

Where a taxpayer relies on a replacement to qualify for BPR, the amount of relief available is generally restricted to the amount that would have been available had the replacement not taken place. For the specific purposes of this rule, however, the following changes are disregarded:

* The formation, alteration or dissolution of a partnership
* The acquisition of a business by a company controlled by the former owner of that business (a.k.a. an 'incorporation')

## 7.19   EXTRA RULES FOR LIFETIME TRANSFERS

Where BPR applied on a lifetime transfer and the transferor dies within seven years, some extra conditions must be satisfied for BPR to also apply at the time of the transferor's death. The conditions are:

i)   The transferee must continue to own the original transferred assets throughout the period from the original transfer to the 'relevant date' (see below)
ii)  The original transferred assets must continue to be relevant business property for BPR purposes on the 'relevant date'

Where the transferee retains only part of the original asset at the 'relevant date', BPR continues to apply to that part, as long as condition (ii) is satisfied.

## The 'Relevant Date' and the 'Relevant Period'

For the purpose of the rules described in this section, the 'relevant date' is the date of the transferor's death or, if earlier, the transferee's death. The 'relevant period' is the period under condition (i): i.e. the period from the original transfer to the 'relevant date'. Of course, the 'relevant date' and 'relevant period' are themselves only relevant if the transferor dies within seven years of the original transfer.

The conditions set out above mean it is generally necessary for the assets to be qualifying business property in the transferee's hands at the time of the earlier of the transferor or transferee's death. This does not apply if the original assets were shares or securities that were either already quoted at the time of the original transfer, or remained unquoted throughout the 'relevant period'.

> ### Wealth Warning
> Where a transferee has a minority holding of unquoted shares, these will cease to be relevant business property if the company obtains a quotation. This could result in a 40% IHT bill if the transferor dies within seven years of the original transfer.

## Replacement Assets

The transferee may retain their BPR entitlement if they dispose of the original assets and acquire replacement assets (as defined in Section 7.18). Qualifying agricultural property (see Section 7.29) also qualifies as a replacement asset for these purposes.

The following further conditions must be met:

a) The replacement assets must be acquired within three years of the transferee's disposal of the original assets
b) Both the transferee's sale of the original assets and their acquisition of the replacement assets must take place on 'arm's length' terms (see Section 2.1)
c) The whole consideration received on the sale of the original transferred assets must be expended in acquiring the replacement assets
d) The transferee must own the replacement assets at the 'relevant date' unless the transferor dies first and within the 'allowed period' (see below)
e) Apart from the 'allowed period', either the original transferred assets or the replacement assets must be owned by the transferee throughout the 'relevant period'
f) The replacement assets must be relevant business property in the transferee's hands at the 'relevant date' (except as noted below)

## The Allowed Period

The three-year period under condition (a) begins when the transferee enters a binding contract to sell the original assets. Fortunately, it is only necessary for them to enter a binding contract to acquire the replacement assets within the requisite period: completion can take place later if necessary. (There's more on binding contracts coming up in Section 7.20)

This three-year period, which is known as the 'allowed period', can extend after the transferor's death, so that the replacement may sometimes take place after the transferor dies. For these purposes, condition (f) is amended so that the replacement assets need to be relevant business property in the transferee's hands when the transferee acquires them.

The legislation seems to suggest only one replacement is allowed under these circumstances, unlike other 'replacements', as considered in Section 7.18.

### Tax Tip

What all this means is, if you receive qualifying business property in a gift from someone else, you may find yourself with an IHT bill if you sell that property within seven years. However, if you can wait at least four years before selling the gifted property, you will have the opportunity to restore your BPR by acquiring replacement business property if your benefactor should pass away unexpectedly.

## Gifts with Reservation

A lifetime transfer of qualifying business property could still be a 'Gift with Reservation of Benefit' (see Section 4.9). This would mean the property effectively remained in the transferor's estate and IHT would be payable if the property did not qualify for BPR at the time of their death.

In particular, excessive salary payments to the transferor could make the transfer a 'Gift with Reservation'. (I.e. excessive salary paid to the transferor following the transfer of a business, partnership share, or shares or securities in a company.) The same would apply to other benefits provided in excess of a normal commercial level, including excessive pension contributions.

## Lifetime Transfers Becoming Chargeable on Death

If the transferee loses the BPR on a transferred asset, as explained above, then IHT will be payable if the transferor dies within seven years. Additional IHT may also be payable on a transferor's death when the transferred asset only qualifies for BPR at 50%. In both cases, any other available reliefs, such as the annual exemption, may be taken into account.

Where the original transfer was a chargeable lifetime transfer (e.g. to a trust), only that transferee will be affected by any loss of BPR.

Where the original transfer was a potentially exempt transfer, the loss of BPR means the whole of the transferor's estate must be recalculated on the basis set out in Section 4.5, but without the BPR originally claimed on the transfer.

## 7.20   HOW TO PRESERVE BUSINESS PROPERTY RELIEF

For anyone with a qualifying business, BPR is incredibly valuable. The trouble is you need to qualify for the relief at the moment a transfer takes place. That moment may be death in many cases and this carries some inherent problems.

Firstly, it is generally pretty unpredictable when this will be. Secondly, it may be some time after you cease to be interested in running a business. Most people will want to retire at some point and, unfortunately, this will often result in the loss of their BPR.

### Selling Up

As soon as you have a binding contract for sale, you are, for IHT purposes, no longer regarded as owning the asset being sold. Instead, you are regarded as owning a right to the sale proceeds. That right is generally not a qualifying asset for BPR purposes. Hence, at one stroke of a pen, you can lose your BPR and substantially increase your family's IHT bill in the event of your death.

### *Example*

*Eddie owns an unquoted trading company, Cochran Ltd. The company is Eddie's only asset so, as things stand, Eddie has no need to worry about IHT.*

*Eddie gets an offer from a French company, Aznavour S.A., to buy Cochran Ltd for £10.325m. He decides to accept the offer, so he flies to Paris, takes the Metro to Aznavour S.A.'s offices and signs a binding contract to sell his company.*

*Leaving the office, Eddie looks the wrong way crossing the street and steps in front of a bus. IHT bill: £4m!*

**This example is based on a true story** and readily demonstrates the ease with which BPR can be lost and the dire consequences that may result. An entrepreneur like Eddie might have been intending to reinvest his sale proceeds in a new business venture and hence might have regained the protection of BPR within a few weeks by virtue of the 'replacement property' rules we examined in Section 7.18. Perhaps Eddie should have considered taking out insurance to cover the IHT risk during this short interval!

When an individual who has sold a qualifying business within the last three years gets a little more warning of their demise, the 'replacement property' rules might provide an answer.

### Tax Tip
The protection of BPR can generally be maintained if the taxpayer reinvests all the sale proceeds from qualifying business property into new qualifying business property within three years.

### Exceptions to the Loss of Business Property Relief on Sale
A binding contract for sale will not result in a loss of BPR if the contract is:

a) For the sale of an unincorporated business to a company that is to carry on that business where the purchase consideration is wholly or mainly shares or securities in that company, or

b) For the sale of shares or securities in a company for the purposes of reconstruction or amalgamation

### Liquidation and Winding Up
BPR is lost on a company's shares if the company is in liquidation or being wound up. There is an exception to this, however, if the winding up is being carried out as part of a scheme of corporate reconstruction or amalgamation (e.g. a company reorganisation or merger of two companies).

### Retirement
BPR is lost as soon as a partner retires from a qualifying partnership business. Any capital the retired partner leaves in the business is simply regarded as a loan and is ineligible for BPR.

One way to avoid this problem is for the partner to continue in partnership, but with a very small profit share. (Remaining in partnership does, of course, have commercial implications, which should also be considered.)

When a sole trader retires there is no business so there can be no BPR. The answer here may be to take on a partner and then, at a later date, to 'semi-retire' – i.e. reduce to a very small profit share in the same manner as described above.

A taxpayer owning qualifying shares or securities in a trading company can happily retire without any loss of BPR as their position depends on their shareholding and not on whether they actually participate in the company's business.

### Tax Tip
Incorporating the business prior to retirement may sometimes be a good way to preserve BPR.

### Buy-Out Clauses on Death: A BIG NO-NO!
It is common business practice for business partners to enter into an agreement whereby their executors will sell their partnership share to the surviving partners in the event of their death.

Similar agreements are also often used by shareholder/directors of unquoted companies whereby their executors sell their shares back to the company, or to their fellow directors, in the event of their death.

While these agreements make a good deal of commercial sense, from a BPR perspective, they represent a disaster waiting to happen. This is because, at the moment of death, a binding sale contract will come into force and the estate will not hold relevant business property but, as we saw above, will instead hold a non-qualifying right to sale proceeds.

To avoid this problem, it is essential to avoid any form of agreement that may form a binding contract on the death of a partner or director.

## Cross Options

A better alternative is to use non-coterminous cross options. In other words, the business partners should enter into an agreement whereby, in the event of a partner's death, their executors will have an option to sell the deceased's partnership share and the surviving partners will have an option to buy it.

Similarly, private company directors would enter into an agreement whereby, in the event of a director's death, their executors will have an option to sell the deceased's shares or securities in the company and either the company itself or the surviving directors will have an option to buy them.

To be on the safe side, it is wise to ensure the options are 'non-coterminous'. Broadly, this means the option to purchase and the option to sell may only be exercised at different times. (E.g. the deceased's executors must exercise the option to sell within six weeks of the deceased's death and the surviving business partners, or directors, must exercise the option to purchase more than six but less than twelve weeks after the deceased's death.)

HMRC has specifically confirmed this approach is acceptable in the case of a business partnership and there is no reason to suppose the same principles would not be equally valid in the case of unquoted company shares or securities.

Using cross options will therefore preserve any BPR entitlement while also satisfying the original commercial objective of allowing the deceased's share of a business to be 'bought out'.

## Other Approaches for Partnerships

HMRC has confirmed the following methods for dealing with a deceased partner's share of a business will preserve any BPR entitlement available:

- Partnership ceases on death, partnership assets to be realised and deceased partner's estate receives appropriate share of proceeds
- Partnership continues and deceased's estate represents the deceased
- Partnership share falls into deceased's estate with surviving partners having an option to purchase at either a valuation or an agreed formula-based price
- The deceased's partnership share accrues to the surviving partners but the deceased's estate is entitled to payment at either a valuation or an agreed formula-based price
- Cross options (as explained above), which must be exercised within a set period following the partner's death

## 7.21    MAXIMISING BUSINESS PROPERTY RELIEF

Where an individual owns and controls a qualifying trading company, the whole value of that company could effectively be exempt from IHT. As that individual nears the end of their life, it may make sense to ensure the value of the company is maximised.

Furthermore, any assets held personally by the individual and used in the company's business would only qualify for 50% BPR. Again, it might make sense to ensure these were held in the company.

The savings that could be achieved can be illustrated with an example.

### *Example*
*Madge is a very wealthy old woman. Among her many assets is her unquoted trading company, Ciccone Ltd. She also owns a CD pressing plant worth £10m, which is used by the company.*

*Ciccone Ltd is currently worth £4m. This value takes account of the fact the company owes £2m for the purchase of new equipment and has a bank overdraft of £1.5m.*

*If Madge were to die with things as they stand, her personal representatives would be able to claim BPR as follows:*

| | |
|---|---|
| *Ciccone Ltd: £4m @ 100%* | *£4,000,000* |
| *Pressing Plant: £10m @ 50%* | *£5,000,000* |
| *TOTAL* | *£9,000,000* |

*Realising she isn't immortal after all, Madge decides to undertake some IHT planning. First, she transfers the pressing plant into the company. She is able to avoid CGT on this transfer by using a 'holdover relief' election. SDLT is, however, payable on the market value of the property. In this case, the SDLT amounts to £489,500.*

*Madge then uses £4m out of her substantial private wealth to subscribe for further new shares in Ciccone Ltd. This enables the company to pay off the bank overdraft, the debt for the new equipment and the SDLT on the property transfer.*

*Ciccone Ltd will now be worth £17.5m and, after just two years, the whole of this value will be covered by BPR.*

*The overall value of Madge's estate will be virtually unchanged except for the £489,500 paid in SDLT. However, this simple piece of planning will save her family £3.6m in IHT!*

Note that it will take two years for Madge's new shares in Ciccone Ltd to qualify for BPR. The transfer of the pressing plant will provide an immediate saving.

**Tax Tip**
New shares issued by way of a rights issue are treated as part of the original shareholding for the purposes of BPR. Hence, a new investment into an existing qualifying trading company, which is structured as a rights issue, may be eligible for full BPR immediately.

**Practical Pointer**
Although the transfer of the pressing plant in the above example can be carried out free of CGT, there may be other important tax consequences if the company subsequently sells the property. The potential advantages or disadvantages of holding property through a company are covered in depth in the Taxcafe.co.uk guide *'Using a Property Company to Save Tax'*.

**Wealth Warning**
The IHT planning undertaken by Madge worked because her company was in debt and was using the pressing plant in its business. If, on the other hand, she had injected so much capital into the company that it had a surplus in excess of its usual trading requirements, there would have been a restriction on her BPR under the 'excepted assets' rules (see Section 7.10).

The restriction would have operated by reference to the amount of the 'non-trading' surplus as a proportion of the company's total net assets. If the surplus were large enough, the company might even have failed the 'wholly or mainly' test (see Section 7.7) and thus ceased to qualify for BPR altogether!


## 7.22 DIRECTOR'S LOAN ACCOUNTS

Most small company owners have a director's loan account with their company. This account represents money due to them from their company (a credit balance) or money they owe to their company (a debit balance).

Director's loan accounts can arise in several ways, including cash injected into the company by the director, cash withdrawn, or an accumulation of non-cash transactions such as unpaid salary, dividends, or rent.

The IHT impact of a director's loan account depends on whether we are looking at a credit balance or a debit balance.

**Credit Balances**
A debt due to you from your own company is a completely separate asset to your company shares. Furthermore, it is highly unlikely this asset will qualify for BPR. As explained in Section 7.8, it is only debts in the form of securities that actually contribute to your control of the company that qualify for BPR.

A credit balance on a director's loan account can, however, readily be converted into a qualifying asset for BPR purposes simply by issuing new shares to yourself in place of the balance on your loan account. If this is done by way of a rights issue then, as explained in Section 7.21, the new shares are treated as part of the original shareholding for the purposes of BPR and may therefore qualify for relief immediately.

There is also the problem that, as a separate asset, your director's loan account may pass to a different beneficiary on your death. This may cause a few practical difficulties in some cases, and may not be what you would ideally like to happen, so it will be sensible to make a specific provision to deal with your director's loan account in your Will.

Alternatively, a director's loan account may sometimes be a useful way to provide your spouse, or another beneficiary, with a source of tax-free income. For example, you could leave company shares qualifying for BPR to one of your children, but leave your director's loan account to your spouse. Future company profits could then be used to repay the director's loan account, giving your spouse an effective source of tax-free income. This is a tax efficient structure but is probably only suitable where the surviving family members are happy to co-operate.

A director's loan account has other advantages during your lifetime, when it is probably preferable to investing in additional shares. As with many things, there are different factors to weigh up and it is perhaps only as you grow older that you might wish to convert your director's loan account into shares. For some of the lifetime benefits of a director's loan account, see the Taxcafe.co.uk guide *'Using a Property Company to Save Tax'*.

### Debit Balances
A debt due from you to your own company will enhance your company's value provided the debt is recoverable (i.e. you have sufficient private assets to repay the debt). Relatively small balances that have arisen through normal everyday transactions should not affect the company's status for BPR purposes. However, large balances may effectively become investment assets in the company's hands, and could either be 'excepted assets' (see Section 7.9), or may even threaten the company's qualifying status under the 'wholly or mainly' test (Section 7.7).

As with any other liability, the director's loan account will need to be repaid out of the assets of your estate in order to be deductible on your death.

Debit balances on director's loan accounts may also have Corporation Tax consequences for the company, as well as personal tax consequences for the director. See the Taxcafe.co.uk guide *'Small Business Tax Saving Tactics'* for further details.

### 7.23  SHELTERING INVESTMENTS WITH BUSINESS PROPERTY RELIEF

BPR on company shares may be reduced, or possibly lost altogether, if a non-trading asset, such as an investment property or quoted share portfolio, were transferred into the company. (Such a transfer may also give rise to CGT liabilities – plus SDLT in the case of a property.)

However, as we have already seen, there would nevertheless remain the possibility of arguing that a 'hybrid business', qualifying under the 'wholly or mainly' principle (see Section 7.7) existed, so that the investment property or quoted share portfolio might be sheltered from IHT within the trading company. But how far can we push this?

If investments are simply being dumped into a trading company, HMRC is unlikely to accept the 'hybrid business' argument and, as we saw in Section 7.7, may argue the company is simply being used as a repository for non-business assets.

The important distinction to remember is that investments can only be sheltered within a trading company qualifying for BPR if they form part of the company's business. A random cobbled together collection of non-trading investments will not be good enough.

The best way to make use of the trading company 'shelter' would therefore be to build an investment 'arm' to the company's business over several years.

It would be vital to ensure this part of the business remained comfortably less than 50% of the company's overall business, bearing in mind the various possible tests set out in Section 7.7.

To maintain full BPR on the company's shares, its investment business 'arm' would need to be an integral part of the company's overall business and it is important to reflect this in the company's records, including management accounts, directors' board minutes, cashflow projections, etc.

### Example
*After making the transfer of the pressing plant and subscribing for new shares, which we saw in Section 7.21, Madge begins to make some quoted investments within Ciccone Ltd. She runs the entire enterprise as a single business, ensuring that management accounts, directors' board minutes and other company documentation all record the fact that the investment arm is an integral part of Ciccone Ltd's business.*

*A few years later, the total value of the company is £35m, including £10m worth of investments and trading assets worth £25m.*

*By building the investment portfolio within Ciccone Ltd instead of privately, Madge has reduced her IHT exposure by another £4m.*

A similar approach could also be taken to shelter investments from IHT within a trading partnership.

It would be difficult for a sole trader to achieve the same result, however, as HMRC would probably view them as having two businesses: one qualifying for BPR and one not. Nevertheless, this problem might perhaps be overcome if the 'investments' were an integral part of the same business.

135

**Tax Tip**

One good way to argue that investments are an integral part of any business is to make investments in companies operating in the same industry. These investments will provide the investor with valuable information on their competitors, including access to their competitors' shareholders' meetings, and there is therefore a strong argument this can be regarded as an integral part of the business.

**Wealth Warning 1**

Under the 'wholly or mainly' test for BPR purposes, a company could still qualify with just under 50% of its activities being non-trading activities. However, for the purposes of a number of CGT reliefs, including entrepreneurs' relief and holdover relief on a gift of shares, the company may lose its trading status if just 20% of its activities are non-trading activities.

This may have significantly adverse consequences for the company's shareholders. The criteria to be used for this 20% test would broadly follow the same headings examined in Section 7.7 and are thus potentially extremely wide.

The loss of entrepreneurs' relief could result in extra CGT of up to £100,000 for each shareholder on a sale of shares in the company. We will look at the importance of holdover relief in Chapter 11.

**Wealth Warning 2**

If making investments via a trading company, it is important to ensure the company's Memorandum and Articles of Association permit this activity. Any activity not so permitted is strictly illegal and thus cannot be regarded as part of the company's business.

## 7.24   CHANGING THE BUSINESS TO SAVE INHERITANCE TAX

It is worth bearing in mind that a business only needs to qualify for BPR throughout the two-year period before the transfer. Hence, the business owner could build up a valuable non-qualifying business over many years and then change it into a qualifying business later. If the owner survives at least two years after the change, they can avoid IHT on the business.

*Example*

*Steve has built up an unquoted property investment company, Tyler Properties Ltd, over many years. He is now 80 years old and wishes to retire. In early 2020, Steve retires and his daughter Liv takes over the running of the company. Steve continues to own the company and Liv is paid a salary.*

*Liv immediately begins to change the company's business to one of property development. This process is completed by March 2021. Sadly, in May 2023, Steve dies and leaves Tyler Properties Ltd to Liv. As the company had carried on a qualifying trading activity for the previous two years, the shares left to Liv are fully covered by BPR and no IHT is due.*

The change in the company's business activity may give rise to some additional Corporation Tax costs. However, where the change takes place gradually, over a number of years, these should not be too severe.

Remember also that the change in activity does not need to be absolute, as it is only necessary for the company to pass the 'wholly or mainly' test (see Section 7.7) during the last two years prior to the transfer.

For IHT purposes, Steve would also have been able to claim BPR on a lifetime transfer of his Tyler Properties Ltd shares any time after the company had been carrying on a qualifying business for two years.

However, this would mean Liv would need to continue the qualifying business for up to another seven years in order to retain BPR (see Section 7.19). This could also lead to a CGT liability for Steve on the share transfer if the company still held any investment assets at that time.

## 7.25   BUSINESS SUCCESSION PLANNING

From a tax perspective, the last thing a dying person should do is sell a business that qualifies for BPR!

The day before the sale, the business would have been completely covered by BPR and available to pass on to their family free of IHT. The day after the sale, the proceeds would be completely exposed to IHT, resulting in the loss of up to 40%.

This is on top of any CGT that arose on the sale. As we shall see in Chapter 11, CGT could also generally be avoided if the family sold the business shortly after the original owner's death.

In practice, unfortunately, and much to HMRC's delight, it will often be necessary to sell the business before the owner's death. Very often, a large proportion of a business's value can be lost when its proprietor dies. After all, it is better to let HMRC take 40% of a great deal than to deny them their share of very little.

Ideally, business succession planning is something that should be looked at much earlier on, when the original proprietor is still hale and hearty and looking forward to a well-deserved retirement. We will return to some of the relevant practical issues involved in passing on a business in Section 10.18.

If a 'deathbed sale' situation does arise, however, one way to avoid the pitfalls described above would be to sell the business in exchange for unquoted shares in a trading company. Full BPR would then be preserved and CGT can also generally be avoided.

## 7.26    SMALLER SHAREHOLDINGS

*Any* shareholding in an unquoted trading company qualifies for 100% BPR. This includes shares in AIM companies. The problem is when one considers the generally volatile nature of unquoted shares, combined with the minimum two-year holding period, putting your wealth into these types of assets just to save IHT is a pretty risky business. Nevertheless, under the right circumstances, it is certainly something to consider. Let's look at an example.

### Example
*Noel wins a substantial sum on the National Lottery. "Great," his brother Liam says, "how 'bout helpin' me out with me business then?" Noel agrees to give Liam £100,000 to help get his new business started. However, if Noel simply gives Liam the money, this will be a potentially exempt transfer and if Noel dies within seven years, it will have to be brought back into his estate.*

*So, what Noel does instead is to subscribe for shares in Liam's company, Wonderwall Ltd. After just two years, the Wonderwall Ltd shares will qualify for BPR and Noel can then give them to Liam free from IHT (subject to the points set out in Section 7.19).*

## 7.27    THE AIM EXEMPTION

I've said it enough times but I know you think it's too good to be true, so here it is again: shares traded on the Alternative Investment Market ('AIM') are eligible for 100% BPR. In other words, IHT really is voluntary and here's how to avoid volunteering in five easy steps:

- i)    Sell everything you've got unless it already qualifies for BPR or APR at 100%
- ii)   Put £325,000 on deposit (perhaps more – see below)
- iii)  Buy an annuity to give yourself sufficient guaranteed income to get by on (this step is optional but sensible)
- iv)   Put everything else into a portfolio of AIM shares
- v)    Survive two years

Widows and widowers with a full TNRB entitlement can increase the deposit under step (ii) to £650,000. Parents and grandparents may be able to exclude their home from step (i) if it will qualify for the RNRB (see Section 3.4), or add equivalent funds to the deposit under step (ii) if the downsizing provisions apply (see Section 12.16).

Too drastic for you? Perhaps, but the point to remember is, although AIM shares are classed as 'unquoted' for most tax purposes, including BPR, they are still traded on the London Stock Exchange and are thus effectively liquid assets (albeit that, due to the relatively low level of trading, it can sometimes be difficult to sell AIM shares at a fair price).

Are they risky? Well, yes, all investments are risky, but AIM shares have often outperformed the FTSE. By 2017 there were approximately 950 companies quoted on AIM with a combined market value of over £100 billion.

Furthermore, the risk is substantially reduced if you invest in a portfolio of shares and there are financial products available to enable you to do this with professional fund managers choosing your AIM investments for you.

The fund managers will monitor the performance of your investments and will make changes to the portfolio to protect your investment and your BPR. Such changes can usually be made without any loss of BPR due to the replacement property rules (see Section 7.18).

And you can afford a bit of risk anyway can't you? Think about it – if you lose, say, 20% of your investment, but save 40% in IHT, your family are still better off aren't they?

Better still, you can even eliminate the risk altogether by investing in a protected IHT service with a built-in life assurance policy. If your investment has fallen in value when you die, the life policy will pay out the shortfall. The life policy itself can be made tax-efficient by being written into trust (see Section 10.14).

All you need do is survive the requisite two years. You can then leave your family up to 67% better off, even if your AIM portfolio has performed badly!

Naturally, a scheme like this does not come cheap and the fund managers' charges can be quite expensive. Furthermore, the life assurance premiums will typically absorb any income from the investment: and you will still have to pay Income Tax on any dividends paid by the AIM companies in your portfolio that total in excess of your 'dividend allowance' (see Appendix A).

However, under the right circumstances, it could be well worth bearing these costs for the sake of the ultimate 40% tax saving. For an elderly person with surplus funds, the potential to avoid IHT after surviving just two years represents a huge incentive.

Furthermore, anyone investing the proceeds from the sale of other qualifying business property within the last three years could obtain BPR immediately, thus exempting their entire investment from IHT even if they die shortly afterwards.

And it's worth remembering an investment in AIM shares is not locked away permanently. If your circumstances change and you need to realise some of those funds, which are no longer 'surplus' to requirements after all, you can simply sell some of your AIM portfolio. This makes an AIM portfolio very attractive to anyone who wishes to save IHT without actually giving any of their money away. The portfolio provides a means to protect some of your wealth from IHT when you are unsure whether you can genuinely afford to live without it.

On the other hand, in view of the costs inherent in a protected AIM portfolio investment, a wealthy person with funds that are quite definitely surplus to requirements and a life expectancy of well over seven years might do better to simply give that surplus away and take out term life insurance to cover the risk of a premature death within seven years.

Nevertheless, while the full five-step plan outlined above may not be for you, there could still be a place for some AIM shares in your IHT planning strategy.

### Wealth Warning 1
While AIM shares are eligible for BPR in principle, it remains important that the companies in which you invest are themselves carrying on qualifying businesses. This will, however, include AIM companies with a 'hybrid business' that passes the 'wholly or mainly' test (see Section 7.7).

### Wealth Warning 2
If your AIM shares get a full listing, your BPR will be lost (unless you control the company). Having said that, if this does happen, you will probably have made a nice profit, so it wouldn't be all bad would it?

### Wealth Warning 3
Capital gains and dividends received on AIM shares are subject to CGT and Income Tax respectively in the normal way. There are no special reliefs applying to AIM shares for these taxes.

## 7.28 AIMING TOO HIGH

As with any other form of qualifying business property, any liabilities incurred after 5th April 2013 and used, directly or indirectly, to purchase qualifying AIM shares must be deducted from the value of those shares for BPR purposes in the event of a transfer of value.

This means it is no longer possible to obtain additional BPR by borrowing against other assets to purchase AIM shares.

In this context, it is important to bear in mind HMRC takes a very broad view of what is meant by 'indirectly'.

### *Example*
*Ella owns a house worth £1.5m and has savings and investments totalling £1.2m. In 2020, she sells her investments and invests the proceeds, together with her savings, into qualifying AIM shares. (I have ignored CGT on the sale of her investments for the sake of illustration, but this needs to be taken into account.)*

*A short time later, Ella mortgages her house for £1m. She gives £600,000 to her grandchildren and uses the remaining £400,000 to replace some of her savings: to assist in funding her mortgage and provide her with a bit of a 'cushion'.*

According to HMRC's guidance, Ella should be treated as having used £400,000 of her mortgage to indirectly finance the purchase of her AIM shares, restricting her BPR to £800,000 (£1.2m – £400,000).

Their logic is that Ella could have achieved substantially the same result by investing just £800,000 of her savings in AIM shares and taking out a mortgage of £600,000 to provide funds to give to her grandchildren.

As always, HMRC's guidance is not actually the law, but it can often be persuasive and, until the matter is actually tested in court, it would be wise to operate on the basis that their interpretation is correct. In other words, it would be sensible for someone in Ella's position to restrict their AIM investment to the amount they can actually afford without taking on any additional borrowing.

## 7.29    AGRICULTURAL PROPERTY RELIEF

APR applies in a broadly similar way to BPR. The following types of property may be covered:

i)   Agricultural land or pasture
ii)  Buildings used for the intensive rearing of livestock or fish
iii) Stud farms
iv)  Farmhouses, cottages and other farm buildings
v)   Woodlands

Property under (iv) or (v) must generally be occupied on a basis ancillary to property also occupied under (i), (ii) or (iii); although buildings used to grow indoor crops, such as mushrooms, may qualify in their own right without the need for any additional agricultural land.

The relief applies to agricultural land anywhere in the UK, the European Economic Area ('EEA'), the Channel Islands, or the Isle of Man. The EEA comprises the 27 member states of the European Union plus Iceland, Liechtenstein and Norway.

To qualify for APR, the land or buildings must either have been:

a)    Occupied (i.e. used) by the transferor for agricultural purposes for a period of at least two years prior to the date of transfer, or
b)    Owned by the transferor and used for agricultural purposes (by anyone) for a period of at least seven years prior to the date of transfer

Occupation by a company controlled by the transferor is treated as occupation by the transferor for the purposes of (a) above. Occupation by a partnership is treated as occupation by the partners.

APR is given at rates of 50% or 100%, depending on the exact circumstances of the transfer and subject to the usual raft of provisions designed to prevent abuse. It is essential that agricultural activities are being carried out on the land at the time of the transfer. Furthermore, the relief is restricted to the 'agricultural value' of the land or property. This is the value of the land or property if transferred subject to a condition it must remain in agricultural use permanently.

Any excess value may be eligible for BPR in some cases. Where the transferor is actively farming the land themselves, this will usually qualify as a trading activity for BPR purposes.

Farming syndicate arrangements are available to provide IHT shelters for investments of £200,000 or more.

A separate IHT deferral relief is available for woodlands in the UK or the European Economic Area that do not qualify for APR.

### Agricultural Liabilities

The rules set out in Sections 7.11 to 7.16 apply equally to liabilities incurred to finance agricultural property, woodlands, or (where appropriate) shares and securities in companies carrying on these activities.

### 7.30 FARMHOUSES

If you ever discuss IHT in your local pub or golf club, some bright spark is bound to tell you they have avoided IHT by buying a farm.

For a start, the mere fact they are around to make this bar room boast means they have not actually avoided IHT yet. More specifically, the problem with a lot of so-called 'farmhouses' is they are really just a country house with some farmland nearby. This alone is not enough to secure APR.

A normal size farmhouse occupied by a working farmer is indeed eligible for APR but it is essential the house is 'of an appropriate character' and occupied for the purposes of farming throughout the two years prior to the relevant transfer (or seven years where occupied by someone other than the owner).

To be occupied for the purposes of farming, the house must be occupied by the person with day-to-day responsibility for running the farm (e.g. a farm manager). A farm owner with only limited involvement in the day-to-day running of the farm does not occupy their home for the purposes of farming. So, simply buying an old farmhouse isn't necessarily enough to claim APR.

Of course, the fact the farmhouse doesn't qualify does not necessarily preclude the rest of the farm from qualifying, so our bar room braggart may not be entirely wrong, but this will generally only be a small comfort, as the majority of the value will usually be in the house.

Even when a farmhouse does qualify for APR, the relief is restricted to its 'agricultural value': the value it would have if sold subject to a covenant requiring it to remain in agricultural use. In some cases, there will be a substantial difference between this and the house's open market value and the excess will not be eligible for APR. Whether any of the excess value is eligible for BPR will depend on the exact circumstances of the case.

The major problem for genuine farmers is that the house must be occupied for the purposes of farming throughout the two years prior to the relevant transfer (or seven years where occupied by someone other than the owner). Elderly farmers who are seeking to retire should therefore consider passing the farmhouse to their children while it still qualifies for relief.

## 7.31    THE SAFETY NET

Given the numerous and highly complex conditions that must be satisfied to obtain BPR or APR, the matter will often be in doubt when the business owner dies.

If the owner simply leaves the business or agricultural property to their surviving spouse, the matter will still not be resolved as this transfer will usually be exempt anyway. However, if the deceased left the property to a discretionary trust in their Will, HMRC would need to examine the case and, hopefully, the matter will soon be resolved. But how does this help?

If BPR or APR is denied, there should be time to appoint the assets to the surviving spouse free from IHT (see Section 17.3). The tax is at least deferred and the executors will know where they stand. Furthermore, the surviving spouse may have time to correct whatever defects were in the property so there is a better chance of claiming relief on their subsequent death.

If it turns out that full BPR or APR *is* available on the first death, there is a chance to do some further planning, as outlined in Sections 7.32 and 14.2.

## 7.32    MAKE HAY WHILE THE SUN SHINES

If a person dies leaving property that is fully exempt under BPR or APR, there is a strong argument to suggest it would be wise to pass this property directly to the deceased's children, rather than risk any possibility that the relevant relief may be lost before the deceased's surviving spouse or partner also dies.

BPR or APR could be lost during the surviving spouse or partner's lifetime due to either a change in legislation or a change in the nature of the business.

In many cases, the fear of losing the relief may place unwelcome constraints on the business. By passing the business directly to the next generation, such constraints are effectively removed (although the problem will of course eventually return).

This approach will not suit every family, of course, and most people will want to be sure their spouse or partner is financially secure before they are happy to pass the family business straight to their children.

For those who literally are 'making hay', i.e. running the family farm, it is often a good idea to pass the farmhouse directly to the children on the first spouse's death since APR may subsequently be lost if the surviving spouse is unable to run the farm on their own.

Furthermore, for all types of business, passing the business directly to the children (or other ultimate beneficiaries) on the first death may help to ensure the widow or widower's estate does not exceed £2m on the second death, thus preventing the loss of their RNRB due to tapering (see Section 3.4).

# Chapter 8

# IHT Planning With Trusts

## 8.1 WHAT IS A TRUST?

In its simplest form, a 'trust' is an arrangement under which someone is given the legal title to an asset and is 'trusted' to hold that asset on behalf of one or more beneficiaries.

Trusts have a long and honourable history as a well-established mechanism for protecting the vulnerable, such as widows, orphans or disabled people. They originated in the Twelfth Century when crusaders would entrust their assets to another person before setting off to fight in the Holy Land.

### Some definitions:

**'Trustee'** - The person trusted to hold the asset
**'Beneficiary'** - The person on whose behalf the asset is held
**'Settlor'** - The person who transferred the asset into the trust
**'Absolutely'** - When assets finally leave the trust and become property of the ultimate beneficiary we say the beneficiary holds those assets 'absolutely'
**'Testator'** - A deceased person who left a valid Will (which may have been used to set up a trust)

Very often, the settlor will also be a trustee. Legally, there is nothing to prevent the settlor from also being a beneficiary, although this usually renders the trust ineffective for IHT planning purposes and can also give rise to some unwanted CGT liabilities on the transfers.

### Settlements and Settled Property
In legal parlance (and within tax legislation), the act of putting assets or funds into a trust is generally referred to as a 'settlement'. When a trust is created, this is also referred to as a 'settlement'.

The assets held within the trust are known as 'settled property'. Every time new assets or funds are put into the trust a new item of 'settled property' is created. Each item of 'settled property' has its own separate identity for IHT purposes and this is especially important when there are changes to the IHT treatment of trusts.

### Example
*On 20th March 2006, Marc set up the Jeepster Discretionary Trust and transferred £1m into it. On 25th March 2006, Marc transferred another £1m into the trust. Although there is only one formally constituted trust, it contains two distinct items of 'settled property', one settled on 20th March 2006 and one on 25th March 2006.*

It is important to remember IHT law applies not only to a trust in its entirety, but also to each individual item of settled property within that trust. In our example, the Jeepster Discretionary Trust is one settlement containing two items of settled property.

A single trust may hold settled property subject to an interest in possession while other property is held on discretionary trust. For IHT purposes, each item of settled property is treated according to the relevant rules relating to that particular item of property.

A trust may therefore be regarded as an envelope, which may contain any number of different items of settled property of differing types.

In most cases, for the sake of simplicity, we will generally assume that each trust has only one type of settled property. Always remember, however, that IHT law applies to each item of settled property in its own right.

Fundamental changes were made to the IHT treatment of trusts in 2006. These changes have far-reaching consequences and it will therefore often make a critical difference whether property was 'settled' before or after the date of the change.

Naturally, when planning for the future, we will only be concerned with the current regime and any potential future changes. Nonetheless, as we shall see later in this chapter, many people will also still be affected by the earlier rules.

Before we move on to look at some of the useful IHT planning techniques that trusts provide, we need to understand more about trusts and how they are treated for tax purposes.

## 8.2   WHAT TYPES OF TRUST ARE THERE?

In essence, there are really only two kinds of trust: an 'interest in possession trust' and a 'discretionary trust'. The distinction between these two main types of trust revolves entirely around whether any beneficiary is entitled to enjoy an 'interest in possession' in any of the settled property within the trust. We will look at what constitutes an 'interest in possession' in Section 8.3. We will also look at what constitutes a discretionary trust in Section 8.4.

For IHT purposes, it is necessary to further sub-divide the two main types into a number of other categories, as follows:

- Bare Trusts
- Charitable Trusts
- Bereaved Minors' Trusts
- Pre-22/3/2006 Interest In Possession Trusts
- Disabled Trusts
- Immediate Post-Death Interests
- Transitional Serial Interests
- 18 to 25 Trusts
- Post-22/3/2006 Interest In Possession Trusts
- Discretionary Trusts

While there are only two fundamental types of trust, each of the ten categories listed above is subject to different rules for IHT purposes.

The question of whether there is an 'interest in possession' in trust property nevertheless remains a crucial factor in determining how the trust will be treated for IHT purposes. Every item of settled property will either be subject to an 'interest in possession' or will be held on discretionary trust.

Various other factors then need to be considered in order to determine which of the categories listed above each item of settled property falls into.

As explained in Section 8.1, a single trust may hold items of settled property that fall into two or more different categories. Hence, we may sometimes get a sort of 'hybrid' trust subject to different rules on its different parts.

Before April 2008, there was another category of trust, an 'accumulation and maintenance trust', which was exempt from the 'relevant property' regime. Such trusts had until 5th April 2008 to convert to a different type of trust, failing which they became a relevant property trust (see Section 8.15).


### 8.3    WHAT IS AN INTEREST IN POSSESSION?

Whenever a specific individual is beneficially entitled, for a specified period, to the income from, or to otherwise enjoy, an asset within a trust, that person has an 'interest in possession'.

Where more than one person is to share the income or enjoyment of the assets for a specified period, this is also an interest in possession. The income may be shared in any proportion specified in the Trust Deed.

If, however, the trustees have discretion over the income paid to the beneficiaries, this would make the trust a discretionary trust.

### Example
*Nicole transfers several rental properties into the All Saints Trust. Under the terms of the trust, the annual rental profits must be paid to the beneficiaries as follows:*

- *Half to Nicole's sister, Natalie*
- *The first £10,000 of the remainder to her friend, Melanie*
- *The remaining balance to her niece, Shaznay*

*Each beneficiary's interest is an interest in possession because each of them receives a specific defined amount under the terms of the Trust Deed that is not dependent on the discretion of the trustees.*

### Life Interests
Where a beneficiary is entitled to an interest in possession for the remainder of their life, we refer to this as a 'life interest' (sometimes known as a 'liferent'). A trust subject to a life interest is often referred to as a 'Life Interest Trust'.

Generally speaking, the IHT treatment of a life interest trust is exactly the same as any other interest in possession trust.

### The Remainder

The 'remainder' is a term used to describe a right to assets that comes into force after an interest in possession ends.

The most common example is when a person leaves a life interest in property to their spouse with the remainder to their children. This means on the spouse's death the property passes absolutely to the children.

### Reversion to Settlor

It is possible to create an interest in possession trust where the remainder interest reverts to the original settlor. This, in itself, does not invoke the 'Gift with Reservation' rules (Section 4.9) as long as the settlor is excluded from any benefit during the period the interest in possession exists (in practice, as discussed in Section 9.8, the settlor's spouse would usually also need to be excluded).

### Income Tax Treatment

All other things being equal, an interest in possession trust is generally to be preferred whenever possible as it enjoys a more beneficial Income Tax regime than a discretionary trust. See Section 8.21 for further details.


## 8.4    DISCRETIONARY TRUSTS

A discretionary trust is basically any trust, or part thereof, where no person is entitled to an interest in possession. The trustees have discretion to decide who to allow the enjoyment of the trust's assets, who to pay the income of the trust to, and how much.

There is usually a defined class of beneficiaries from whom the trustees can choose, such as 'all my grandchildren', for example.

It is possible for a discretionary trust to have just one beneficiary, as long as there is a theoretical possibility of there being at least one other additional beneficiary at some time and the trustees have discretion over whether, and when, to pay out income.

The assets of a discretionary trust will always be 'relevant property' (see Section 8.17) unless the trust qualifies as:

- A bereaved minor's trust (Section 8.9),
- An 18 to 25 trust (Section 8.14),
- A disabled trust (Section 8.11), or
- A charitable trust (Section 3.5)

## 8.5    INHERITANCE TAX REGIMES FOR TRUSTS: AN OVERVIEW

In essence, there are three IHT regimes for settled property within trusts:

- The relevant property regime,
- Trust property included in the beneficiary's estate, and
- Exempt trusts

Where settled property falls into the relevant property regime, it is subject to IHT charges in its own right, as detailed in Sections 8.17 to 8.20. Such settled property is referred to as 'relevant property' for IHT purposes.

Most other categories of settled property are treated as if they belong absolutely to the beneficiary and are included in the beneficiary's estate for IHT purposes, as explained in Section 2.6.

The scope of the third regime, 'exempt trusts', was severely curtailed by the changes made by Gordon Brown in 2006 but, as the name implies, it provides complete exemption from IHT for certain types of trust.

The various categories of trust fall into these three regimes, as follows:

**Relevant Property:**
> Discretionary Trusts
> Post-22/3/2006 Interest in Possession Trusts (Note 1)
> 18 to 25 Trusts (Note 2)

**In Beneficiary's Estate:**
> Pre-22/3/2006 Interest in Possession Trusts
> Disabled Trusts
> Immediate Post-Death Interests
> Transitional Serial Interests
> Bare Trusts

**Exempt:**
> Bereaved Minors' Trusts
> 18 to 25 Trusts (Note 2)
> Charitable Trusts

This table is naturally a simplification of the position, but hopefully useful.

**Notes**
1.    A new interest in possession created on or after 22nd March 2006 that does not qualify under any other category of trust will fall into the relevant property regime. Typically, this will now occur in the case of most lifetime transfers into trust, or new interests in possession coming into force on the termination of a previous interest.
2.    18 to 25 trusts are effectively exempt until the beneficiary attains the age of 18 and then fall into the relevant property regime thereafter.

## 8.6    TRANSFERS INTO TRUST

### On Death
Transfers into trust made on the transferor's death are generally chargeable to IHT in the same way whatever type of trust is involved.

The regimes described in the previous section determine how the settled property is treated later; they do not usually alter the amount of IHT arising on the transferor's death.

The only exceptions are charitable trusts and the fact the spouse exemption applies to an immediate post-death interest for a surviving spouse (see Section 8.12). In all other cases, transfers into trust arising on death form part of the estate in the normal way and will be subject to IHT as usual.

### Transfers on Death and the Residence Nil Rate Band
Transfers of qualifying property, on death, into a trust for the benefit of one or more of the deceased's direct descendents, will qualify for the RNRB, where available, provided one of the following types of trust are used:

- Bare Trust
- Bereaved Minors' Trust
- Disabled Trust
- Immediate Post-Death Interest
- 18 to 25 Trust

### Lifetime Transfers
As we saw in Section 4.2, most lifetime transfers into trust are now chargeable lifetime transfers. Lifetime transfers to disabled trusts or bare trusts are, however, potentially exempt transfers and transfers to charity are exempt.


## 8.7    THE TRUST HIERARCHY

All trusts must take their place in what I call the 'Trust Hierarchy'. Every trust will be categorised as the highest type within the hierarchy for which it qualifies. For example, a trust that qualifies as an Immediate Post Death Interest (ranked sixth in the hierarchy) cannot be an 18 to 25 Trust (ranked eighth) even if it would otherwise qualify.

The trust hierarchy is as follows:

1. **Charitable Trusts**
2. **Bare Trusts**
3. **Bereaved Minors' Trusts**
4. **Pre-22/3/2006 Interest in Possession Trusts**
5. **Disabled Trusts**
6. **Immediate Post-Death Interests**
7. **Transitional Serial Interests**
8. **18 to 25 Trusts**
9. **Relevant Property Trusts**

Readers will note that two of our categories from Section 8.2 are absent here. Discretionary trusts and post-22/3/2006 interest in possession trusts (not falling into any other category) will both be relevant property trusts.

The first step in our trust hierarchy deals with Charitable Trusts, which have exempt status.

We will now proceed to examine each of the remaining steps of our trust hierarchy in turn. Remember throughout this process that any trust that qualifies at one point in the hierarchy cannot also qualify lower down the hierarchy.

> **Tax Tip**
> As we shall see in the sections that follow, several categories of trust must be created immediately on the settlor's death. However, in Chapter 17, we will see both Deeds of Variation and distributions from most trusts made within two years of the settlor's death will be treated as if they had occurred immediately on death. Hence, in practice, most of the trusts that in theory need to be set up immediately on death can often be set up any time within two years afterwards.

## 8.8 BARE TRUSTS

Assets that are simply held in someone else's name are held on 'bare trust', sometimes also known as an 'absolute trust'. A bare trust only exists where the beneficiary has full beneficial ownership of the trust assets and has an immediate and absolute right to both capital and income.

Most commonly, a bare trust exists when an adult holds property on behalf of a minor who will become absolutely entitled to the asset on reaching the age of 18 (sometimes 16 in Scotland). Bare trusts for minors occur frequently because persons under the age of 18 cannot take legal title to property in England or Wales. The position in Scotland is slightly different and legal title is sometimes possible at 16. Bare trusts may sometimes continue beyond this point until the beneficiary calls for the trust assets to be transferred to them.

Assets held on bare trust are not regarded as 'settled property' for IHT purposes and are simply treated as belonging to the beneficiary. We will see some useful consequences of this in the next chapter.

## 8.9 BEREAVED MINORS' TRUSTS

The 'trust for a bereaved minor', to give it its proper name, is a very restrictive class of trust. Where the appropriate rules are met, trust property will be exempt from IHT and there will be no charges if a beneficiary dies or assets are transferred out of the trust. The basic conditions are:

i)   The beneficiary of the trust must be under 18 years of age
ii)  At least one of the beneficiary's parents is dead
iii) The trust was set up under:
     a.   Intestacy,
     b.   The criminal injuries compensation scheme, or
     c.   The Will of a deceased parent
iv)  The beneficiary must be absolutely entitled to the trust assets by the age of 18 at the latest
v)   Trust assets may only be applied for the benefit of the minor until he or she reaches the age of 18
vi)  Trust income may either be applied for the benefit of the minor or given directly to them. (The minor may have an interest in possession, if the settlor so desires.)

For the purposes of these rules, a 'parent' includes a natural parent, a step-parent, an adopted parent and any other person with 'parental responsibility' (e.g. a legal guardian).

While the above rules are clearly designed for a single beneficiary, a trust may still qualify with two or more beneficiaries, as long as each of them obtains absolute entitlement to their share of the trust assets at the age of 18.

The major problem with this type of trust is the beneficiary must gain absolute possession of the assets at the age of 18. Many people are horrified at the prospect of the entire family fortune suddenly being at the whim of someone so young. The risk of them frittering everything away before they have the wisdom to look out for their own future is all too obvious.

Thankfully, these concerns were at least partly recognised when the concept of the '18 to 25 Trust' was introduced. We will come on to these trusts in Section 8.14, but it is worth noting that a bereaved minor's trust can be converted to an '18 to 25 Trust' without charge.

### Small Payments for Non-Qualifying Purposes
Small payments that do not qualify under points (v) or (vi) above are permitted. These are limited to the lower of £3,000, or 3% of the value of settled property in the trust, each year.

### 8.10   OLD INTEREST IN POSSESSION TRUSTS

Prior to 22nd March 2006, whenever a beneficiary had an interest in possession they were treated, for IHT purposes, as if they owned the asset outright. Subject to certain exceptions, the termination of their interest, on death or otherwise, represented the transfer of the underlying asset for IHT purposes.

Interests in possession already in existence on 21st March 2006 continue to be treated as part of the beneficiary's estate for IHT purposes.

### Wealth Warning
The old rules only apply to **'settled property'** transferred into trust before 22nd March 2006. Any new lifetime transfers of assets into an existing trust will constitute new settled property and will be subject to the current rules.

The consequences arising when an interest in possession already in existence on 21st March 2006 comes to an end differ according to whether this occurred before or after 6th October 2008 (see Sections 8.13 and 8.16).

### Changes to Terms
Where the terms of a pre-22/3/2006 interest in possession trust are altered after 5th October 2008, including a change to the period of the interest, this will result in the settled property subject to that interest in possession becoming 'relevant property'.

The trust would then be subject to the IHT charges explained in Sections 8.18 and 8.19. However, where there is no change to the actual beneficiary, there would not be a chargeable lifetime transfer and hence no 'entry charge'.

### Extended 'Old' Interest in Possession Trusts
During the transitional period that ended on 5th October 2008, it was possible to extend the life of the trust by altering the terms applying to the existing beneficiary or by transferring the interest to a beneficiary with a longer life expectancy. See Section 8.13 for further details.


## 8.11 DISABLED TRUSTS

Assets within a trust for the benefit of a qualifying disabled person are exempt from the 'relevant property' provisions and are instead treated as part of the beneficiary's estate.

Self-settlement by a person with a condition expected to lead to a qualifying disability is permitted. This extension only applies to self-settlements; other settlors must wait until the beneficiary's condition deteriorates enough for them to qualify under the general rules.

A disabled trust may be either a discretionary trust or an interest in possession trust. Further rules apply to the use of funds held by a discretionary trust.

The rules governing disabled trusts are mainly designed to cover beneficiaries with a mental disability but will often also cover a person with a terminal illness.

### Practical Pointer
This provides the opportunity for the settlor to put property into trust during their terminal illness. While this will not save any IHT, it will enable the trustees to manage all or part of the estate following the settlor's death without having to wait for the grant of probate or confirmation.

## 8.12 IMMEDIATE POST-DEATH INTERESTS

An interest in possession created immediately on death, either by Will or intestacy, is termed an 'Immediate Post-Death Interest' and forms part of the beneficiary's estate for IHT purposes.

The settled property subject to the immediate post-death interest will therefore be included in the beneficiary's own IHT calculation if they should die while still entitled to the interest in possession or within seven years of the termination of that interest.

Most importantly, this means the spouse exemption is available on the creation of an immediate post-death interest. This provides tremendous additional potential for tax planning using the spouse exemption and we will explore this further in Section 9.9.

Furthermore, where an immediate post-death interest ends during the beneficiary's lifetime and property passes to a Bereaved Minor's Trust under the terms of the original settlor's Will, this will be a potentially exempt transfer. Combining this with the spouse exemption provides a potential opportunity to pass assets tax free to minor children. We will explore this in Section 9.10.

An immediate post-death interest may also be set up so that the settled property transfers to a bereaved minor's trust or '18 to 25 trust' for the benefit of the original testator's children on the death of the original beneficiary (IHT is payable on the original beneficiary's death in the normal way in this case).

When a testator adds new settled property to an existing interest in possession trust this will also be treated as an immediate post-death interest.

A TNRB may be set against the value of an immediate post-death interest brought into the spouse's estate on their death.

## 8.13 TRANSITIONAL SERIAL INTERESTS

Where an interest in possession in a settlement made before 22nd March 2006 was replaced by a new interest in possession in the same settled property within the same trust before 6th October 2008, the old rules continue to apply to that new interest in possession. The replacement interest is termed a 'Transitional Serial Interest' and will form part of the beneficiary's estate for IHT purposes. (Unless the new interest in possession qualifies under a higher category in the hierarchy, such as a Bereaved Minors' Trust, for example.)

### *Example*
*Maurice died in 2005 and left a life interest in all his assets to his brother, Robin. Under the terms of Maurice's Will, on Robin's death, the assets are to remain in trust for the benefit of Maurice's nephew, Andy. Robin died in September 2008, so the old rules continue to apply to Andy's interest in possession.*

Alternatively, Robin might have chosen to renounce his life interest in favour of Andy. If Robin had done this before 6th October 2008, this would have represented a potentially exempt transfer (as the old rules still applied) and the trust assets would form part of Andy's estate.

### Changes to Terms

Where the terms of a pre-22/3/2006 interest in possession trust were altered before 6th October 2008, including a change to the period of the interest, this will also constitute a Transitional Serial Interest.

### No Second Chances!

When a transitional serial interest comes to an end itself and is replaced by a new interest in possession, the new interest will be relevant property and will be taxed as set out in Sections 8.17 to 8.19. This will include cases where changes are made to the terms of the transitional serial interest, including the period of the interest. Further details of the consequences arising on termination of a transitional serial interest are set out in Section 8.16.

### Spouses and Civil Partners

Where a pre-22/3/2006 interest in possession comes to an end on the beneficiary's death and a new interest in possession in favour of the deceased's spouse comes into being, this new interest will be a transitional serial interest. The spouse exemption will apply to the settled property that falls into the deceased's estate under these circumstances. This continues to apply to pre-22/3/2006 interests in possession transferring to a spouse on the death of a beneficiary at any time.

The same treatment does not apply when a transitional serial interest comes to an end on a beneficiary's death and the spouse exemption is not available to a new interest in possession arising at that time.


### 8.14  18 TO 25 TRUSTS

To meet the concerns raised by many bodies in the wake of the original Budget 2006 announcements, a further category of trust was created: the '18 to 25 Trust'.

The '18 to 25 Trust' is essentially the same as a Bereaved Minors' Trust (Section 8.9) in all respects except the beneficiary must become absolutely entitled to the trust property by the age of 25 at the latest, rather than by 18.

Between the ages of 18 and 25, the beneficiary must either be entitled to an interest in possession or else the trust funds must be accumulated for their benefit (subject to the exception for small non-qualifying payments described in Section 8.9).

An '18 to 25 Trust' only retains its IHT exempt status until the beneficiary is 18. Thereafter, the trust assets effectively become 'relevant property'.

There is no IHT charge when the trust assets become 'relevant property' on the beneficiary's 18th birthday, but the exit charges explained in Section 8.19 will then apply as if the trust had been set up on this date.

This means there will be a maximum exit charge of 4.2% if the trust assets pass to the beneficiary at the age of 25 (in addition to the IHT already paid on the parent's death – making a total charge of up to 44.2%!).

More details of the exit charges applying to '18 to 25 Trusts' are given in Section 8.19. Exit charges also apply in the same way if the beneficiary of an '18 to 25 Trust' dies after the age of 18.

An '18 to 25 Trust' cannot arise if an immediate post-death interest is created instead, as this takes precedence under the trust hierarchy. An immediate post-death interest will often be preferable, as this avoids the exit charge that would apply to an '18 to 25 Trust'.

## 8.15  RELEVANT PROPERTY TRUSTS

Any trust not falling under another category in the trust hierarchy is subject to the relevant property regime, which we will examine in detail in Sections 8.17 to 8.20. This includes most lifetime settlements, even those conferring interests in possession on the settlor themselves (known as 'self-settlements'), or on their spouse, and 'reverter to settlor' trusts (see Section 8.3).

Before 2006, only discretionary trusts were subject to the relevant property regime. For this reason, the regime was sometimes referred to as 'the discretionary trust regime'. Discretionary trusts generally continue to fall within the relevant property regime unless they qualify under one of the other categories set out in Section 8.7.

When settled property falls within the relevant property regime, IHT charges may arise when the settlement is made, when assets come out of the trust, and every ten years in between (so it's 'in, out, and, every ten years, shake it all about').

Remember, as explained previously, this may apply to any new settlement, not just a newly constituted trust. There is, however, a partial exception for life policies held in trust and we will return to this in Section 10.13.

### Transfers on Death

Most interests in possession created on death will qualify as 'immediate post-death interests', as explained in Section 8.12, and should therefore escape the relevant property regime. Dangers arise, however, where the interest in possession does not arise immediately on death. In particular, a new interest in possession that replaces an 'immediate post-death interest' may fall within the relevant property regime (unless, as always, it qualifies under a higher category in the hierarchy).

## 8.16 END OF TRUST INTERESTS WITHIN BENEFICIARY'S ESTATE

As we saw in Section 8.5, there are five types of trust that are regarded as forming part of the beneficiary's estate.

Property within these trusts is subject to IHT at 40% when the beneficiary's interest comes to an end by reason of their death (subject to the exemptions explained in Chapter 3 and the 'reverter to settlor' exemption explained below).

Under certain circumstances, property within a pre-22/3/2006 interest in possession trust may be eligible to pass into an immediate post-death interest trust, a bereaved minor's trust or an '18 to 25 Trust' on the original beneficiary's death.

### Interests Ending During the Life of the Beneficiary

If the beneficiary becomes absolutely entitled to the trust property, this will be a non-event for IHT, as the property remains within the same estate.

If the original settlor or the beneficiary's spouse becomes absolutely entitled to the property, or it goes to charity, the transfer will be exempt.

In other cases, when the beneficiary's interest ends during their lifetime, a potentially exempt transfer will take place if:

- One or more individuals become absolutely entitled to the trust property
- Property transfers to a bare trust
- Property transfers to a disabled trust
- Property subject to an immediate post-death interest transfers to a bereaved minors' trust

All other transfers on termination of a beneficiary's interest during their lifetime will be chargeable lifetime transfers and the transferred property will fall into the relevant property regime.

If the original beneficiary retains an interest in former trust property, this may constitute a 'Gift with Reservation'. See Section 4.9 for further details.

### Reverter to Settlor Trusts

When property reverts to the original settlor on the termination of a pre-22/3/2006 interest in possession trust, the resultant transfer of value is exempt from IHT. This exemption only applies when the property passes back to the settlor absolutely.

## 8.17    THE RELEVANT PROPERTY REGIME

To make life easier, for the rest of this guide I will refer to any trust that falls into the relevant property regime as a 'relevant property trust'. A relevant property trust is treated as a separate and distinct person in its own right for IHT purposes. This has the following major consequences:

- Lifetime transfers into a relevant property trust are chargeable transfers, not potentially exempt transfers
- Transfers into a relevant property trust will generally be ineligible for the spouse exemption
- Assets within a relevant property trust are not generally included in a beneficiary's estate for IHT purposes
- No charges arise on the death of a beneficiary or termination of their interest in the trust's assets, but
- A charge may arise when assets leave the trust (see Section 8.19)
- There is no 'revert to settlor' exemption (see Section 8.16)
- Ten-year anniversary charges apply (see Section 8.18)

In essence, IHT may arise when assets go into a relevant property trust, when they come out of it, and every ten years while they're in it. Nevertheless, a relevant property trust's 'separate life' does give rise to some very useful tax-planning opportunities, which we will consider further in Chapters 9 and 12.


## 8.18    TEN-YEAR ANNIVERSARY CHARGES

Unfortunately, to counter the possible advantages of a relevant property trust's 'separate life', these trusts are subject to an IHT charge on every tenth anniversary of their creation. We will now examine how this charge is calculated. It gets rather complex but we will work through a practical example at the end to illustrate the main points.

The anniversary charge is calculated as follows:

i)   Take the total value of all the relevant property in the trust on the anniversary date.
ii)  Add any settlements made into other trusts (except charitable trusts or an immediate post-death interest for the settlor's spouse) by the same settlor on the same date as any settlements into this trust where that date is either the date on which the trust was first set up, or any date falling after 9th December 2014.
iii) Calculate the amount of IHT payable on a hypothetical chargeable lifetime transfer of a sum equal to the total of (i) and (ii) on the anniversary date, taking account of:
   a.  The NRB, but not any other exemptions, and
   b.  Any chargeable transfers made by the settlor in the seven years prior to setting up this trust (including any potentially exempt transfers becoming chargeable on the settlor's death).
iv)  Using the amount derived at step (iii), the 'Effective Rate' of IHT on the hypothetical lifetime transfer is calculated.

v) The 'Effective Rate' is multiplied by 3/10ths and then applied to any amounts in (i) above derived from assets held by the trust throughout the ten-year period.

vi) For amounts in (i) derived from assets held for less than ten years, the charge is reduced by one fortieth for every complete calendar quarter those assets were not held as relevant assets of the Trust.

vii) The rate applying to charges under (vi) may be increased to take account of further chargeable lifetime transfers made by the settlor (other than to the trust itself), including any potentially exempt transfers becoming chargeable on the settlor's death.

For charges arising before 10th December 2014, only settlements made into other trusts on the same day as the trust was first set up needed to be included in step (ii). This treatment continues for trusts set up under Wills executed before 10th December 2014 where the testator died before 6th April 2017.

## Now *that* calls for an example!

As usual, all exemptions/reliefs other than the NRB are ignored for simplicity.

### Example

*On 1st April 2011, Mel set up the Spice Discretionary Trust for her granddaughters, Emma and Melanie. She immediately transferred assets worth £80,000 into the trust. No IHT was payable at that time as the transfer amount was below the NRB.*

*On the same day, Mel transferred £50,000 into an interest in possession trust for her niece, Victoria. Previously, on 26th November 2010, Mel had given her sister Geri £135,000. Sadly, Mel passed away in January 2017 but, fortunately, the NRB covered her lifetime transfers.*

*On 1st April 2021, the assets in the Spice Discretionary Trust are worth £330,000. The anniversary charge is calculated as follows:*

| | |
|---|---|
| *Value of relevant property on anniversary date:* | *£330,000* |
| *Other settlement made the same day:* | *£50,000* |
| *Previous chargeable transfers:* | *£135,000* |
| *(i.e. the potentially exempt transfer to Geri,* | |
| *which became chargeable on Mel's death)* | |
| *Cumulative total for hypothetical transfer:* | ***£515,000*** |
| | |
| *Less NRB* | *£325,000* |
| *Gives:* | *£190,000* |
| *IHT at lifetime rate (20%)* | ***£38,000*** |
| | |
| *'Effective Rate' of IHT on the hypothetical transfer:* | |
| *(£38,000 divided by £330,000 PLUS £50,000)* | *10%* |
| | |
| *Rate for anniversary charge: 3/10ths of 10%* | *3%* |
| | |
| *IHT Payable:* | |
| *3% x £330,000* | ***£9,900*** |

*The result of this rather tortuous calculation is that IHT of only £9,900 is payable on the assets in the Spice Discretionary Trust. Remember, had these assets been in Mel's estate at the time of her death, up to £132,000 would have been payable.*

**The Impact of 'Same Day Settlements'**
The position in our example would have been better if Mel had waited until the next day to make the gift into Victoria's interest in possession trust. In fact, the ten-year anniversary charge applying to the Spice Discretionary Trust would then have been just £8,400.

As explained above, the 'Effective Rate' applying to each trust is increased as a consequence of both chargeable transfers in the previous seven years and other settlements into trust made on the same day.

Naturally, it is easy to avoid making a lifetime settlement on the same day as a settlement into another trust, but it is difficult to avoid this happening where settlements are made on death. This was the reason for the changes introduced in 2014 that have effectively blocked a well-known planning strategy known as 'pilot trusts'. In short, 'pilot trusts' no longer work!

**Undistributed Versus Accumulated Income**
Trust income that has simply not yet been distributed to beneficiaries at the anniversary date is not included in 'relevant property' for the purposes of the ten-year anniversary charge. (Nor for any 'exit charges' – see Section 8.19.) However, once the trustees have 'accumulated' that income, it does become part of the relevant property of the trust. Broadly, it is then treated like a new settlement made on the date of the 'accumulation' (although there is no chargeable lifetime transfer).

Where the trustees have a duty to accumulate the trust income, it is treated as being accumulated as soon as it is received. Where the trustees have no power to accumulate income (e.g. in the case of an interest in possession trust) it will not usually be treated as accumulated at any time (but see further below).

In other cases (e.g. most discretionary trusts), the general rule is income is 'accumulated' when the trustees decide not to distribute it to beneficiaries.

Any income that has not been distributed or formally accumulated after five years is deemed to have been accumulated for IHT purposes.


## 8.19   EXIT CHARGES

Transfers of assets out of a relevant property trust may also give rise to IHT charges. These 'Exit Charges' are based on broadly similar principles to the ten-year anniversary charge. The 'Effective Rate' arrived at in each case is multiplied by three-tenths, and then also multiplied by one-fortieth for every complete calendar quarter expiring since the most recent ten-year anniversary, or since the creation of the trust in the case of transfers taking place within the first ten years.

For an Exit Charge arising in the first ten-year period, the hypothetical lifetime transfer used to derive the Effective Rate is based on the value of the assets in the trust at its commencement, plus any further settlements made into the trust between then and the date of the transfer.

### Example
*Let's assume the same facts as the example in Section 8.18 above, except that:*
  i)   *In 2016 Mel transfers another £30,000 into the Spice Discretionary Trust*
  ii)  *On 29th June 2020, the trustees gave £20,000 to Emma out of capital*

*The exit charge on Emma's gift is calculated as follows:*

| | |
|---|---|
| Value of property settled on 1st April 2011: | £80,000 |
| Other settlement made the same day: | £50,000 |
| Previous chargeable transfers: | £135,000 |
| Value of property settled in 2016: | £30,000 |
| Cumulative total for hypothetical transfer: | **£295,000** |

| | |
|---|---|
| Nil rate band | £325,000 |

| | |
|---|---|
| IHT Payable: | **NIL** |

> ### Tax Tip
> As this example demonstrates, IHT can often be avoided when the trust's assets are distributed to beneficiaries before the first ten-year anniversary of the trust. We will look at the opportunities this provides in more detail in Chapter 9.

To continue our look at exit charges, let's slightly revise our example.

### Example Revised
*Let's now assume the gift to Geri that became chargeable on Mel's death was actually £235,000. What does this do to Emma's exit charge?*

*The cumulative total for the hypothetical transfer is now £395,000.*

| | |
|---|---|
| Deducting the NRB of £325,000 leaves: | £70,000 |
| IHT at lifetime rate (20%) | £14,000 |

| | |
|---|---|
| 'Effective Rate' of IHT on the hypothetical transfer: | |
| £14,000 divided by £160,000* | 8.75% |
| (* £80,000 + £50,000 + £30,000) | |

| | |
|---|---|
| Rate for exit charge: | |
| 8.75% x 3/10 x 36/40 | 2.3625% |

| | |
|---|---|
| IHT Payable: | |
| 2.3625% x £20,000 | **£473** |

**Points To Note**

i) If Emma bears the tax, the exit charge will be £473, as above. However, if the trust were to bear the tax, 'grossing up' would apply. The 'grossing up' rate in this case would be 2.3625/97.6375 (100 – 2.3625), giving rise to a 'grossed up' charge of £484.

ii) Only 36 calendar quarters are counted here. The 37th quarter does not end until 30th June 2020. As the transfer to Emma took place before that date, this quarter had not yet expired. If the transfer had been made two days later, we would have needed to include the 37th quarter.

Later Exit Charges are based on the Effective Rate applying at the previous ten-year anniversary, as adjusted for any further settlements into the trust since then.

Distributions of income out of the trust do not give rise to Exit Charges. Care must be taken, however, that the income is not allowed to 'accumulate' first before distribution.

**Exit Charges on '18 to 25 Trusts'**

The Exit Charge applying to an '18 to 25 Trust' (see Section 8.14) is based on the number of complete calendar quarters that have expired since the later of:

i) The date of the settlor's death, and
ii) The beneficiary's 18th birthday

**Tax Tip**
Exit charges can be kept slightly lower if beneficiaries become absolutely entitled to the settled property before the expiry of an additional calendar quarter following the later of (i) and (ii) above.

In general, therefore, when setting up an '18 to 25 Trust', it will make sense to allow the beneficiaries to become absolutely entitled to their inheritance two days before one of their birthdays (somewhere between their 19th and 25th birthday, as desired). By following this advice, the maximum charge of 4.2% should never arise!

**Penal Exit Charges**

Bereaved minors' trusts and '18 to 25 Trusts' are both subject to a penal exit charge regime which, broadly speaking, will apply if trust assets are not distributed to the beneficiary by the age of 18 or 25 respectively. The maximum potential charge under this regime is 21%. The exit charge does not apply to distributions of assets due to the death of the beneficiary before attaining the relevant age (i.e. 18 or 25), or to the conversion of a bereaved minors' trust to an '18 to 25 Trust' (or vice versa).

## 8.20 DEATH OF SETTLOR

When a settlor dies, potentially exempt transfers made within the last seven years of their life become chargeable transfers. This may lead to retrospective increases to the amount of any exit charges or ten-year anniversary charges where the settlor has also made transfers of value into a relevant property trust within that same seven-year period.

## 8.21 INCOME TAX AND TRUSTS

As I said in Section 8.3, interest in possession trusts generally have a better Income Tax position than discretionary trusts. Discretionary trusts pay Income Tax at the 'trust rate' (currently 45%) on all trust income in excess of a small basic rate band of just £1,000 (except for dividend income, which has its own 'dividend trust rate', currently 38.1%).

In other words, after the first £1,000 of trust income, a discretionary trust is taxed as if it were an individual with income in excess of £150,000.

Some of the Income Tax paid by the trust can be recovered by the beneficiaries when income is paid out. However, at best, there remains a significant cashflow disadvantage and, at worst, the trust's Income Tax burden effectively becomes permanent when income is retained in the trust.

An interest in possession trust, on the other hand, is generally taxed at basic rate only. The beneficiary entitled to the income then includes that income in their own tax calculation and pays any higher rate Income Tax due.

Looked at another way, an interest in possession trust is given the 'benefit of the doubt' and taxed at basic rate, with any extra tax due paid by the beneficiary. A discretionary trust is treated as a 'worst case scenario' and, apart from the first £1,000, taxed as if it were a wealthy individual, with the resultant excess tax then being reclaimed by the beneficiary.

There is an exception for 'trusts for vulnerable individuals' under which a discretionary trust can be taxed as if its income belonged directly to the 'vulnerable' beneficiary. This generally only applies to disabled trusts, trusts for bereaved minors and a few other cases where the beneficiary is aged under 18.

See Section 10.17 regarding lifetime settlements made for the benefit of your own minor children.

Charitable trusts are generally exempt from Income Tax unless they undertake trading activities.

# Chapter 9

# More Advanced Planning With Trusts

## 9.1 THE RELEVANT PROPERTY TRUST SHELTER

Because relevant property trusts are effectively treated as separate persons for IHT purposes, they provide an opportunity to shelter assets in a vehicle that exists outside any individual's estate. (Subject, of course, to the anniversary and exit charges explained in Chapter 8.)

In Section 8.15, we saw that relevant property trusts may be created through most lifetime transfers into trust (but see Section 9.8 below). To create a relevant property trust on death will usually require a discretionary trust.

In effect, and subject to any other transfers you may be making, there is the opportunity to transfer assets equal in value to the NRB into relevant property trusts every seven years free from IHT.

In fact, taking the annual exemption and the fact the NRB will hopefully begin to increase again one day into account, it should be possible to accumulate a considerable amount of value within the relevant property trust. Let's look at an example with a wealthy couple starting their IHT planning next year. Throughout this example, we will follow the assumptions set out in Section 3.2 regarding the future projected level of the NRB, *BUT* it is important to note these are only forecast projections used for the sake of illustration.

### *Example*
*Salvatore and Cherilyn are a wealthy married couple with adult children. Neither of them has made any transfer of value prior to 6th April 2021. On that date they set up the Caesar & Cleo Family Trust with their children as beneficiaries and each transfer £331,000 into it. The first £6,000 of each person's transfer is covered by their annual exemptions for 2021/22 and 2020/21 (see Section 5.2) and the remaining £325,000 by their NRB.*

*Hence, while there is a chargeable lifetime transfer, no IHT is payable at this stage. A total of £662,000 is now 'sheltered' in the trust.*

*On 6th April 2022, and then again on 6th April 2023, Salvatore and Cherilyn are each able to put a further £3,000 into the trust. Each transfer is covered by their annual exemptions so by 6th April 2023 a total of £674,000 has been transferred to the trust free from IHT.*

*From 2024/25 onwards, the Government finally starts to increase the NRB again, starting with an increase to £334,000 for the 2024/25 tax year. On 6th April 2024, Salvatore and Cherilyn are therefore each able to put a further £12,000 into the trust. £3,000 of each transfer is covered by the annual exemption, leaving a chargeable lifetime transfer of £9,000. This brings each person's cumulative* chargeable transfers up to £334,000 (£325,000 plus £9,000), which is covered by the NRB for 2024/25. A total of £698,000 has now been transferred to the trust free from IHT.

The couple follow the same principle in each of the following three years, bringing the total cumulative amount transferred into the trust free from IHT as at 6th April 2027 up to £770,000.

After 6th April 2028, however, the first transfers made on 6th April 2021 will not need to be counted in calculating the couple's cumulative chargeable transfers.

On 7th April 2028, Salvatore and Cherilyn will therefore each be able to transfer £338,000 into the Caesar & Cleo Family Trust free from IHT. This is because, at this point, each person's cumulative chargeable lifetime transfers in the last seven years are just £36,000.

The projected NRB at this point is £371,000, meaning each of them can make a new chargeable transfer of £335,000 without giving rise to any IHT. Adding the annual exemption gives a total tax-free transfer of £338,000 each. These latest transfers bring the total value transferred into the trust to date up to £1.446m.

Following the same principles for the next two years produces the following results:

| Date | Transfer (Each) | Total Value Transferred To Date (Both) |
|------|-----------------|----------------------------------------|
| 7th April 2029 | £13,000 | £1,472,000 |
| 7th April 2030 | £13,000 | £1,498,000 |

Great – almost £1.5m has now been 'sheltered'. However, on 6th April 2031, our 'shelter' springs a leak – the ten-year anniversary charge. To calculate this charge, let's assume all the trust's income has been distributed to the beneficiaries each year, but the assets in the trust have grown at the rate of 7.5% per annum (compound). This produces a total value for the trust assets at 6th April 2031 of £2.428m.

The transfers made by each of the settlors will be treated separately, so each has their own NRB (which is now £401,000 per our projections).

The 'Effective Rate' is derived by taking 20% of the value of trust assets in excess of two NRBs as a percentage of the value of those assets. In this case, the 'Effective Rate' is 13.39% (£2.428m – 2 x £401,000 = £1.626m x 20% = £325,200, which, divided by £2.428m, produces a rate of 13.39%).

This rate is multiplied by 3/10ths and then one-fortieth of this result is deducted for each calendar quarter the relevant assets were not in the trust. The assets in the trust from the outset are therefore subject to a charge of 4.018%. The assets that have been in the trust for nine years suffer a charge of 3.619%, those held for eight years suffer 3.214%, and so on.

In total, the anniversary charge amounts to £69,277. This represents just 2.85% of the value of the assets in the trust. If Salvatore and Cherilyn still held those assets personally, they would be exposed to potential IHT charges of 40%, or £971,200. The potential saving is therefore huge.

Note that I have made a fairly conservative assumption regarding future increases to the NRB: namely that it will merely rise in line with the CPI after the expiry of a projected fifteen year 'freeze' to 5th April 2024.

However, it is possible the NRB may be subject to more significant increases at some stage in the future. If so, the value of the planning technique described in the example will be substantially enhanced.

## 9.2    SERIAL TRUSTS

There is one major drawback to the method used by Salvatore and Cherilyn in the previous section. By using just one trust, they had access to just one extra NRB each. It would be better to set up a new trust every seven years and thus continually increase the number of NRBs available.

Hence, what Salvatore and Cherilyn should have done is to set up the Caesar and Cleo No. 2 Family Trust on 7th April 2028 and make their next seven years' worth of transfers into that trust. Then, on 8th April 2035, they could set up the Caesar and Cleo No. 3 Family Trust, and so on, for as long as they are able. For a start, this more sophisticated approach would have reduced the charge arising on 6th April 2031 to £41,779.

The longer-term calculations for this planning technique get quite horrendous but, if Salvatore and Cherilyn are lucky enough to survive until 8th April 2041 then, using our projection methodology set out in Section 9.1 above, they would have the following assets in trust:

| | |
|---|---|
| Caesar and Cleo Family Trust: | £2.945m |
| Caesar and Cleo No. 2 Family Trust: | £2.128m |
| Caesar and Cleo No. 3 Family Trust: | £1.533m |
| Total: | £6.606m |

These figures take account of anniversary charges of £41,779 in 2031, £48,267 in 2038 and £121,632 in 2041. The total IHT paid so far is thus £211,678. This compares with potential IHT of over £2.6m had these assets still been held by Salvatore and Cherilyn personally.

## 9.3    HOW USEFUL IS THE RELEVANT PROPERTY TRUST SHELTER?

You don't need to be in a couple to use the technique described in Sections 9.1 and 9.2. It works just as well for an individual: you just have to halve all the numbers. It must be admitted, however, that there are some restrictions to this technique and we will examine these in Section 9.8.

You may also wonder whether using relevant property trusts to shelter assets is really effective in view of the anniversary and exit charges. It is worth bearing in mind, however, that the tenth anniversary charges arising under the method given in Section 9.2 work out at less than 3%.

Twentieth anniversary charges (if the assets are still in trust) will tend to be higher, say around 4%, and, if you get to a thirtieth anniversary, we can expect charges approaching 5%. These are all based on our projected growth rate per Section 9.1. More growth would mean higher charges, but the overall saving compared with leaving the assets in the individuals' estates would also be greater. However high the growth, anniversary charges will always be less than 6%, as this is the theoretical maximum.

In general, the anniversary charges within the trusts are likely to work out at less than 0.5% per annum on average. Even if there were no growth in value within the trusts, this means you would need to survive more than eighty years after starting the plan before the anniversary charges exceeded the IHT saved on your death.

However, in fact, because of the dynamic nature of the plan and the anticipated growth in value of the assets within the trusts, the ultimate savings will continue to grow year on year for as long as you live. Following the method (and assumptions) set out in Sections 9.1 and 9.2, I have calculated the projected IHT savings for a couple based on the number of years they survive after starting the plan:

| Years Survived | Total Net Assets In Trust £000s | Total Net Assets In Estate £000s | Saving £000s |
|---|---|---|---|
| 1 | £717 | £691 | £26 |
| 2 | £776 | £726 | £50 |
| 3 | £856 | £783 | £73 |
| 4 | £942 | £843 | £99 |
| 5 | £1,034 | £908 | £126 |
| 6 | £1,131 | £976 | £155 |
| 7 | £1,888 | £1,441 | £447 |
| 8 | £2,051 | £1,551 | £500 |
| 10 | £2,426 | £1,804 | £622 |
| 12 | £2,882 | £2,110 | £772 |
| 14 | £4,054 | £2,851 | £1,203 |
| 16 | £4,756 | £3,321 | £1,435 |
| 18 | £5,599 | £3,886 | £1,713 |
| 20 | £6,565 | £4,540 | £2,025 |
| 25 | £10,580 | £7,210 | £3,370 |
| 30 | £16,207 | £11,031 | £5,176 |

**Notes**

i) In compiling the above figures, it is assumed the trusts are wound up at the time of the couple's death. This does not necessarily need to happen, but I have done so here to make the comparison fair. The 'Total Net Assets In Trust' are the remaining funds distributed to beneficiaries less the IHT charges suffered at this time.

ii) 'Total Net Assets In Estate' is the total net sum left in the estate after IHT from the same assets if these had been retained personally. To create a fair 'like with like' comparison, it is assumed the deceased's NRB is used against these assets.

iii) 'Saving' is, broadly speaking, the overall net tax saving. To be more accurate though, it is actually the additional net amount left to the beneficiaries after IHT.

iv) It is assumed neither member of the couple makes any other transfers of value outside the relevant property trust plan.

v) The above table takes the simplistic view that both members of the couple die at the same time. In reality this is unlikely to be the case, but the table still serves as a fair illustration of the savings that might be achieved.

vi) A single individual following the same technique would produce savings equal to half of those shown above.

vii) As explained in Section 9.1, the savings could be far greater if there are more substantial increases in the NRB at some point in the future.

viii) The savings shown above are based on using 'serial trusts', as outlined in Section 9.2.

It is interesting to note that the projected savings start almost immediately, with £26,000 saved even if the couple die after just one year. This arises because, once the assets are in the trust, any capital growth is immediately safeguarded from inclusion in your estate.

The savings steadily increase over time but there are significant additional increments in the total saving at each seventh anniversary, as a new NRB effectively becomes available.

This table is a perfect illustration of the benefit of starting IHT planning as early as possible. The table is not given in tax terms due to the cashflow impact of ten-year anniversary charges, which render a direct 'tax paid' comparison slightly unfair after the first ten years. Nevertheless, it does ably demonstrate that an excessive concern over anniversary and exit charges is generally unwarranted!

## 9.4 HOW TO AVOID ANNIVERSARY AND EXIT CHARGES

Anniversary and exit charges can easily be avoided by:

a) Distributing all trust assets to the beneficiaries before the tenth anniversary of the trust's creation, and

b) Ensuring the cumulative value of 'relevant transfers' does not exceed the NRB when the assets are distributed

Remember that the value of 'relevant transfers' for this purpose includes:

i) All transfers of relevant property into the trust
ii) Accumulated income within the trust (see Section 8.18)
iii) Chargeable transfers made in the seven years before setting up the trust (including potentially exempt transfers becoming chargeable on death)
iv) Other settlements of relevant property made on the day the trust was set up, or on the same day as any other settlements into this trust after 9th December 2014

We will see a simple example of how anniversary and exit charges may be avoided in Section 9.6.

Even when following the above strategy, up to ten years of 'capital growth' in the value of the trust assets can be accumulated free from IHT.

However, in order to achieve the significant longer-term benefits outlined in Section 9.3, or to maintain some of the practical advantages discussed in Section 9.5, it may actually be preferable, in the long run, to suffer ten-year anniversary charges.


## 9.5 WHY NOT JUST GIVE ASSETS TO THE BENEFICIARIES?

As we know from Chapter 4, assets can be passed directly to other individuals as potentially exempt transfers and all that is required is to survive seven years to ensure no IHT is payable. In the right circumstances, this is naturally a much simpler way to avoid IHT.

However, using a relevant property trust will often have significant practical advantages over giving assets directly to your ultimate beneficiaries, including:

- Control: Although you cannot benefit from the gifted assets (see Section 9.8), you will be able to retain control over them.
- Assets in the relevant property trust are outside any person's estate. This will avoid the danger of unexpected IHT liabilities arising if your beneficiaries should pre-decease you.
- Relevant property trusts can be used as a vehicle to 'skip a generation' (or even two) and pass family wealth directly to grandchildren or great-grandchildren, while still providing the settlor's children with income during their lifetime.
- The income from, or enjoyment of, assets can be given to your beneficiaries at an early age without exposing them to the risk of losing the underlying capital due to their own inexperience, a bad marriage, or some other misfortune.

On top of these practical issues there is also the fact that assets can be transferred into a relevant property trust free from CGT and we will look at this in the next section.

## 9.6　HOW TO AVOID INHERITANCE TAX AND CAPITAL GAINS TAX AT THE SAME TIME

As explained in Section 4.10, the transfer of assets other than cash will generally be treated as a sale at market value for CGT purposes.

However, because a transfer to a relevant property trust is a chargeable transfer for IHT purposes, the transferor is given the ability to 'hold over' any capital gains arising on the assets transferred.

This means no CGT is payable on the transfer and the trust is treated, for CGT purposes, as having acquired the asset at the same price as that originally paid by the transferor.

Furthermore, when, at a later date, the trust then transfers the asset to the ultimate beneficiary, the trustees and the beneficiary may, once again, claim that the capital gain should be 'held over'.

Hence, by this method, appreciating assets may be passed on free of both IHT and CGT.

### Example
*Eric has an investment property worth £325,000, which he wishes to pass to his adult daughter, Patty. Eric is concerned he will have a substantial CGT bill if he gives the property directly to Patty.*

*Instead, therefore, Eric sets up the Slowhand Trust with Patty as the beneficiary. He then transfers the property to the trust and elects to hold over the capital gain arising. Eric has made no previous transfers of value, so his chargeable transfer of £325,000 is covered by his NRB.*

*A couple of years later, the trust transfers the property, now worth £375,000, to Patty. Patty and the trustees jointly elect to hold over the capital gain arising, with the result that Patty is deemed to have acquired the property for the price Eric originally paid.*

*There is no exit charge on the transfer to Patty as the NRB covers the £325,000 that the property was worth when Eric put it into the trust. The fact that the property is now worth £375,000 is irrelevant.*

### Points to Note

i) Only the transferor needs to elect to hold over the gain going into the trust, whereas the trustees and the beneficiary must jointly elect to hold over the gain when the asset is transferred out of the trust.
ii) Increases in the value of trust assets after transfer into the trust will not give rise to any additional charges as long as those assets are distributed to beneficiaries within ten years of the trust's formation.
iii) A simple interest in possession trust will usually suffice for the purpose of this technique.

### Wealth Warning 1

Where gains have been held over on the transfer of residential property, neither the trust nor the beneficiary will be entitled to any principal private residence relief on the property for CGT purposes.

See also the comments in the next section regarding SDLT where there is a mortgage on the property.

### Wealth Warning 2

Gains cannot be held over when assets leave the trust within three months of the initial settlement or within three months of an anniversary charge. This is because the hold over relief is only available where an IHT charge arises, so there must be a technical liability for an 'exit charge' (see Section 8.19); although there is no problem if this actually works out at nil.

## 9.7    INVESTMENT PROPERTY TRUSTS

The technique described in the previous section, which allows assets to be passed on free from both IHT and CGT, is well suited to an investment property business. The restriction on principal private residence relief will often be irrelevant in the case of investment properties. In addition to adult children, the technique works just as well when the trust is used to pass property to an unmarried partner, grandchild, nephew, niece, other relative, or friend. It is not generally possible to use it to pass existing investment property to your own minor children, however, as CGT holdover relief would not be available.

Where two settlors jointly transfer property into the trust, two NRBs will be available. A couple could therefore use this technique to transfer up to £650,000 worth of rental property to their adult child free of both CGT and IHT. All they need to do is survive the requisite seven years.

After seven years, the couple will each have a new NRB available and could therefore do it all over again. A couple with a life expectancy of over 21 years could conservatively expect to be able to pass over £3m worth of rental property to their adult children free from tax!

### The Impact of Mortgages

When undertaking this planning technique, it is important to take any outstanding loans or mortgages secured against the property into account. Such loans are a useful means to provide greater flexibility for IHT planning but represent a potential hazard for CGT purposes and a major drawback as far as SDLT is concerned.

For IHT purposes, when a property is transferred subject to a mortgage, the value of the transfer is only the net equity in the property. This provides a useful mechanism to 'tweak' the transfer value if required.

Conversely, however, any mortgage or other loan assigned to the trust or beneficiary will be deemed to represent consideration paid for the property transferred. For CGT purposes, it is not possible to hold over any part of the gain that would have arisen on a sale of the property for the amount of this deemed consideration.

Furthermore, where the deemed consideration is £40,000 or more (or more than £150,000 for a commercial property) SDLT will generally be payable.

### *Example*

*Paul and Linda jointly own a residential investment property worth £800,000 and wish to pass it to their adult daughter, Stella. They bought the property for just £200,000 and it currently has no outstanding loans against it.*

*A direct transfer of the property to Stella would give Paul and Linda a total CGT bill of up to £168,000 (£600,000 x 28%). Fortunately, neither Paul nor Linda has made any other transfers in the last seven years. The couple therefore decide to transfer the property into an interest in possession trust for Stella's benefit in March 2021 and to elect to hold over the gain arising for CGT purposes. As things stand, however, this would give rise to an immediate IHT charge at 20% on the excess of the property's value over £662,000 (see Section 9.1), i.e. £27,600.*

*Paul and Linda therefore decide to mortgage the property prior to the transfer and assign the loan to the trust. This will reduce the property's net equity value at the time of the transfer and thus reduce or eliminate the IHT charge.*

*CGT should not present a problem unless Paul and Linda take out a loan of more than their original purchase price of £200,000. However, if they take out a loan of £40,000 or more, SDLT will be payable on the transfer. The loan required to eliminate any IHT charge on the initial transfer is £138,000 (£800,000 - £662,000). The loan required to be sure of also avoiding any exit charge when the property is ultimately passed to Stella is £150,000 (£800,000 - £650,000). The required loan would therefore produce a SDLT charge of £4,400 or £5,000 (see the Taxcafe.co.uk guide 'How to Save Property Tax' for SDLT rates).*

*On the other hand, restricting the loan to just £39,999 to avoid SDLT would still leave an IHT charge of £19,600 on the initial transfer (£800,000 - £39,999 - £662,000 = £98,001 x 20%) plus an additional small exit charge (up to £660 for each year the property is in the trust) when the property passes to Stella absolutely.*

*Paul and Linda therefore decide to take out a loan of £138,000 and the trust pays SDLT of £4,400 on the transfer.*

*Two years later, the trust transfers the property to Stella and she and the trustees jointly elect to hold over the gain arising. Most of the property's equity value on the original transfer (£662,000) is covered by Paul and Linda's NRBs, leaving just £12,000 exposed to an exit charge at 1.2% (two years represents eight calendar quarters so the charge works out at 20% x 3/10 x 8/40 = 1.2%). Stella therefore pays an exit charge of £144.*

*Stella will have to pay a further £4,400 in SDLT, due to the outstanding mortgage, bringing the total tax cost of the whole exercise up to £8,944 (£4,400 x 2 + £144).*

I have assumed Stella already owns another residential property, so the additional 3% SDLT charge applies on both property transfers. I also assumed it would be possible to assign the loan to the trust. If this is not possible, alternative methods are available, such as having the trust take out a mortgage for the requisite amount and use these funds to buy the property. The tax effects would be the same.

Despite the drawback of SDLT, the example demonstrates the huge tax-saving potential of using trusts to pass investment property to adult children or other beneficiaries. In this case, the couple faced an unpleasant choice between an immediate CGT charge of £168,000 and an eventual IHT bill of at least £320,000. By using a trust, they were able to pass a valuable investment property to their daughter almost tax free. In many cases, the same result can be achieved completely tax free.

## 9.8    SETTLOR-INTERESTED TRUSTS

Where the settlor, their spouse, or a dependent minor child of the settlor, can benefit in any way from a trust, that trust is a 'settlor-interested trust'. CGT holdover relief is not available for transfers of assets into a 'settlor-interested trust'. Gifts of land and buildings, or other appreciating assets, to such trusts may thus give rise to an immediate CGT charge. Additionally, if a trust becomes settlor-interested at any time within six years after the end of the tax year in which holdover relief was previously claimed, the relief is withdrawn and a CGT charge will arise.

Assets in a 'settlor-interested trust' are subject to the 'gifts with reservation' rules (Section 4.9) unless the settlor themselves is excluded from benefit. Strictly speaking, a benefit derived by the settlor's spouse does not necessarily give rise to a 'gift with reservation', but there is often a danger the settlor may share such a benefit. Hence, in practice, it is usually wise to ensure the settlor's spouse is also excluded from benefit. Unless the settlor is completely excluded from benefit, in theory and in practice, the trust will be ineffective for IHT planning purposes.

## 9.9    PASSING ASSETS TAX-FREE TO ADULT CHILDREN AND OTHER BENEFICIARIES

As we saw in Section 8.12, it is possible to leave assets to an immediate post-death interest trust in favour of your spouse free from IHT. This has the tremendous advantage that you can benefit from the spouse exemption and yet still be certain your assets will eventually pass to your children (or other intended beneficiaries). As explained in Section 8.3, this is achieved by bequeathing the 'remainder' to your ultimate intended beneficiaries. In many cases, you may want the immediate post-death interest to persist for the remainder of your spouse's life. This means IHT will arise on their death. Alternatively, if the immediate post-death interest is terminated during the spouse's lifetime, the assets can be passed to the ultimate beneficiaries as a potentially exempt transfer that will become fully exempt seven years later, as long as the spouse survives to the end of this period.

This is a useful variation on the technique explained in Section 6.15, as it provides certainty the assets will pass to your intended beneficiaries. It is important to retain the assets in the trust for at least two years and a day after your death. In fact, it may be wise to keep them in the trust a little longer than this (say three years) as HMRC frequently challenges life interests of only just over two years under the associated operations rules (see Section 10.19).

Generally, it is preferable to avoid any fixed arrangements for the trust's early termination and leave it to your widow or widower to give up their interest voluntarily. This may not always be desirable, however, and we will look at some alternative options in Section 9.10 (plus one set out below).

Assets must pass to adult children or other beneficiaries absolutely in order to be a potentially exempt transfer. Unlike the technique described in Section 9.10 (for minor children), it is not possible to use an '18 to 25 trust' to pass assets to young adult children tax-free, as the transfer from the immediate post-death interest would be a chargeable lifetime transfer.

For example, the deceased might leave an interest in possession to their surviving spouse, which terminates on their child's 21st birthday, when the assets pass absolutely to the child. As long as the deceased's spouse survives until the child's 28th birthday (i.e. seven years later), the whole process should take place free from IHT.

As this is a more 'common-sense' approach than passing assets to a minor, there is probably little risk of an attack under the associated operations rules.

## 9.10   PASSING ASSETS TAX-FREE TO MINOR CHILDREN

In many cases, where someone dies leaving both a spouse and minor children, they will be content for their assets to remain in their widow or widower's hands until the children reach adulthood. For advice on how to get those assets into the children's hands tax-free after they reach the age of 18, see Sections 6.7, 6.15 and 9.9.

In some cases, however, the deceased may prefer their assets to pass to their children sooner, particularly if their spouse is unlikely to survive until the children are over 25 (i.e. more than seven years after the children reach adulthood), if they are separated from their spouse, or if their spouse is not their children's other parent.

As explained in Section 8.12, where an immediate post-death interest ends during the beneficiary's lifetime and property passes to a bereaved minor's trust under the terms of the settlor's Will, this will be a potentially exempt transfer. This provides the opportunity to pass assets tax-free to minor children.

### *Example*
*James wishes to leave his estate to his five-year-old daughter Beatrice. If he left the estate directly to Beatrice or a trust for her benefit, the IHT arising would be colossal.*

*Instead, therefore, James leaves just £325,000 (his NRB) to a bereaved minor's trust for Beatrice and everything else to an immediate post-death interest trust in favour of his estranged wife, Heather. Heather's immediate post-death interest lasts for a fixed period of three years, after which the estate passes into Beatrice's bereaved minor's trust.*

*The bulk of James's estate initially passes into Heather's immediate post-death interest tax free under the spouse exemption and, three years later it passes into the trust for Beatrice as a potentially exempt transfer.*

*As long as Heather outlives James by at least ten years, his entire estate can pass to Beatrice tax free.*

Technically, taking the strict letter of the legislation, Heather's interest would only need to last two years and a day, but I made it three years in the example since, as explained in Section 9.9, a shorter period could lead to a risk of challenge under the associated operations rules (see Section 10.19). The legacy to Heather could then be ignored and James's entire estate (except his NRB) could be subject to IHT.

Whether three years is even long enough is not clear, as any fixed period for Heather's interest may make the transfer to Beatrice's trust too much of a certainty for HMRC's liking. Clearly though, the longer Heather's interest lasts, the more robust the arrangement will be (but bear in mind the transfer to Beatrice's trust needs to take place before she is 18: after that, the assets would need to pass to her absolutely, as explained in Section 9.9).

Nonetheless, the associated operations rules are usually only used in blatant cases of tax avoidance, so a more subtle version of this approach is more likely to work, especially where the couple are still living together immediately before the transferor's death.

Immediate post-death interest trusts in favour of a surviving spouse that terminate on their remarriage are commonplace and would not generally be challenged. Other conditions that might terminate the spouse's interest, such as emigration or bankruptcy, for example, might also be acceptable.

The difficulty in a case like James's is he will want some certainty that the estate will pass to the child reasonably soon. A clause terminating the surviving spouse's interest when the child reaches a certain age might be subtle enough for the scheme to work (again, this needs to be before the child reaches 18 if you wish to use a bereaved minor's trust; otherwise the method described in Section 9.9 should be used instead).

Whatever method is used to trigger the termination of the spouse's interest, it must last at least two years and a day, and there will often need to be a risk that it could last a few years more for this strategy to be effective. This could mean the loss of several years' income for the ultimate beneficiary: although if it prevents them losing 40% of the capital, it could be worth it.

The surviving spouse may sometimes be prepared to give up their interest voluntarily. This would not create a bereaved minor's trust, but could result in a bare trust in favour of the child with similarly beneficial results. The implications of such a voluntary transfer were discussed in Section 6.15.

Note, as the transfer from the immediate post-death interest to the bereaved minor's trust or bare trust is a potentially exempt transfer, holdover relief is not available for CGT purposes. Hence, the method may not be entirely 'tax free', as CGT would arise on the increase in value of any non-cash assets in the trust since the original owner's death.

## 9.11    DISCOUNTED GIFT TRUSTS

A useful type of trust used in IHT planning for many years is the 'Discounted Gift Trust' or 'Reversionary Interest Trust'. These trusts are usually provided by life insurance companies and different companies tend to give their trusts their own names but the basic principles employed are broadly similar.

A discounted gift trust is actually not a single trust, but a series of mini-trusts. The transferor gives a substantial sum to the discounted gift trust, which is then divided up among the mini-trusts with the following rights:

Mini-Trust 1: income accumulated for one year, after which the original funds in the Trust are returned to the transferor.
Mini-Trust 2: income accumulated for two years, after which the original funds in the Trust are returned to the transferor.
Mini-Trust 3: income accumulated for three years, after which the original funds in the Trust are returned to the transferor.

And so on ...

The accumulated income in the trusts is held for the benefit of the transferor's eventual beneficiaries. The effect of this is that the transferor continues to receive an 'income' stream from their investment, despite the fact much of it is no longer in their estate for IHT purposes.

The statistical value of the reversionary interests in the mini-trusts does still have to be included in the transferor's estate, but this is less than the amount of the original investment and steadily reduces as time passes.

Actually, what the transferor is receiving is not, strictly speaking, income at all, but a return of capital. This has the added advantage of being free from Income Tax too!

The insurance companies providing these investments were quick to adapt to the changes made in 2006 and continue to provide discounted gift trust schemes using absolute trusts. This reduces the flexibility of the scheme but prevents a chargeable lifetime transfer from arising on the initial investment.

Another form of discounted gift trust using relevant property trusts can also be set up but this will give rise to a chargeable lifetime transfer when the initial investment is made. Nevertheless, the structure may still sometimes work satisfactorily for investments that do not exceed the NRB.

## 9.12  LOAN TRUSTS

Another popular scheme provided by many life insurance companies is the 'Loan Trust'. In essence, the transferor does not make any transfer of value to the trust but simply lends funds to it. As there is no transfer of value, there can be no IHT charge.

Funds invested within the trust will (one hopes) experience capital growth, but the beauty of this scheme is that the capital growth is outside the original transferor's estate. All that the original transferor is due is a repayment of the original loan and hence this is the only value remaining in their estate.

The loan can be interest-free if desired (see Section 2.11) and the transferor may progressively withdraw their original loan capital. This capital can be spent on the transferor's own living expenses, thus gradually removing its value from their estate. Alternatively, the transferor could gift the benefit of the loan to another individual as a potentially exempt transfer (Section 4.3).

Meanwhile, the capital growth and accumulated income within the trust belongs to the beneficiaries and is thus also kept out of the transferor's estate.

A loan trust may be set up as an absolute trust in order to avoid any danger of becoming a relevant property trust. An absolute loan trust would be exempt from any anniversary or exit charges. Otherwise, as a relevant property trust, there would be some risk of anniversary and exit charges, but these could generally be avoided by ensuring the trust assets are distributed before the trust's net value exceeds the NRB (see Section 9.4 for further advice on avoiding anniversary and exit charges).

## 9.13  EXCLUDED PROPERTY TRUSTS

Those who did not have a UK 'Domicile of Origin' (see Section 15.2) but who have subsequently acquired actual or deemed UK domicile, or who have elected to 'opt-in' for IHT purposes (see Section 6.19), may generally exclude non-UK assets transferred into a trust for their benefit before they acquired UK domicile, or deemed UK domicile, or opted in.

Where such assets are still held in the trust at the relevant time, they may be excluded from the value of the beneficiary's estate for IHT purposes. Property held in such trusts is known as 'excluded property'.

This treatment even extends to property transferred into the trust by the beneficiary themselves: since the 'excluded property' rules take precedence over the 'Gifts with Reservation' provisions (see Section 4.9).

Hence, any person who is shortly about to become UK domiciled or deemed UK domiciled (see Section 2.2), or who is planning to 'opt-in' (see Section 6.19), could transfer any non-UK assets into a trust for their own benefit before this occurs and thus prevent those assets from becoming subject to UK IHT.

An excluded property trust can also be used to shelter non-UK assets inherited from a non-UK domiciled person and may be put in place via a deed of variation where appropriate.

Note that property held in trust ceases to be excluded property at any time when a non-UK domiciled settlor acquires deemed UK domicile as a consequence of resuming UK residence where they had been born in the UK with a UK domicile of origin (see Section 2.2).

As explained in Section 2.11, any liabilities incurred, directly or indirectly, to finance excluded property must be deducted from the value of that property and cannot be deducted from other chargeable assets.

See also Section 2.2 regarding indirect holdings of UK residential property.

Lastly, note that further new restrictions are to apply to excluded property trusts from the date of Royal Assent to Finance Act 2020. Professional advice is essential.

# Chapter 10

# Practical Aspects of IHT Planning

## 10.1 THE BIGGER PICTURE

No-one should do IHT planning; they should do 'Estate Preservation Planning'. What is important is not just saving IHT but preserving family wealth for the benefit of the next generation. Saving IHT is just one part of preserving wealth and it is important never to lose sight of this bigger picture.

When we come to the bigger issue of estate preservation, there are many other factors to be taken into account. In this chapter we will look at some of these other factors, as well as some practical aspects of IHT planning itself.

## 10.2 COMMERCIAL ISSUES & OTHER TAXES

From early on in my career I was taught 'never to let the tax tail wag the commercial dog'. In other words, it is almost always more important to get the commercial aspects right before letting tax planning dictate your actions.

For example, putting all your savings into a share of *'Dave's Dodgy Autos'* might be a great way to avoid IHT, but what's the use of that if Dave runs off to South America with all your money? After all, when all is said and done, Boris Johnson and Rishi Sunak will only take 40%, so they are (just slightly) better than Dodgy Dave.

On the other hand, as we saw in Section 7.27, saving 40% may still be beneficial overall, even in some slightly uncommercial situations. It's a question of getting the right balance and is best expressed as follows:

> ### Bayley's Law
> *"The truly wise taxpayer does not seek merely to minimise the amount of tax paid but rather to maximise the amount of wealth remaining after all taxes have been accounted for."*

After commercial issues, the next important issue to watch out for is other taxes. When undertaking tax planning, it is essential to consider all taxes, not just the one you're trying to save.

IHT planning will often involve transferring assets and this can have important implications for Income Tax, Corporation Tax, Stamp Duty (on shares and securities), or SDLT (on land and buildings).

However, the tax that interacts most frequently with IHT is CGT, and we will look at that particular 'clash of the titans' in Chapter 11.

## 10.3    VALUATIONS

Valuation is a key part of IHT. We are frequently concerned with the value of land, buildings, unquoted shares, or unincorporated businesses.

Very often, the value of an asset owned by an individual is dependent on what proportion of a larger asset they own. We saw an example of this with Bjorn's chairs in Section 2.1. In practice, the most significant examples are in the case of unquoted shares. A controlling (i.e. over 50%) shareholding in a private company might be worth £5,000 per share, for example, while a small minority holding in the same company might be worth just £600 per share.

These changes in proportionate value can have major implications for any transfers of value that result in the transferor's shareholding falling into a lower value category.

### *Example*
*Mick owns a thousand ordinary shares in Fleetwood Ltd out of the company's total issued share capital of 10,000 shares. There is only one class of shares. It has been established that shareholdings of 10% or more (but less than 25%) can be valued at £2,000 per share but holdings of less than 10% are worth only £600 per share. Hence, at present, Mick's shareholding is valued at £2m (1,000 x £2,000).*

*Mick decides to give one share to his daughter, Stevie. This reduces the value of his remaining holding of 999 shares to £599,400 (999 x £600). The gift to Stevie is therefore treated as a transfer of value of £1.4006m (£2m - £599,400) despite the fact her share is worth just £600.*

*This preposterous result could be absolutely disastrous for Stevie. If Mick should die within three years of making this gift, Stevie could face an IHT bill of up to £560,240. All for a share worth just £600! Let's hope BPR is available on these shares and Stevie does nothing to mess it up. She certainly needs to hope Fleetwood Ltd isn't floated on the stock exchange within the next seven years (Section 7.19).*

There are clearly times when a gift should not be accepted!

### Key Thresholds for Unquoted Shares

Valuing unquoted company shares is a highly complex matter, but it is perhaps worth pointing out the requirements of company law relating to shareholders' resolutions effectively create some key thresholds where increases in share values can be expected to apply. These thresholds are:

* 10%
* 25%
* 50%
* Over 50% (no-one else can have 50%)
* Over 75% (no-one else can have 25%)
* Over 90% (no-one else can have 10%)
* 100% (no-one else can interfere at all!)

## 10.4 RELATED PROPERTY

When valuing assets for IHT purposes, an individual's assets are treated as if they are part of a larger holding made up of all the assets held by the individual and their spouse; plus any assets held by a charity or similar exempt body at any time within the last five years that were originally transferred to that body by the individual or their spouse.

*Example*
*Christine and John are an unmarried couple. Christine owns 3,000 of the 10,000 issued shares in Fleetwood Ltd; John owns 2,200. It has been established that shareholdings of 10% or more (but less than 25%) can be valued at £2,000 per share; holdings of 25% or more (but less than 50%) can be valued at £5,000 per share; and holdings of over 50% are worth £10,000 per share. Hence, at present, Christine and John's shareholdings are valued as follows:*

*Christine:*     *3,000 x £5,000 = £15m*
*John:*        *2,200 x £2,000 = £4.4m*

*Christine and John have a son, Lindsay, and eventually intend to leave their shares to him. As things stand, this would give rise to transfers of value totalling £19.4m.*

*Christine and John decide to get married. The related property provisions mean their shares must now be valued as an appropriate proportion of a combined shareholding of 5,200 shares worth £52m (5,200 x £10,000). Their shareholdings are therefore now valued as follows:*

*Christine:*     *£52m x 3,000/5,200 = £30m*
*John:*        *£52m x 2,200/5,200 = £22m*

*Leaving their shares to Lindsay will now give rise to transfers of value totalling £52m, or £32.6m more than before they married, thus potentially costing up to £13.04m in extra IHT (£32.6m x 40%).*

Christine and John will, of course, have gained the benefit of the spouse exemption and that may be worth more to them. Furthermore, if the shares qualify for BPR, the increase in value may not cause any problems. Nonetheless, while marriage is nearly always beneficial for IHT purposes, the example shows there could be some exceptions.

### Practical Problems and Solutions

These 'related property' provisions can cause unexpected problems, with small gifts sometimes being given large hypothetical values for IHT purposes. However, the impact of the 'related property' rules can be reduced if transfers are timed carefully. This is particularly relevant to unquoted shareholdings held by married couples where BPR may not be available.

*Example*
*Jack and Diane are a married couple and both own shares in Mellencamp Ltd, an unquoted investment company.*

*Jack owns 2% of the company and his shares are worth just £2,000*
*Diane owns 49% of the company and her shares are worth £245,000*

*Under the related property rules, however, their shares must be valued as part of a combined shareholding of 51%. This shareholding, being enough to provide control of the company, is worth £510,000.*

*The couple now wish to give their son John a 25% share in the company.*

*Jack transfers his 2% stake to John first. This represents a transfer of value of £20,000 (2/51 x £510,000). Diane then transfers a further 23% to John. This represents a transfer of value of £115,000 (23/49 x £245,000), bringing the total to £135,000.*

*If Diane had made her transfer first, this would have been a transfer of value of £230,000 (23/51 x £510,000). Jack's subsequent transfer would then have been a transfer of value equal to 2/28ths of the value of a 28% shareholding, let's say £10,000 for the sake of argument.*

*Hence, by making the smaller transfer first, the couple have reduced the effective transfer of value by £105,000, achieving a potential IHT saving of up to £42,000 (at 40%).*

## 10.5   JOINTLY HELD PROPERTY

Any form of property can be held jointly, including bank accounts, shares and securities or land and buildings.

The key point to note about jointly held property is that, on a joint owner's death, their share may sometimes pass by survivorship and not by intestacy or under the deceased's Will. This has major implications for IHT planning, as you may not be free to transfer your share of jointly held property in the most tax-efficient manner.

After the joint bank account, the next most common form of jointly held property in the UK is land and buildings, sometimes referred to as 'real property'. In fact, most couples in the UK now own their home jointly.

In England and Wales, there are two different legal forms for jointly held property, 'Joint Tenants' or 'Tenants in Common'.

### Joint Tenants

In a joint tenancy the ownership of each joint owner's share passes automatically on death to the other joint owner (or joint owners). This is what is meant by 'survivorship'. Furthermore, neither joint owner is normally able to sell their share of the property without the consent of the other.

This may restrict the scope for IHT planning with the property and joint tenancies are therefore generally less desirable than tenancies in common purely from a tax planning perspective.

Having said that, however, the security provided by the right of 'survivorship' will often be of more value to many couples.

## Tenants in Common

Under a tenancy in common, the joint owners are generally each free to do as they wish with their own share of the property and there is no right of survivorship. The joint owners' shares in the property need not be equal.

A tenancy in common therefore opens up a wide range of IHT planning opportunities that may not always be available under a joint tenancy.

## Practical Implications

As explained above, each person's share in a joint tenancy will usually pass to the other joint owner by survivorship. In the case of the family home, the surviving joint owner will usually be the widow or widower of the deceased. Following the introduction of the TNRB (see Chapter 6), this will usually be the best result anyway.

Nevertheless, for the reasons explained in Section 6.8, this may sometimes still be bad IHT planning.

It is, however, possible to 'break' a joint tenancy via a deed of variation (see Section 17.1) executed within two years after a joint owner dies.

Alternatively, it may be preferable to sever the joint tenancy during both owners' lifetimes as this provides more certainty to the intended IHT planning. It is not always wise to rely on being able to use a deed of variation to rectify the situation!

Once a joint tenancy has been severed or broken, whether during the owner's lifetime or via a deed of variation, it becomes a tenancy in common.

A share in property held under a tenancy in common may be passed to anyone, under the terms of the deceased's Will, or possibly via a deed of variation, as explained in Section 17.1.

Hence, whenever undertaking any IHT planning on the family home in England or Wales that involves passing a share of the property to anyone other than the surviving spouse, it may be wise to first ensure the property is held under a tenancy in common and not a joint tenancy.

Breaking a joint tenancy to create a tenancy in common can be achieved at a reasonably modest cost and should, in itself, be tax free, as it is not treated as a disposal for CGT purposes, nor an acquisition for SDLT purposes.

### Wealth Warning
If you change your property to a tenancy in common and then draw up your Wills to put the appropriate IHT planning measures in place, remember to make sure you also buy any new property as tenants in common if you move house!

### Scotland

In Scotland, joint ownership of real property mainly comes in a form known as 'Pro Indivisio' ownership, which operates in a broadly similar manner to a tenancy in common.

A form of beneficial joint tenancy is also available in Scotland using a 'survivorship destination'. This cannot be severed unilaterally, which can sometimes lead to practical difficulties if one joint owner decides they wish to pass their share to someone other than their fellow joint owner.

A 'survivorship destination' can, however, be broken by a deed of variation where the surviving joint owner is prepared to co-operate.

Nonetheless, relying on using a deed of variation when the time comes may not always be wise so it may make sense to break the 'survivorship destination' during both owners' lifetimes to better facilitate any IHT planning that involves passing a share of the property to someone other than the surviving joint owner.

And be careful when you move house too!

### 10.6    VALUING JOINTLY HELD PROPERTY

A useful benefit of jointly held property is the fact that a discount often applies to the value of a joint owner's share of the property.

#### *Example*
*Two sisters, Mel and Kim, live together in Appleby Manor, which they own jointly. Sadly, Kim dies in September 2020, when Appleby Manor is worth £1.5m. Kim's half share is not valued at £750,000, as one might expect, but at a discount of 15%, i.e. £637,500. This discount produces an effective IHT saving of £45,000.*

The discount applies to reflect the practical difficulty in selling a joint owner's part share of a property. The discount also reflects the fact that the other joint owner has a right to occupy the property and is therefore akin to a 'sitting tenant', thus further reducing the value of a joint share in the property.

The 15% discount used above was established by an IHT case back in 1982. In a more recent case, it was suggested a discount of just 10% might now be more appropriate, especially where the surviving joint owner is not likely to remain in occupation of the property. Nevertheless, conventional wisdom seems to be that a 15% discount is still appropriate in the case of residential property occupied by the surviving joint owner. A lower rate of discount may be appropriate in other cases but it is certainly still worth claiming.

HMRC takes the view that the related property rules (see Section 10.4) prevent any discount from applying where a property is held jointly by spouses.

Unfortunately, due to the different nature of joint property titles in Scotland, the usual discount does not generally apply to property in Scotland.

## 10.7  OTHER JOINTLY HELD ASSETS

A jointly held bank or building society account in England or Wales passes in its entirety to the surviving joint account holder on the other account holder's death.

In Scotland, a joint account holder's share of a joint account usually falls into their general estate to be dealt with according to the terms of their Will or under the laws of intestacy (see Section 10.10).

In either case, the deceased's share of the joint account is included in their estate for IHT purposes (although it will usually be exempt if it passes to their spouse). The deceased's share will generally be taken to be half of the account balance and no discount can apply.

Other jointly held property, such as paintings, antiques and personal effects may be subject to a substantial discount due to the fact that a joint owner is generally unable to sell such property.

> **Tax Tip**
> Unmarried couples can save substantial amounts of IHT by jointly holding tangible moveable property (such as antiques) and separately passing each joint share to their intended beneficiaries (but not each other).


## 10.8  MORTGAGES

It is important to be aware that any transfer of property subject to a mortgage will require the lender's consent. If the transferee takes over the mortgage, the outstanding borrowings will be deemed to constitute purchase consideration and may give rise to a SDLT charge if they are £40,000 or more; or more than £150,000 in the case of commercial property.


## 10.9  RESIDENTIAL CARE FEES

While IHT is a major worry, many people are more concerned about losing their property to the local authority in order to pay nursing home or residential care fees in their old age. In some cases, the local authority may even be able to force a sale of a property that has previously been given away if they can show this was done to avoid payment of the fees.

In some instances, it has been accepted that, where a property has been given away for IHT planning purposes, the local authority were unable to claim the taxpayer's motive was to avoid the care fees. Nevertheless, this approach is not entirely reliable, as many families have found to their cost (see further in Section 11.8).

A better approach is often to take out long term care insurance or even emergency care assurance. The latter approach generally requires the payment of a single lump sum premium in exchange for an annuity covering the residential care fees. The amount of the premium is generally equal to around two to three years' worth of the care fees.

Emergency care assurance is a useful strategy employed by many families who wish to have certainty about the cost of looking after their elderly relative.

If necessary, the premium can be funded by way of a loan secured against the relative's former home, thus enabling the family to keep the property and perhaps even benefit from the CGT uplift on death (see Section 11.2).

## 10.10  WILLS AND INTESTACY

Most people are pretty relaxed about dying intestate (without a Will) until they realise what would actually happen. Most of us know we should make a Will, but a great many of us put it off until it's too late.

Quite apart from any IHT planning, a Will is sensible as, without a valid Will, your assets will be divided up according to the ancient laws of intestacy and this may well be very different to what you would have liked. More importantly, a Will is essential for nominating the future guardians of your children if, as Oscar Wilde would have put it, they are careless enough to lose both parents.

In the tables that follow, 'issue' generally means your children but, if your children pre-decease you, their children will take their place. For example, if you have three children and one of them pre-deceases you, leaving two children of their own, the share going to 'your children' will be divided so that one third of that share goes to each of your surviving children and one sixth goes to each of your grandchildren by your deceased child.

### Dying Without a Will: England and Wales
If you are domiciled in England and Wales, and die without a Will, your estate will be divided as follows:

### 1. If you leave a spouse and issue
The first £250,000 and all personal possessions go to your spouse. 50% of the balance is divided equally between your children. The remaining 50% is held on trust, with your spouse having a life interest and the remainder going to your children.

### 2. If you leave a spouse but no issue
If you have no surviving parents, siblings, nephews or nieces, your entire estate goes to your spouse. Otherwise, your spouse's share is restricted to £450,000 plus all personal possessions and 50% of the remaining balance.

The other 50% of the balance goes to your parents if they survive you, to your siblings if both of your parents pre-decease you, or to your nephews and nieces if your siblings also pre-decease you.

185

### 3. If you leave issue but no spouse
Your estate is divided equally between your children.

### 4. If you leave no spouse or issue
Your estate goes to the nearest relatives to survive you, using the following order of precedence:
  - i) Your parents
  - ii) Your siblings, or their issue (i.e. your nieces and nephews)
  - iii) Your grandparents
  - iv) Your aunts and uncles

### 5. If no near-relatives survive you
Your entire estate goes to the Crown!

### Dying Without a Will: Scotland
There are proposals for major reforms to the laws of succession in Scotland, although it is uncertain whether these will be adopted. At present, if you are domiciled in Scotland and die without a Will your estate will be divided as follows:

### 1. If you leave a spouse and issue
Your spouse gets:
  - i) Your interest in any dwelling (i.e. the family home) up to a value of £300,000. If the family home's value exceeds this amount, the spouse's entitlement is limited to the right to receive the sum of £300,000
  - ii) Personal possessions up to the value of £24,000
  - iii) The first £42,000 of the remaining estate
  - iv) One third of any other moveable property (i.e. anything other than land and buildings)

Your children then get the remainder of your estate.

### 2. If you leave a spouse but no issue
Your spouse gets your interest in any dwelling and personal possessions as per (i) and (ii) above, plus:
  - i) The first £75,000 of the remaining estate
  - ii) One half of any other moveable property (i.e. anything other than land and buildings)

The rest of your estate falls into your 'free estate' and is dealt with as set out below. If you have no surviving parents, siblings, nephews or nieces, your spouse will effectively receive your entire estate.

### 3. If you leave issue but no spouse
Your estate is divided equally between your children.

### 4. If you leave no spouse or issue
Your entire estate will be dealt with under the rules for a 'free estate'.

**Free Estate**

In dealing with your free estate, any claimant's children or remoter issue may take the place of a claimant who pre-deceased you, except where the deceased claimant was your spouse or parent. If you are survived by at least one parent and at least one sibling (or their issue), 50% of your free estate goes to your parents and 50% to your siblings or their issue.

In any other case, the free estate goes to the nearest relatives to survive you, based on the following order of precedence:

  i)   Your siblings
  ii)  Your parents
  iii) Your surviving spouse (for cases under (2) above)
  iv)  Uncles and aunts
  v)   Grandparents
  vi)  Grandparents' siblings
  vii) Great-grandparents, etc.

If you have no relatives, as set out above; yes, you've guessed it, everything goes to the Crown.

So, as you can see, whether you live in Swansea, Penzance or Aberdeen (and probably Belfast too, although I don't have those rules available), you really shouldn't be relaxed about dying without a Will.

It is not unknown for widows to be forced to sell the family home due to the operation of the above rules and, without proper provision children could end up being taken into care.

The statutory rules set out above take no account of common-law partners, step-children or many other important personal relationships. A remote cousin could get everything in priority to a fondly loved step-child!

The Crown could even get your house in priority to a common-law partner you've lived with for decades. And you thought IHT was bad enough!

## 10.11   STATUTORY RIGHTS

In England, Wales or Northern Ireland, you may generally distribute your entire estate as you wish under the terms of your Will. Surviving spouses may, however, apply to the courts for an increased share of the estate where the amount provided to them in the Will does not represent adequate financial provision for their care and maintenance. In essence, this is something akin to posthumous divorce proceedings.

Similar applications may be made on behalf of dependent minor children of the deceased.

A different system operates in Scotland where 'legal rights' take priority over the terms of the deceased's Will unless waived by the beneficiaries concerned. Legal rights for beneficiaries of a deceased domiciled in Scotland are:

**Surviving spouse:** Where there are no issue of the deceased, one half of the deceased's moveable property, otherwise one third.

**Surviving issue:** Where there is no surviving spouse of the deceased, one half of the deceased's moveable property, otherwise one third.

Remember, the question of whether you are domiciled in Scotland is the same as any other domicile issue (see Chapter 15). Hence, you may have lived in London for many decades, but, if you or your parents were born in Scotland, you could still be domiciled in Scotland and your spouse and children will still have 'legal rights' as set out above.

Current proposals for the reform of the laws of succession in Scotland include a proposal to abolish legal rights for adult children. Again, however, it is uncertain whether this proposal will be adopted.


## 10.12   LIFE INSURANCE

One simple way to prevent your estate from being excessively inflated on your death is to ensure all forms of life insurance cover you have are written in favour of other family members. Such policies are effectively held on bare trust (see Section 8.8). In that way, the proceeds will never fall into your estate but will go, instead, to your intended beneficiaries free of IHT.

This should also extend to the 'Death Benefit' under any pension schemes where possible (see Section 10.15).

Ideally, if they can afford to do without it, your spouse should not be the beneficiary under any of your life policies. In practice, this suggestion may sometimes be somewhat impractical, especially when you have a young family, but it is worth reviewing the position as you get older.

Payments of regular insurance premiums will usually be covered by the annual exemption or the exemption for normal expenditure out of income (see Section 5.7), so these do not usually present a problem.

Depending on the exact circumstances, and for the reasons outlined in Section 4.4, a large lump-sum premium paid on a policy written in favour of another individual may represent a potentially exempt transfer, a chargeable lifetime transfer, or a mixture of both.


## 10.13   LIFE POLICIES WRITTEN IN TRUST

By writing a life policy 'into trust', you will be using a form of interest in possession trust rather than a bare trust. This retains the advantage of keeping the proceeds of the policy out of your estate but also means you can vary the intended beneficiaries over the course of your lifetime. Furthermore, this also ensures no IHT arises if any of those beneficiaries should pre-decease you.

For these reasons, it generally made sense to write life policies 'into trust' before March 2006.

For many policies written into trust before 22nd March 2006, it is 'business as usual' and their beneficial treatment still continues. HMRC has even confirmed that the payment of a regular premium on a policy already held by a pre-22/3/2006 interest in possession trust will generally continue to be classed as a potentially exempt transfer if not already exempted under some other provision. One change of beneficiary between 22nd March 2006 and 5th October 2008 will have turned the trust into a transitional serial interest (see Section 8.13) and it will effectively retain its beneficial treatment. Any other changes of beneficiary, however, will bring it into the relevant property trust regime (see Sections 8.17 to 8.19).

Life policies written into trust after 22nd March 2006 will generally fall into the relevant property trust regime. This also applies where changes are made to existing policies and those changes were not already permitted under the terms of the policy on 22nd March 2006.

Where a life policy falls into the relevant property trust regime, it may potentially be subject to entry, exit and anniversary charges.

Payments of regular premiums will usually be covered by the annual exemption or the exemption for normal expenditure out of income (see Section 5.7), so these do not usually present a problem in themselves.

Any large lump-sum premium payments, however, will be chargeable lifetime transfers and will give rise to immediate IHT liabilities where the policyholder's NRB has been exhausted.

Ten-yearly anniversary charges will be applied to the policy (Section 8.18). Generally, the policy's value for this purpose will be taken to be the cumulative amount of premiums paid to date, although in cases where the policyholder is in poor health at the anniversary date, it is feared HMRC may argue a greater value should be used to reflect the likelihood of the policy's imminent maturity. (An image of a vulture has suddenly jumped into my mind!)

Worst of all, of course, an exit charge of up to 6% (see Section 8.19) will apply when the policyholder dies. That's still a lot better than 40% though!

## 10.14  INSURING FOR INHERITANCE TAX LIABILITIES

Much of the IHT planning discussed elsewhere in this guide depends on the transferor surviving a certain period after a transfer, or some other transaction, has been made. Often the period concerned will be seven years, but survival to other anniversaries can often also be critical. When death occurs before the expiry of the critical period, unexpected tax bills can arrive as a nasty surprise. It is often a good idea, therefore, to take out some term life insurance on the transferor to guard against this possibility.

### Wealth Warning

Make sure the transferor themselves is not the beneficiary of the term insurance as this will inflate the value of their estate and lead to an effective 'grossing up' of IHT liabilities.

## 10.15 PENSIONS

In recent years pensions have become a lot more attractive when it comes to leaving money to your family. After you die your pension savings can be transferred tax free to any member of your family (or anyone else for that matter). Under the old rules a 55% 'death tax' was generally payable.

### Death Before Age 75

Your pension savings can be paid tax free to any beneficiary. It doesn't matter whether you've started withdrawing money from the pension scheme or not. Your beneficiaries can withdraw your pension savings as a tax-free lump sum or keep the money invested in a drawdown plan and make tax-free withdrawals as and when they like. The drawdown investments will continue to grow tax free.

### 75 or Older

Your beneficiaries can inherit all your pension savings but they will have to pay Income Tax on any money they withdraw. They can keep the money invested where it will continue to grow tax free for as long as they like.

There are no restrictions on the amount of income they can withdraw, i.e. the whole pension pot can be paid out in a single tax year, although this could result in a large Income Tax bill.

### Inheritance Tax

Pension savings are typically held in trust outside your estate and are thus free from IHT in most cases. This is because the pension scheme administrator normally has discretion over who inherits your pension pot. However, they will typically be guided by your wishes, which can be stated on a simple expression of wishes form. Because these forms are usually not legally binding (although rarely ignored) your pension savings will not form part of your estate for IHT purposes.

See the Taxcafe.co.uk guide *'Pension Magic'* for more information.

## 10.16 LOTTERY SYNDICATES

Lottery, pools and other gambling syndicates are 'breeding grounds' for potential IHT problems. Just imagine this:

### *Example*
*Donny wins £15m on the National Lottery. It's in all the newspapers, so you can bet HMRC knows about it. He gives £3m to each of his brothers, Wayne, Merrill, Jay*

*and Jimmy. Tragically, just a few weeks later, Donny is killed water skiing in Utah.*

*HMRC demands almost £6m in IHT from Donny's family as the transfers to his brothers were made only weeks before his death. "But we were in a syndicate," protest the brothers. "Prove it!" replies HMRC.*

The simple answer to this problem is to make sure you have documentary evidence of any syndicate arrangements.

We can take the principle of the lottery syndicate a step further. A few years ago, I heard that an 84 year-old lottery winner had given away his entire £13m win to a combination of charities and family and friends.

Like most other people (I suspect), my first thought was "what a nice chap", but then the cynic in me took over and I began to wonder if there was perhaps an IHT planning motive present here.

But, at 84, our lottery winner's life expectancy was around five and a half years. Hence, while his charitable transferees are in the clear, his family and friends would be well advised to keep 40% of their gifts to one side in case their benefactor doesn't last too long.

Our winner could, however, have planned things better. Let's suppose he had previously drawn up a lottery syndicate agreement with his family and friends and agreed to share any winnings with them. Naturally, his family and friends would also agree to contribute to the weekly lottery stake. However, in practice, the transferor would then pay the weekly stake himself.

The transferor's payment of the weekly stake would represent a transfer of value, but it should be sufficiently small to be exempt as 'normal expenditure out of income', or else be covered by the annual exemption.

I would suggest this course of action makes sense for any elderly person playing the lottery (or 'doing the pools', etc.)

### 10.17 MINOR PROBLEMS

You may have noticed I tend to base most of my examples around gifts to adult children. This is because making transfers of value to minor children carries a few extra complications.

### Gifts to Minors by Parents
Any gift from a parent to, or for the benefit of, their own minor child is subject to the Income Tax 'settlements' legislation. This means the parent is subject to tax on any income derived from the gifted assets (subject to a general exemption for income not exceeding £100 per annum and the further exemptions for Child Trust Funds and Junior ISAs explained below).

> #### Tax Tip
> The Income Tax burden can often be reduced by making sure the parent with the lower level of income makes the gift.

The child does have their own annual exemption and basic rate band for CGT purposes, so some savings can be generated on capital gains, such as where funds are invested in a stock market portfolio on behalf of the child.

Assets gifted to a child, or purchased with gifted funds, are usually held on bare trust, with one parent acting as trustee. Bare trusts are treated as if the child owned the assets directly for IHT purposes (Section 8.8); although it is important not to fall foul of the 'gifts with reservation' rules (Section 4.9).

The best way for a parent to make large IHT effective gifts to minor children is generally to use relevant property trusts (see Sections 9.1 to 9.3). Such trusts will be 'settlor-interested trusts' (Section 9.8). Hence, given the inability to hold over capital gains, it will generally make sense to make cash settlements into the trust.

When using a 'settlor-interested' trust, it is essential to ensure the parent making the settlement cannot benefit. If both parents are making a settlement into the trust then neither can benefit. Even when there is only one settlor, it is generally wise to ensure their spouse cannot benefit. If a settlor can or, in practice, does benefit from a trust, the assets and funds within the trust will be treated as 'gifts with reservation' (see Section 4.9) and the trust will be rendered ineffective for IHT planning purposes. See Section 9.8 for further guidance. For smaller gifts, either a Child Trust Fund or a Junior ISA may be the best vehicle to use (see further below).

### Grandparents, Aunts, Uncles, Etc

Other family members may generally make gifts to minor children without facing the problems set out above. Hence, you could make gifts to your grandchildren, or your nephews and nieces, and these will usually simply be potentially exempt transfers; or you could transfer assets into trust for these children and holdover any capital gains arising. Similarly, your parents, or your siblings, could make gifts to your children, or into a trust for their benefit, with the same results. Be careful to avoid any kind of reciprocal arrangements, however, as these might trigger the 'associated operations' rules (see Section 10.19).

Furthermore, don't forget the 'gifts with reservation' rules (Section 4.9) can apply to a gift to any person, or any trust where you are not excluded from benefitting.

### Will Trusts for Minors

HMRC appears to take the view that a minor cannot have an immediate post-death interest (see Section 8.12), as the Trustee Act 1925 would make such a trust discretionary in nature. Anyone intending to leave assets to trust for the benefit of a minor should therefore consider using a bereaved minor's trust, an '18 to 25 Trust', or even just a bare trust.

A bare trust carries some advantages for Income Tax and CGT purposes, as the minor's own allowances could be set against income and capital gains. A similar result may be obtained via the 'trusts for vulnerable individuals' exception (see Section 8.21) but this carries a few limitations that will not always be desirable.

## Child Trust Funds and Junior ISAs

Every child born in the UK between 1st September 2002 and 2nd January 2011 should have a Child Trust Fund. Junior ISAs are available to all UK resident minors who were not eligible for a Child Trust Fund.

Parents, family, and friends of minor children may put up to £9,000 in total into the child's Junior ISA or Child Trust Fund in 2020/21 (similar amounts are expected to apply in each future year). Monies are invested in a long-term investment account to grow free from Income Tax or CGT, like a normal ISA.

On maturity, funds within a Child Trust Fund may be transferred to an ISA in the child's name. Junior ISAs automatically convert to a normal ISA when the child reaches 18. No withdrawals are permitted before this time.

Payments into Child Trust Funds or Junior ISAs are potentially exempt transfers unless covered by an exemption, such as the annual exemption or the exemption for normal expenditure out of income.

Funds within a Child Trust Fund or Junior ISA form part of the child's estate and, crucially, **not** their parent's. They remain subject to IHT, however, in the tragic event that the child should die before the age of 18 (yes, if a child's estate exceeds the NRB, they are subject to IHT like anyone else. Vultures!)

### 10.18   INCOME, CAPITAL AND CONTROL

One of the major practical problems that stands in the way of effective IHT planning is the fact the prospective transferor usually wishes to shed capital (in order to save IHT), but needs to retain income (in order to survive!)

On top of this, the prospective transferor will often wish to retain control of the underlying assets.

In Chapter 9 we saw how relevant property trusts could be used as a means to retain control. We also saw how discounted gift trusts and loan trusts provided effective means to retain an 'income' stream. However, the 'gift with reservation' rules (see Section 4.9) generally make it very difficult to retain both income and control while still giving away capital effectively.

Where BPR is available (see Chapter 7), the taxpayer is in the happy position that retaining control of their capital and keeping their income will not give rise to an IHT liability.

For investments or businesses that do not qualify for BPR, possible methods to get around this fundamental dilemma include:

- Using a family investment company (see Chapter 13)
- Holding property through a partnership or Limited Liability Partnership
- Family debt schemes (see Section 6.16)

Some of these methods also provide opportunities to pass on capital in small parcels, thus making effective use of the IHT and CGT annual exemptions (but see Section 10.19).

Finally, an additional problem that often arises is that the elderly sometimes hang on to control too long. We'll look at possible solutions in Section 16.15.

## 10.19 ASSOCIATED OPERATIONS & THE GENERAL ANTI-ABUSE RULE

Where there are two or more transfers of the same property, or two or more transactions that affect the same property, HMRC may invoke the associated operations rules.

Broadly speaking, where these rules are applied, the transfers or transactions are treated as if just one transfer from the original transferor to the ultimate recipient had taken place, thus undoing any tax planning the intermediate steps aimed to achieve.

HMRC's powers under the associated operations rules are extremely wide-ranging and, as we have seen several times throughout this guide, there are many IHT planning techniques that might potentially be caught. Nevertheless, where there are sufficiently good non-tax reasons for carrying out the transactions involved, the application of the associated operations rules may still be avoided.

Time is a good defence against the associated operations rules: the longer the gap between one transaction and the next, the less likely the planning measures are to be attacked. Uncertainty is also important. Where subsequent transfers are uncertain of being carried out at the time of an earlier transfer, they are far less likely to be deemed associated operations.

It is also worth noting that, as a general principle, death itself is not regarded as an associated operation or a step in a tax avoidance scheme (perhaps because, while the event itself is certain, the timing is not). This saves many planning techniques from being caught by the associated operations rules.

The general anti-abuse rule ('GAAR') is targeted at 'artificial' and 'abusive' or 'aggressive' tax avoidance schemes that go beyond the scope of normal tax planning and use loopholes in tax legislation in a way not intended by Parliament. We are told 'normal' tax planning should not be affected.

Where the GAAR applies, any tax advantage gained through the use of the 'abusive' scheme will be reversed.

To date, HMRC have not applied the GAAR to any of the IHT planning strategies in this guide. It seems unlikely that the GAAR could affect any IHT planning techniques not already at risk of attack under the associated operations rules. Nonetheless, there is a risk that some more advanced IHT planning techniques might one day be challenged under the GAAR.

## 10.20  DISCLOSURE OF TAX AVOIDANCE SCHEMES

There is a legal obligation to disclose certain types of IHT planning techniques under the 'DOTAS' (disclosure of tax avoidance schemes) regime. In other words, the taxpayer using the technique must advise HMRC they have done so. Disclosure does not necessarily mean the scheme doesn't work, but it may lead to greater scrutiny from HMRC.

Only the more advanced techniques are affected, specifically those which:

- Reduce or eliminate the entry, anniversary or exit charges where assets or funds are placed in a relevant property trust (see Chapter 8)
- Reduce or eliminate charges on company participators (not referred to in this guide, but potentially an issue for family investment companies: see Chapter 13)
- Avoid the 'gifts with reservation of benefit' rules (see Section 4.9), without leading to a pre-owned assets charge (see Section 10.21)
- Reduce the value of a person's estate without creating a chargeable lifetime transfer or potentially exempt transfer

The arrangements must also involve one or more 'contrived or abnormal' steps to require disclosure. Writing a Will is never regarded as 'abnormal', so anything put in place purely through a Will need not be disclosed.

By and large it is only commercial products, such as those covered in Sections 7.27, 9.11, and 9.12, or complex arrangements, such as those in Section 12.13, Chapter 13, and Sections 14.1 and 14.2, which may need to be disclosed. These generally require professional advice. Hence, *my* advice is:

### Practical Pointer
Whenever an IHT planning technique is complex enough to require professional advice, seek advice regarding whether the scheme needs to be reported under DOTAS at the same time.

## 10.21  THE PRE-OWNED ASSETS CHARGE

An Income Tax charge may be levied on the former owner of an asset who continues to benefit from that asset. The charge may also extend to a donor who benefits from the use of assets purchased with funds they had previously gifted.

While this is an Income Tax charge, its purpose is to deter IHT planning. Hence there is a general exemption for assets already caught under the 'gifts with reservation' rules (see Section 4.9) or that are otherwise still included in the donor's estate.

Assets subject to the charge are known as 'pre-owned assets' and, broadly, the charge taxes the 'annual value' of these assets as a benefit-in-kind. For land and buildings, the annual value is the property's open-market rental value. For most other assets it is based on a fixed sum of 5% of their capital value.

The initial values to be used are those prevailing on the date the asset first falls within the provisions. These values can be used for five years before the asset must be revalued.

Any amounts the former owner is paying for the use of the asset may be deducted from the annual value in arriving at the taxable benefit. These payments must be made under a legal obligation so, in the case of property, a formal lease is required.

The charge is designed to hit back at a number of IHT planning schemes but, technically, could also catch many unintended, innocent victims, as there is no 'motive' test. Furthermore, there is no exemption for an unexpected change of circumstances in the same way as there is for 'gifts with reservation' (see Section 4.9).

### Practical Pointer
HMRC have been accused of 'institutional disinterest' in the pre-owned assets charge as it is really designed to deter IHT planning and they seem to have very little interest in actually collecting it. Nonetheless, where the charge is technically due, it remains the taxpayer's duty to report it.

### Wealth Warning
Subject to the 'practical pointer' above, technically speaking, one of the greatest risk areas is gifts between unmarried partners. For example, if an individual gives their partner some money to help with the purchase of a property that they then live in together, that property is caught by the charge. Furthermore, the charge still applies even if the couple subsequently get married.

Such problems can usually be avoided by either purchasing the property in joint names or by marrying before the gift is made: although these simple strategies will not be available in every case.

### Exemptions
Thankfully, there are a few exemptions from the charge, including:

i)      Gifts to your spouse; or to a former spouse under the terms of a court order (including gifts to a trust for their benefit: although the exemption ceases to apply if their interest comes to an end before their death)
ii)     Gifts for 'maintenance of family' (see Sections 5.5 and 5.6)
iii)    Gifts wholly covered by the annual exemption or small gifts exemption
iv)     Sales of your entire interest in an asset made on commercial, arm's length terms (even if made to a connected party)
v)      Sales of a part interest in an asset made on normal, commercial, arm's length terms to an unconnected party, or for consideration not in the form of money, or assets readily convertible into money (see Appendix B for a list of 'connected persons')

| vi) | The donor's total annual taxable benefits **before** deducting contributions paid by the donor do not exceed £5,000. This is an 'all or nothing' exemption so, if total taxable benefits exceed this amount, the **whole** sum (less donor contributions) is taxed |
| --- | --- |
| vii) | The asset was acquired with funds derived from an outright gift of money seven years or more before the donor first enjoyed any benefit |
| viii) | The original gift was to a charity or other exempt body (see Section 3.5) |
| ix) | The donor has retained a suitable interest in the gifted asset, such as a parent who has given a joint share in a property to an adult child who lives there with them |

Furthermore, the charge does not apply to non-UK residents, or to assets that would not be chargeable to UK IHT, such as foreign assets formerly held by, or purchased with funds donated by, a non-UK domiciled individual (who is also not deemed UK domiciled and has not 'opted in': see Sections 2.2 and 6.19 respectively).

The charge does not apply where the donor's enjoyment of an asset is minor and incidental, such as social visits to the current occupier of a property. The charge can only apply to property if the donor is in 'occupation' and HMRC's guidance suggests this requires an element of 'control and exclusion': for example, the ability to access the property freely, or store items at the property. However, use of a property that fulfils these criteria will amount to 'occupation', even if only occasional.

Finally, there is a 'Get Out Of Jail - But Not Free' card, in the shape of an option to elect out of the pre-owned assets charge by allowing the relevant asset to be included in the donor's estate for IHT purposes. The asset is then treated as a 'gift with reservation' (see Section 4.9) and effectively remains in the donor's estate for as long as they continue to enjoy a benefit. The election should be made by 31st January following the tax year in which the charge would have first arisen, although HMRC generally accept late elections. Once made, the election is irrevocable.

The most likely application of the pre-owned assets charge is in the case of the family home, so we will consider this issue further in Chapter 12.

# Chapter 11

# Interaction with CGT

## 11.1 A QUICK CAPITAL GAINS TAX UPDATE

Before we look at that 'clash of the titans' created by the interaction between CGT and IHT, it may be useful if I provide a quick update on the current CGT regime.

Individuals currently pay CGT at five rates:

- 10% where entrepreneurs' relief or investor's relief is available (see Section 11.5)
- 18% on gains on residential property made by basic rate taxpayers
- 28% on gains on residential property made by higher rate taxpayers
- 10% on other gains made by basic rate taxpayers
- 20% on other gains made by higher rate taxpayers

Basic rate taxpayers pay the reduced rates to the extent of any basic rate tax band remaining available. Generally speaking, therefore, once your combined taxable income and gains for the tax year exceed the higher-rate tax threshold (£50,000 for 2020/21), you must pay CGT at either 20% or 28%, as appropriate, on any further amount of capital gains arising in the same tax year.

### *Example*
*Beyoncé has taxable income of £38,000 for 2020/21. After deducting her personal allowance of £12,500, she is liable for Income Tax on £25,500. This means £12,000 of her £37,500 basic rate band for 2020/21 remains available.*

*In February 2021, Beyoncé makes a capital gain of £37,300 on a residential investment property. After deducting her annual CGT exemption of £12,300 she is left with a taxable gain of £25,000.*

*The first £12,000 of Beyoncé's taxable gain is taxed at 18% and the remaining £13,000 is taxed at 28%.*

Anyone with taxable income in excess of the higher-rate tax threshold simply pays CGT at 20% or 28% on all their capital gains after deducting the annual CGT exemption. (Except where entrepreneurs' relief or investor's relief is available – see Section 11.5)

For further details of the current CGT regime, see the Taxcafe.co.uk guide *'How to Save Property Tax'*.

## 11.2   THE UPLIFT ON DEATH

Do you remember my opening comments in Section 4.5? I'll refresh your memory: "For CGT purposes, death is often a very good tax-planning strategy."

The reason for this rather dark-humoured remark is one simple fact. On death, the CGT base cost of all the deceased's assets is uplifted to their market value at that date.

### Example

*In 1985, Jerry set up Killer Ltd with an investment of just £10,000. By July 2020, his controlling interest in Killer Promotions PLC (the same company) is worth £100m. Jerry's CGT bill on a sale of these shares would be almost £20m.*

*Sadly, Jerry dies in August 2020, and leaves his entire Killer Promotions PLC shareholding to his son Lee. Lee sells the shares for £102m in March 2021. His CGT bill will be just £400,000 at most.*

Lee is treated as if he acquired the shares in August 2020 for a price of £100m. We call this the CGT 'uplift on death'. His taxable gain on the sale in March 2021 is therefore just £2m.

## 11.3   THE CAPITAL GAINS TAX vs INHERITANCE TAX DILEMMA

While death is very good CGT planning, lifetime transfers generally pose a problem. As explained in Section 4.10, a lifetime transfer of anything other than cash will give rise to a CGT disposal, which is deemed to take place at market value.

Hence, in our example above, if Jerry had given the Killer Promotions PLC shares to Lee before he died, he may have given himself a £20m CGT bill!

This creates a bit of a dilemma: the best way to save IHT is often to make lifetime transfers, whereas the best way to save CGT is to hold on to assets until death.

What we really want to do is minimise the overall tax burden (or, to be more precise, follow **Bayley's Law**, as per Section 10.2). To do this, we need to start by considering what reliefs the assets concerned will qualify for, both under the IHT regime and the CGT regime.

The three major areas to consider are:

- Business assets
- Transfers to spouses
- The family home

We will look at each of these areas in turn. 'Other assets' that do not fall under any of these headings are dealt with in Sections 11.9 and 11.10.

## 11.4    GIFTS OF BUSINESS ASSETS

Where a qualifying business asset is transferred by way of gift, the capital gain arising may be held over. This provides an effective CGT deferral but does mean the uplift on death will be lost.

### *Example*
*Kurt set up Nevermind Ltd in 2001 with a share capital of just 100 £1 ordinary shares. The shares currently qualify for both holdover relief and entrepreneurs' relief (see Section 11.5).*

*In December 2020, Kurt gives 25 shares to his unmarried partner Courtney and they elect to hold over the capital gain arising. In effect, this means Courtney is treated as if she acquired the shares for £1 each: the same price Kurt paid for them.*

*Kurt dies in March 2021 and, fearing a drop in value, Courtney decides to sell her Nevermind Ltd shares at their current value of £50,000 per share, or £1.25m in total.*

*Courtney's base cost for her shares is just £25, so she ends up with a capital gain of £1,249,975. Her CGT bill, at 20%, is therefore £249,995 (assuming she is a higher-rate taxpayer and has used her annual exemption elsewhere).*

Sadly, despite its name, holdover relief on gifts of business assets does not actually apply to assets used in a 'business', but generally only to assets used in a trade. What will qualify as a 'trade' can be very difficult to define, but it certainly does not include property investment businesses.

Broadly, the assets that qualify for holdover relief will be:

* Assets used in a qualifying trade (including goodwill)
* Unquoted shares in a trading company
* A holding of at least 5% of a quoted trading company

This time, 'unquoted' does not include shares traded on AIM.

To be a trading company, the underlying business must not include any 'substantial' element of non-trading activities. This is usually taken to mean non-trading activities amount to no more than 20% of the business, using the tests set out in Section 7.7.

Property used in a qualifying furnished holiday letting business (see the Taxcafe.co.uk guide *'How to Save Property Tax'* for details) also qualifies, even though this is not strictly a trade for tax purposes. Additionally, anything that qualifies for APR (Section 7.29) also qualifies for CGT holdover relief.

### Partial Holdover

While a lifetime transfer inevitably means the transferee will not benefit from the CGT uplift on death, it is sometimes possible to achieve a partial uplift without incurring an immediate CGT liability.

This is because where assets are actually sold to the transferee, but for a price less than their full market value, the gain held over is the difference between the sale price and the market value of the assets. The net result is the transferee is now deemed to have acquired the assets for the price actually paid on the transfer.

Where the transferor's annual CGT exemption is available, a tax-free uplift of up to £12,300 (at 2020/21 rates) can usually be achieved.

### Example Revisited

*Let us suppose Kurt actually sold his 25 Nevermind Ltd shares to Courtney for £12,325. By using a holdover relief election, Kurt's capital gain can be reduced to just £12,300, which is covered by his annual CGT exemption. Assuming Kurt had no other capital gains during 2020/21, the transfer could therefore still be made free of CGT.*

*After paying Stamp Duty at 0.5% of £62, Courtney would have a base cost for the shares of £12,387 instead of just £25 as before.*

*When Courtney later sold her shares, her capital gain would be reduced to £1,237,613 giving her a CGT bill of £247,523.*

*This simple mechanism would therefore save Courtney £2,472 in CGT; or a net £2,410 after taking account of the Stamp Duty cost.*

Where land and buildings are transferred using this strategy, the SDLT cost will need to be taken into account and this will often be quite significant (see the Taxcafe.co.uk guide *'How to Save Property Tax'* for details).

The sale proceeds on the transfer will, of course, remain in the transferor's estate. However, the proceeds could be left outstanding as a loan and the benefit of the loan could be given to another individual as a potentially exempt transfer (using a variation of the 'family debt scheme' in Section 6.16). The potentially exempt transfer would be exempt after seven years.

The loan may be deductible from the transferee's estate, but this will depend on whether it is repaid out of the assets of their estate (see Section 2.11) and on whether the property transferred qualified for BPR or APR (see Section 7.11).

### Restrictions and Formalities

Holdover relief on 'Gifts of Business Assets' is not available for:

- A transfer of shares or securities to a company
- Any transfer to a settlor-interested trust (see Section 9.8)

A claim for holdover relief requires a joint election by the transferor and the transferee (or by the transferor alone where the transferee is a trust).

## 11.5 BUSINESS PROPERTY RELIEF AND ENTREPRENEURS' RELIEF

As we have already seen, the uplift on death provides enormous potential to save CGT. Whether that saving is achieved at an IHT cost, however, is highly dependent on whether BPR or APR is available.

Another important factor for business assets is the question of whether entrepreneurs' relief is available for CGT purposes.

### Entrepreneurs' Relief

Where a disposal of business assets qualifies for entrepreneurs' relief, the rate of CGT applying is reduced to 10%. Each individual may only claim entrepreneurs' relief on a maximum cumulative lifetime total of £1m of capital gains (£10m for disposals arising before 11th March 2020). Thereafter, the CGT rate will revert to the normal rates set out in Section 11.1.

The qualifying rules for entrepreneurs' relief are entirely different to the rules for BPR or holdover relief, so it is essential to consider each relief separately in every case.

Broadly speaking, entrepreneurs' relief is available on the disposal of:

i) The whole or part of a qualifying business
ii) Assets formerly used in a qualifying business that has ceased or been disposed of
iii) Shares or securities in a 'personal company'

A qualifying business for this purpose is generally a trade, although, once again, qualifying furnished holiday letting businesses (see the Taxcafe.co.uk guide *'How to Save Property Tax'* for details) also qualify.

A 'part' of a business can only be counted for these purposes if it is capable of operating as a going concern in its own right and HMRC interprets this point very strictly. However, an 'interest' in a business, such as a partnership share, may qualify.

A disposal of assets formerly used in a qualifying business must take place within three years after the cessation or disposal of the business.

In all cases, the individual making the disposal must have owned the qualifying business for at least the 'qualifying period' (see below) prior to its disposal, or cessation, as the case may be.

### The Qualifying Period

The 'qualifying period' for a number of the tests referred to throughout this section is generally two years, but is just one year where the business ceased before 29th October 2018 (or the disposal took place before 6th April 2019).

## Personal Company

The definition of a 'personal company' for the purposes of entrepreneurs' relief is broadly as follows:

i) The individual holds at least 5% of the ordinary share capital
ii) The holding under (i) provides at least 5% of the voting rights
iii) The company is a trading company (using the same 20% rule as we saw in Section 11.4)
iv) The individual is an officer or employee of the company (an 'officer' includes a non-executive director or company secretary)
v) The individual's shareholding gives them at least a 5% interest in both the distributable profits and net assets of the company
    OR
    On a disposal of all the company's ordinary shares, the individual would be entitled to at least 5% of the proceeds

Each of these rules must be satisfied for at least the qualifying period prior to the disposal in question or, if earlier, the cessation of the business. In the latter case, the disposal must again take place within three years after cessation. Furnished holiday letting is again accepted as trading.

## Associated Disposals

Entrepreneurs' relief may sometimes extend to assets owned personally but used in the trade of a 'personal company', or a partnership in which the owner is a partner. A number of restrictions apply to these 'associated disposals', however. Broadly, the relief is only available where the owner is also disposing of at least a 5% stake in the company or partnership, or is disposing of their entire remaining stake, having held at least a 5% stake at some time in the past.

The assets must have been used in the company or partnership's business for at least the qualifying period immediately prior to the sale of the business stake or, if earlier, cessation of the business. In the latter case, the disposal must again take place within three years after cessation. Assets purchased after 12th June 2016 need to have been owned for at least three years at the date of disposal.

The relief is restricted where the asset has not been used in the business throughout the seller's ownership or where any payment has been received for the use of the asset after 5th April 2008.

## Investor's Relief

Investor's relief is available to investors subscribing for new issues of ordinary shares in unlisted trading companies after 16th March 2016. Shares must be held for at least three years commencing from 6th April 2016 in order to qualify and the investor must **not** be an officer or employee of the company.

Shares qualifying for investor's relief are subject to a CGT rate of 10%. The relief is subject to a lifetime limit of £10m of capital gains: this is a separate allowance to the limit applying to entrepreneurs' relief.

Where an individual holds shares qualifying for investor's relief, the implications for IHT planning discussed in this guide will be the same as in the case of shares qualifying for entrepreneurs' relief.

### Interaction between Business Property Relief and Entrepreneurs' Relief or Investor's Relief

The interaction between these important reliefs has enormous consequences for estate preservation planning. There are three possible combinations we need to consider, so let's examine each in turn.

### Business Property Relief & Either Entrepreneurs' Relief or Investor's Relief Available

These assets can be passed on free from IHT and it will therefore often make sense for the transferor to hang on to these assets and transfer them on death to obtain the CGT uplift with no IHT cost.

If it is not possible to hang on to the original assets until death, the same result can sometimes be achieved by exchanging these assets for 'replacement assets', as explained in Section 7.18. To avoid any CGT liabilities on the exchange, the 'replacement assets' generally need to be one of the following:

i) Shares issued in exchange for shares in the transferor's own company (e.g. a 'takeover')
ii) Shares issued in exchange for the transfer of an unincorporated business into a company
iii) Business property acquired within the three year period following the disposal of the original assets. (E.g. buying business premises to replace previous premises used in the same business or the acquisition of property for use in a new qualifying business.)

Any new business under (iii) will need to qualify as a trading business. A qualifying furnished holiday letting business would also suffice for this purpose from a CGT perspective, but is unlikely to qualify for BPR (see Section 7.5).

Assets that qualify for holdover relief on 'Gifts of Business Assets' (see Section 11.4) can generally be transferred during the transferor's lifetime without any CGT liability. However, while this avoids CGT on the transfer, it also denies the transferee the benefit of the 'uplift on death'.

On the other hand, a transfer of assets qualifying for entrepreneurs' relief or investor's relief will be subject to CGT at a rate of just 10%. In many cases, it will make sense **NOT** to claim holdover relief on the transfer, so the transferee may benefit from an increased CGT base cost on the assets. This is particularly relevant where the transferee is considering a sale of the asset in the near future (although the potential impact of such a sale when the transferor dies within seven years needs to be considered – see Section 7.19).

## Business Property Relief but Not Entrepreneurs' Relief or Investor's Relief

These assets can be passed on free from IHT but would often attract an immediate CGT charge of up to 20% or 28% in the case of a lifetime transfer.

If the Killer Promotions PLC shares in our example in Section 11.2 qualified for BPR, Jerry would have been able to leave them to Lee free of IHT. As we saw in Section 11.2, Lee was treated as if he had bought the shares at market value at the date of Jerry's death, thus drastically reducing his CGT bill.

In this situation, it will therefore generally make sense to hang on to the assets and only transfer them on death. CGT uplift will be obtained and both IHT and CGT can be avoided if the transferee sells the assets shortly afterwards. At the very least, there should be a substantial reduction in CGT, as we saw in Section 11.2.

Again, it may be possible to achieve the same results when the assets are exchanged for 'replacement assets' before death. The opportunity to avoid CGT on such an exchange is more limited, however, and item (iii) outlined above may no longer apply in some cases.

Lifetime transfers of these assets will often give rise to immediate CGT liabilities, as holdover relief on 'Gifts of Business Assets' (Section 11.4) may not be available. Even where it is available, the 'uplift on death' will be lost and the transferee will most likely suffer CGT at up to 20% or 28% on the held over gain when they ultimately sell the asset (although there will be a few instances where the transferee is eligible for entrepreneurs' relief and thus pays CGT at just 10%).

**Entrepreneurs' Relief or Investor's Relief but Not Business Property Relief** (Although it is difficult to foresee a situation where an individual qualifies for investor's relief, but not BPR, on the same shareholding)

This scenario could apply where:

   i)   A qualifying business has ceased within the last three years
   ii)  A furnished holiday letting business qualifies for entrepreneurs' relief but not for BPR
   iii) An individual has shares or securities in a quoted company that qualifies as their 'personal company' for the purposes of entrepreneurs' relief

In these cases we face a major dilemma. A lifetime transfer (before the expiry of the three year period in the first case) will give rise to a maximum CGT charge of just 10%, but the opportunity to achieve the CGT uplift on death will be lost and the transferee may face a charge of up to 20% or 28% on the future growth in the asset's value. On the other hand, if the assets are still held at the time of death, IHT will be fully chargeable.

Furthermore, in the first case, it is unlikely the assets will be eligible for holdover relief on 'Gifts of Business Assets' (see Section 11.4). Even where this relief is available, it only provides a CGT deferral and the 'uplift on death' will be lost.

In practice, it may be difficult to establish the best course of action but an early transfer will often produce an overall saving.

### *Example*
*Sanjeev has a large estate well in excess of the NRB, including a 5% shareholding in a quoted trading company that qualifies for entrepreneurs' relief. Sanjeev's base cost in these shares for CGT purposes is £2m.*

*In February 2021, Sanjeev transfers his shares to his daughter Meera when they are worth £3m. He decides not to claim holdover relief in order to secure the benefit of entrepreneurs' relief. His resultant CGT bill is therefore £100,000 (he has used his annual exemption elsewhere). In March 2028, Sanjeev dies when the shares are worth £5m. As the transfer to Meera took place more than seven years previously, no IHT is due. If Sanjeev had still held the shares at this time, the IHT arising would have been £2m.*

*Meera now sells the shares, giving rise to a capital gain of £2m and a CGT bill, at 20%, of £400,000 (she is a higher-rate taxpayer, has used her annual exemption elsewhere, and is not eligible for entrepreneurs' relief). Hence, while father and daughter between them have paid £500,000 in CGT, the overall net tax saving for the family is £1.5m.*

*In fact, if we take account of the additional IHT saved due to the £100,000 reduction in the value of Sanjeev's estate when he paid his CGT bill, the overall net saving is actually £1.54m.*

Clearly, in this example, it was worth incurring a relatively low CGT cost, as the asset was successfully removed from Sanjeev's estate by way of a potentially exempt transfer more than seven years before his death. On the other hand, if Sanjeev had died immediately after his transfer to Meera, there would have been no IHT saving (other than the £40,000 saved due to Sanjeev's CGT bill). The CGT liability would have been incurred needlessly when Meera could have had a CGT uplift on her father's death.

Furthermore, if Sanjeev had left a surviving spouse, the transfer to Meera would have used up his NRB, leaving no TNRB to be used against the spouse's estate.

Between these two extremes lie an almost infinite variety of outcomes. As a general guide, I have produced the table below. It follows broadly the same lines as the example, but with a few minor modifications. It is based on the following assumptions:

i) There is an existing gain of £1m giving rise to a CGT liability of £100,000
ii) The asset is currently worth £3m and its future value will increase at a rate of 7.5% per annum (compound)
iii) The transferee will sell the asset immediately after the transferor's death and will not be entitled to entrepreneurs' relief
iv) The transferee is a higher-rate taxpayer
v) Both the transferor and transferee will use their CGT annual exemption elsewhere
vi) The transferor will not hold over the gain arising on the transfer
vii) The asset is not residential property
viii) The NRB and any TNRB to which they are entitled would have been fully utilised against other property within the transferor's estate if the transfer had not taken place
ix) The transferor survives just beyond the relevant anniversary
x) The NRB in future years is as per our forecast in Section 3.2

| Transferor Dies After | Value on Death | IHT on Transfer* | CGT on Final Sale | IHT if Still in Estate | Net Saving or (Cost)** |
|---|---|---|---|---|---|
| < 1 year | £3,000,000 | £1,200,000 | £0 | £1,200,000 | (£60,000) |
| 1 year | £3,225,000 | £1,200,000 | £45,000 | £1,290,000 | (£15,000) |
| 2 years | £3,466,875 | £1,200,000 | £93,375 | £1,386,750 | £33,375 |
| 3 years | £3,726,891 | £986,000 | £145,378 | £1,490,756 | £299,378 |
| 4 years | £4,006,407 | £773,440 | £201,281 | £1,602,563 | £567,841 |
| 5 years | £4,306,888 | £562,320 | £261,378 | £1,722,755 | £839,058 |
| 6 years | £4,629,905 | £352,640 | £325,981 | £1,851,962 | £1,113,341 |
| 7 years | £4,977,147 | £0 | £395,429 | £1,990,859 | £1,535,429 |
| 8 years | £5,350,433 | £0 | £470,087 | £2,140,173 | £1,610,087 |
| 9 years | £5,751,716 | £0 | £550,343 | £2,300,686 | £1,690,343 |
| 10 years | £6,183,095 | £0 | £636,619 | £2,473,238 | £1,776,619 |

* Includes the additional tax on the estate arising as a result of the transfer (i.e. due to the transfer using up the deceased's NRB in the event of their death within seven years). For this purpose, it is assumed no TNRB is available to the deceased.

** Net saving/(cost) takes account of the CGT paid on the original transfer less the IHT saving arising as a result of this cost.

As we can see, under this scenario, the transferor only needs to survive for two years to make the transfer worthwhile.

The above savings are based on the assumption that the transferor's NRB (and any TNRB available) would be used up on other assets within their estate. This will not be the case if they would have otherwise left everything to their UK domiciled spouse and the points to be considered in this situation are covered in Chapter 6.

## Transferees Eligible for Entrepreneurs' Relief

A lifetime transfer becomes even more attractive where the transferee will also be eligible for entrepreneurs' relief on the transferred asset. In our example above, this might apply if the company Sanjeev held his shares in became Meera's 'personal company' after the transfer.

In practice, this could generally be achieved by ensuring that at least 5% of the ordinary shares are transferred and the transferee is, or becomes, an officer or employee of the company.

The following table sets out the position arising under the same scenario as before except the transferee now qualifies for entrepreneurs' relief on the transferred asset.

| Transferor Dies After | Value on Death | IHT on Transfer | CGT on Final Sale | IHT if Still in Estate | Net Saving or (Cost) |
|---|---|---|---|---|---|
| < 1 year | £3,000,000 | £1,200,000 | £0 | £1,200,000 | (£60,000) |
| 1 year | £3,225,000 | £1,200,000 | *£46,688 | £1,290,000 | (£16,688) |
| 2 years | £3,466,875 | £1,200,000 | £46,688 | £1,386,750 | £80,063 |
| 3 years | £3,726,891 | £986,000 | £72,689 | £1,490,756 | £372,067 |
| 4 years | £4,006,407 | £773,440 | £101,281 | £1,602,563 | £667,841 |
| 5 years | £4,306,888 | £562,320 | £161,378 | £1,722,755 | £939,058 |
| 6 years | £4,629,905 | £352,640 | £225,981 | £1,851,962 | £1,213,341 |
| 7 years | £4,977,147 | £0 | £295,429 | £1,990,859 | £1,635,429 |
| 8 years | £5,350,433 | £0 | £370,087 | £2,140,173 | £1,710,087 |
| 9 years | £5,751,716 | £0 | £450,343 | £2,300,686 | £1,790,343 |
| 10 years | £6,183,095 | £0 | £536,619 | £2,473,238 | £1,876,619 |

* It's assumed in the case of the transferor's death after one year that the transferee keeps the shares for another year to qualify for entrepreneur's relief.

Remember the £1m cumulative lifetime limit for entrepreneurs' relief applies to each individual. Hence, a transferor and transferee may be able to obtain combined relief on up to £2m between them. In this scenario, the transferee is paying CGT at 10% on the first £1m of the shares' growth in value after the transfer and at 20% on any excess.

## Residential Property

Finally, let's look at the same scenario where the transferred asset is residential property that qualifies for entrepreneurs' relief but not BPR. This might be the case for a portfolio of qualifying furnished holiday letting properties, for example (see Section 7.5 regarding the status of furnished holiday lettings for BPR purposes).

We will assume here that the transferee will not qualify for entrepreneurs' relief: perhaps, for example, they might convert the properties to normal residential lettings after the transfer. If the transferee did qualify for entrepreneurs' relief the outcome would be the same as in the previous table.

| Transferor Dies After | Value on Death | IHT on Transfer | CGT on Final Sale | IHT if Still in Estate | Net Saving or (Cost) |
|---|---|---|---|---|---|
| < 1 year | £3,000,000 | £1,200,000 | £0 | £1,200,000 | (£60,000) |
| 1 year | £3,225,000 | £1,200,000 | £63,000 | £1,290,000 | (£33,000) |
| 2 years | £3,466,875 | £1,200,000 | £130,725 | £1,386,750 | (£3,975) |
| 3 years | £3,726,891 | £986,000 | £203,529 | £1,490,756 | £241,227 |
| 4 years | £4,006,407 | £773,440 | £281,794 | £1,602,563 | £487,329 |
| 5 years | £4,306,888 | £562,320 | £365,929 | £1,722,755 | £734,507 |
| 6 years | £4,629,905 | £352,640 | £456,373 | £1,851,962 | £982,949 |
| 7 years | £4,977,147 | £0 | £553,601 | £1,990,859 | £1,377,258 |
| 8 years | £5,350,433 | £0 | £658,121 | £2,140,173 | £1,422,052 |
| 9 years | £5,751,716 | £0 | £770,480 | £2,300,686 | £1,470,206 |
| 10 years | £6,183,095 | £0 | £891,267 | £2,473,238 | £1,521,971 |

## 11.6   TRANSFERS TO SPOUSES OR CIVIL PARTNERS

As we know, transfers to your spouse are usually exempt from IHT. Furthermore, subject to the wealth warning below, transfers to your spouse are also usually exempt from CGT. However, only transfers on death will benefit from the CGT uplift explained in Section 11.2. It therefore makes sense to hold on to assets that are subject to CGT, and which you ultimately intend to leave to your spouse, so they can benefit from the uplift on death.

Alternatively, a lifetime transfer of assets to your spouse could be used to get a CGT uplift on their death. You need to be pretty sure the assets are going to come back to you though!

### Wealth Warning
Unlike the IHT exemption, the CGT exemption for transfers between spouses ceases to apply at the end of the tax year in which they separate. Separated couples who have not yet obtained a decree absolute are eligible for the IHT relief but not the CGT relief.

## 11.7   CAPITAL GAINS TAX AND THE FAMILY HOME

I could write an entire chapter on this subject alone. In fact, I have, but that chapter already appears in the Taxcafe.co.uk guide *'How to Save Property Tax'*.

To put it simply, your home is exempt from CGT for as long as you live in it as your only or main residence, and for at least nine months thereafter (eighteen months for disposals before 6th April 2020). Full exemption will generally apply as long as you moved into the property within two years of acquisition and did not use it for anything else in the interim. Other periods of absence may result in a partial loss of your exemption, although additional reliefs are sometimes available.

Each married couple or single individual may have just one main residence for CGT purposes at any given time.

Hence, as far as CGT is concerned, a lifetime transfer of your qualifying main residence while you are still living there, or within the next nine months thereafter, will usually be exempt.

So, what's the problem? Well, apart from the IHT problems that we will look at in the next chapter, there are two major CGT problems with giving away your main residence:

- The transferees lose the ability to benefit from the CGT uplift on death, and
- Unless they move into the property, the transferees also lose any main residence exemption

In essence, the transferees will be treated for CGT purposes as having acquired the property at its market value on the date of transfer and will be exposed to CGT on any growth in value thereafter.

**Practical Implications**

A sale of the parent's home at any time within nine months of them ceasing to occupy it as their main residence (eighteen months for a sale before 6th April 2020) would generally be fully exempt from CGT if they were still the owner at that time. This additional nine or eighteen month period is extended to three years if the owner is disabled or resident in a care home.

Furthermore, if the parent retained the property until death, it would be subject to the uplift on death, giving the children complete exemption from any gain arising during the parent's lifetime, even if the parent had been absent from the property for a longer period.

Conversely, if a child owns their parent's current or former home, but does not occupy it as their main residence, it is effectively treated like an investment property and is fully exposed to CGT on a subsequent sale.

The capital gain in such cases will be based on the property's increase in value since the time the child acquired it, not since the time of the parent's death. The relevant transfer may have been several years earlier, when the property's value was considerably less, thus leading to a much larger taxable gain.

The interplay between CGT and IHT can produce one of three results:

i) The IHT saving may outweigh the CGT exposure that has been created. This is fine and means the planning is still worthwhile
ii) The IHT saving comes at the price of a similar level of potential CGT liability. Such instances may still be worthwhile, as they may still produce a significant cashflow saving by deferring the tax arising. (This will often be the case where the beneficiaries have no intention of selling the property, or at least not for some considerable time)
iii) The IHT saving results in a significantly greater amount of potential CGT. This, clearly, would be foolhardy if the beneficiaries are contemplating any sale of the property in the foreseeable future

The introduction of the RNRB (see Section 3.4) has significantly altered the potential outcomes of this 'interplay' in many cases. Far more cases will now fall into the third category, meaning that retaining the property in the parent's ownership until death will often be the most sensible thing to do.

In fact, in most cases where a married couple, widow, or widower, intends to leave the family home to their children, there will be little point in trying to avoid IHT on it, as properties worth up to £1m will often be fully covered by the available exemptions. My advice to most such people is therefore to focus their IHT planning on other assets and keep the family home where it is.

But there remain many exceptions to this, and we will look at these in the next chapter.

> **Wealth Warning**
> Where the parent still resides in the property, a simple transfer will usually be a 'gift with reservation'. As we shall see in the next section, it would generally be wise to refrain from making any transfer that would be a 'gift with reservation', as there would be no IHT advantage but all the CGT disadvantages would remain. We will look at ways to resolve this problem in the next chapter.

## 11.8  CAPITAL GAINS TAX AND GIFTS WITH RESERVATION

As explained in Section 4.9, when a transfer falls foul of the 'gifts with reservation' rules, it will be ineffective for IHT purposes until such time as the relevant 'reservation' comes to an end.

This has absolutely no impact on the CGT treatment of the asset. The transfer that was subject to a 'gift with reservation' may still give rise to CGT liabilities based on the market value of the asset transferred, and the new legal owner of the transferred asset will lose the benefit of any reliefs to which the transferor may have been entitled, including main residence relief on the transferor's home.

Generally, with few exceptions, this situation should be avoided as it usually creates CGT problems without saving any IHT.

### Example
*Tina is an elderly divorcee. In 1999 she gave her house to her son, Robert, but continued to live there until April 2018, when she moved into a nursing home. The house was worth £275,000 in 1999 but had increased in value to £725,000 by 2018.*

*Tragically, Tina dies in March 2021, leaving only a few small possessions with no material value and just enough cash to pay her last month's nursing home fees and funeral expenses. However, as she only moved out of her house in 2018, its value at that date must be brought back into her estate, thus resulting in an IHT bill of £160,000.*

*To help pay the IHT, Robert sells the house in August 2021. Let's assume the house is still worth £725,000 at this point.*

*For CGT purposes, he is treated as having acquired the house for just £275,000, thus giving rise to a CGT bill of £122,556 on top of the IHT bill.*

*(His annual CGT exemption of, say, £12,300 is deducted from his capital gain of £450,000; he is a higher-rate taxpayer, so the balance of £437,700 is taxed at 28%).*

I have seen this type of situation countless times and it's an absolute tragedy. Had Tina simply held on to the house, Robert would actually have paid **LESS** IHT, since the RNRB would have been available, and his IHT bill would have been reduced to £90,000.

He would also have paid little or no CGT on a sale of the property shortly after Tina's death.

Hence, the transfer in 1999 has effectively cost Robert almost £200,000 in unnecessary extra tax.

Many families have attempted this type of planning to their cost. To make it even worse, many of these transfers were done to avoid paying residential care fees (see Section 10.9) but, as a result of a number of rule changes and successful cases taken by the local authorities this part of the plan has often failed as well.

In the vast majority of cases, gifts with reservation are to be avoided like the plague!

## 11.9   EXEMPT TRANSFERS

There are a few classes of assets other than cash that are exempt from CGT. For IHT planning purposes, these assets can often be regarded much like cash, since a lifetime transfer will not give rise to any CGT liability, but could save IHT if the transferor survives seven years (or even just three in some cases).

The following assets may be exempt from CGT:

- Enterprise Investment Scheme shares (only the shares themselves, not any gain 'held over' and only if certain qualifying conditions are met, including a minimum holding period of at least three years, sometimes longer)

- Tangible movable assets worth less than £6,000 (also known as 'chattels', this includes items like paintings, antiques and silverware)

- Government securities (also known as 'Gilts')

- Foreign currency held by an individual

- Motor vehicles

- Tangible wasting assets with an expected life of less than 50 years (machinery, computers, household equipment, etc.)

- Medals and certain other awards (although, as stated in Section 3.8, these are usually exempt from IHT when still held by the original recipient)

Note that exemption from CGT does not necessarily provide exemption from other taxes. Anyone trading in any of these items would be classed as a 'dealer' and subject to Income Tax and National Insurance on their profits.

As far as chattels are concerned, a lifetime transfer means foregoing the CGT 'uplift on death', so it might lead to increased CGT liabilities at a later date for the transferee where the assets are later worth over £6,000. The transfer is likely to remain advantageous overall though if an IHT saving is achieved.

Married persons must bear in mind these transfers could lead to a reduction in their spouse's TNRB if the transferor does not survive seven years. The pros and cons of this were discussed in Chapter 6. Items like motor vehicles and other wasting assets will also generally reduce in value, meaning the loss of TNRB will be greater than the ultimate reduction in the transferor's estate, leaving the family worse off on a death within seven years.

### Other Ways to Make Transfers free of Capital Gains Tax

Other ways to make lifetime transfers free from CGT include:

- Using the annual CGT exemption (£12,300 for 2020/21)
- Transferring assets while you are non-UK resident (you must be non-resident for at least five years and this doesn't work for land and buildings located in the UK; foreign tax implications must also be considered)
- Cashing in an ISA and passing over the proceeds

As always it remains important to remember the loss of the CGT uplift on death and, for married persons, the potential impact on your spouse's TNRB.

### 11.10   OTHER ASSETS

So what about those other assets, which do not qualify as business assets or main residences, which aren't exempt, and which you're not planning to give to your spouse? Here we are considering assets that do not qualify for BPR, entrepreneurs' relief, investor's relief, or holdover relief on a gift.

This will make a lifetime transfer less attractive from a CGT perspective. Nevertheless, the opportunity to save IHT by way of an early transfer remains.

## Assets Other Than Residential Property

We'll return to the scenario in our first table in Section 11.5, except for one change: entrepreneurs' relief is **not** available to the transferor. On this basis, the position arising on assets other than residential property is as follows:

| Transferor Dies After | Value on Death | IHT on Transfer | CGT on Final Sale | IHT if Still in Estate | Net Saving or (Cost)* |
|---|---|---|---|---|---|
| < 1 year | £3,000,000 | £1,200,000 | £0 | £1,200,000 | (£120,000) |
| 1 year | £3,225,000 | £1,200,000 | £45,000 | £1,290,000 | (£75,000) |
| 2 years | £3,466,875 | £1,200,000 | £93,375 | £1,386,750 | (£26,625) |
| 3 years | £3,726,891 | £986,000 | £145,378 | £1,490,756 | £239,378 |
| 4 years | £4,006,407 | £773,440 | £201,281 | £1,602,563 | £507,841 |
| 5 years | £4,306,888 | £562,320 | £261,378 | £1,722,755 | £779,058 |
| 6 years | £4,629,905 | £352,640 | £325,981 | £1,851,962 | £1,053,341 |
| 7 years | £4,977,147 | £0 | £395,429 | £1,990,859 | £1,475,429 |
| 8 years | £5,350,433 | £0 | £470,087 | £2,140,173 | £1,550,087 |
| 9 years | £5,751,716 | £0 | £550,343 | £2,300,686 | £1,630,343 |
| 10 years | £6,183,095 | £0 | £636,619 | £2,473,238 | £1,716,619 |

* Net saving/(cost) takes account of £200,000 CGT paid on the original transfer less the resultant IHT saving arising due to the reduction in the value of the transferor's estate.

Apart from entrepreneurs' relief being unavailable, all notes and assumptions made for the first version of this table in Section 11.5 apply. I also assume the transferor is a higher-rate taxpayer. In this scenario, such a transfer remains beneficial as long as the transferor survives at least three years.

## Residential Property

The position is altered if the assets are residential property, as these are subject to higher CGT rates. Based on the assumptions set out above, but assuming the assets transferred are residential property, the position is as follows:

| Transferor Dies After | Value on Death | IHT on Transfer | CGT on Final Sale | IHT if Still in Estate | Net Saving or (Cost) |
|---|---|---|---|---|---|
| < 1 year | £3,000,000 | £1,200,000 | £0 | £1,200,000 | (£168,000) |
| 1 year | £3,225,000 | £1,200,000 | £63,000 | £1,290,000 | (£141,000) |
| 2 years | £3,466,875 | £1,200,000 | £130,725 | £1,386,750 | (£111,975) |
| 3 years | £3,726,891 | £986,000 | £203,529 | £1,490,756 | £133,227 |
| 4 years | £4,006,407 | £773,440 | £281,794 | £1,602,563 | £379,329 |
| 5 years | £4,306,888 | £562,320 | £365,929 | £1,722,755 | £626,507 |
| 6 years | £4,629,905 | £352,640 | £456,373 | £1,851,962 | £874,949 |
| 7 years | £4,977,147 | £0 | £553,601 | £1,990,859 | £1,269,258 |
| 8 years | £5,350,433 | £0 | £658,121 | £2,140,173 | £1,314,052 |
| 9 years | £5,751,716 | £0 | £770,480 | £2,300,686 | £1,362,206 |
| 10 years | £6,183,095 | £0 | £891,267 | £2,473,238 | £1,413,971 |

* Net saving/(cost) takes account of £280,000 CGT on the original transfer less the resultant IHT saving arising due to the reduction in the value of the transferor's estate.

As we can see, under this scenario, it will take three years before a lifetime transfer of residential property provides any advantage.

The position would be different if the property qualified for main residence relief in the hands of either the transferor or the transferee. The situation for a main residence was examined in Sections 11.7 and 11.8, and will also be the focus of Chapter 12.

> **Tax Tip**
> In conclusion, the tables in this section, and in Section 11.5, tell us that early transfers of assets that are appreciating in value will often lead to significant overall tax savings in the end.
>
> However, married persons must remember the tables take no account of the impact of these transfers on the deceased's spouse's TNRB: see Chapter 6 for a thorough examination of this issue.

## 11.11 CAPITAL GAINS TAX AND TRUSTS

A trust for a 'vulnerable' individual may elect to be taxed as if any capital gains arising belong directly to the beneficiary (except that any capital losses made by the individual cannot be set off against the trust's gains).

However, as explained in Section 8.21, this will generally only apply to disabled trusts, trusts for bereaved minors and a few other trusts where the beneficiary is under 18.

Most other trusts (apart from bare trusts and charitable trusts) are subject to CGT at the higher rates of 20% or 28% and generally have an annual CGT exemption equal to half that applying to individuals (hence currently £6,150); although this is reduced where the settlor has set up more than one trust.

In Chapter 8, we considered the various different types of trust and saw some of them had their own 'separate life' for IHT purposes and some did not.

With the exception of bare trusts, however, trusts are treated as a separate legal entity for CGT purposes. This effectively means, subject to any exemptions or reliefs that may be available:

- Transfers into a trust are treated as disposals made at market value, and
- Transfers to beneficiaries from a trust are again treated as disposals at market value

In the case of a bare trust, it is only the transfer to the trust that represents a disposal for CGT purposes. Thereafter, the assets of the trust are generally treated as belonging to the beneficiary for the purposes of both IHT and CGT.

### The Capital Gains Tax Uplift on Death

Assets subject to an interest in possession that fall into a beneficiary's estate for IHT purposes (see Chapter 8) will generally qualify for the same CGT uplift on the death of the beneficiary as assets held absolutely (see Section 11.2). However, the uplift does not apply where property reverts to the original settlor absolutely on the beneficiary's death (but does if the settlor only obtains an interest in possession).

The CGT uplift on death also generally applies to assets in a bereaved minor's trust, or an '18 to 25 Trust', on the death of a beneficiary under the age of 18.

### Held Over Gains

When an interest in possession that is not within the relevant property trust regime (see Chapter 8) ends on the death of the beneficiary and a capital gain was held over when the same assets entered the trust (see Sections 9.6 and 11.4), that held over gain becomes chargeable.

The held over gain can usually be held over again provided that IHT is chargeable on the occasion of the beneficiary's death or the assets qualify as business assets for hold over relief purposes, as explained in Section 11.4.

### Hold Over Relief on Absolute Entitlement

CGT hold over relief is generally available when the beneficiary of a relevant property trust, a bereaved minor's trust or an '18 to 25 Trust' becomes absolutely entitled to trust assets.

There is no restriction on holdover relief when assets are *leaving* a settlor-interested relevant property trust.

> **Tax Tip**
> In some cases, it may be worth changing the terms of a pre-22/3/2006 interest in possession trust so that it becomes a relevant property trust (see Chapter 8). Although this will expose the trust to anniversary and exit charges, the ability to hold over any capital gain arising when assets leave the trust may produce greater CGT savings than any resultant IHT cost.

# Chapter 12

# The Family Home

## 12.1 WHEN OUR MAIN ASSET BECOMES OUR MAIN LIABILITY

For most of us, the family home is our major asset. In the past, it has also often been the main cause of IHT liabilities.

Now, with both the TNRB (see Section 6.3) and the RNRB (see Section 3.4) available in many cases, there will be many people for whom the family home is no longer a problem from an IHT point of view.

Many people now have exemptions totalling £1m available to cover their family home, made up as follows:

| | |
|---|---|
| Nil rate band | £325,000 |
| Transferable NRB | £325,000 |
| Residence NRB | £175,000 |
| Transferable RNRB | £175,000 |
| | |
| Total exemption available: | £1,000,000 |

As discussed in Section 11.7, many married couples, widows, or widowers, intending to leave their home to their children no longer need to worry about IHT on the family home and would be better advised to focus on IHT planning for other assets.

It is also important to remember giving your home away may mean you are unable to benefit from the RNRB. Selling your home will have a different effect, however, and we will return to this subject in Section 12.16.

But, not everyone fits neatly into the Government's 1950s-style vision of a world where everyone gets married, raises a family and lives happily ever after – until the time comes to hand 40% of everything over to them!

There are many people who will still not enjoy the £1m of exemption George Osborne promised us back in 2007. These people may therefore still benefit from carrying out some IHT planning on the family home.

### Who is Still Exposed to Inheritance Tax on the Family Home?

Those who still face potential IHT liabilities on the family home include the following:

- Those with a home worth in excess of £1m
- Single, divorced or unmarried people. You have to become a widow/widower in order to benefit from the TNRB or transferable RNRB. This does not apply to everyone! Those who never become a widow or widower will only be able to enjoy maximum total exemptions of £500,000 (at current rates)
- Widows and widowers with a property worth in excess of £325,000 and who do not have the benefit of a full TNRB. Those whose former spouse used some or all of their NRB will not be able to enjoy the full £1m of exemption detailed above unless they remarry. In some cases, they may also be unable to claim any of their former spouse's RNRB. See Chapter 6 and Section 3.4 for more details
- Those with estates worth in excess of £2m and a home worth in excess of £650,000; or £325,000 if they never become a widow or widower. These people will lose some or all of their RNRB due to the tapering provisions (see Section 3.4)
- Those who do not intend to leave their family home to direct descendants. Not everyone has children, and not everyone who does intends to leave their home to those children. If you do not leave your home to your direct descendants (see Section 3.4 for details), or to the right kind of trust for their benefit (see Section 8.6), then you will not be entitled to the RNRB. This will leave your home exposed to IHT on any value in excess of £650,000; or £325,000 if you never become a widow or widower.

As we can see, there are many people who still need to take action to protect the family home from IHT.

As already mentioned in Section 4.9, the major stumbling block to effective IHT planning with the family home is caused by the 'gifts with reservation' provisions. Furthermore, whenever the transferor of **any** asset (but, most particularly, the family home) continues to enjoy the benefit of that asset, there is also the possibility of an Income Tax charge under the pre-owned assets regime (see Section 10.21). We will consider any specific risks posed by the pre-owned asset charge as we look at the planning techniques set out in Sections 12.2 to 12.14; then summarise the position more generally in Section 12.15.

Despite these drawbacks, there are still a number of methods for saving IHT on the family home. Many of the methods described in this chapter will also have CGT implications for the transferee. These are discussed in more detail in Section 11.7.

The methods described in Sections 12.7 to 12.10 are only beneficial for married couples where one or both spouses already have a TNRB available (see Section 6.8).

Any methods that involve mortgages, loans, or other borrowings will only work if those liabilities are repaid out of the assets of the deceased's estate, or if there is a valid commercial reason for non-repayment (see Section 2.11 for further details).

## 12.2 MOVE OUT THEN GIVE IT AWAY

If you can afford to, and are willing to do it, you can simply move out of the property then give it away. The gift is a potentially exempt transfer that will escape IHT as long as you survive seven years. Furthermore, as long as you make the gift within nine months of the date you move out of the property, it will also be exempt from CGT under principal private residence relief.

If you are prepared to do this, you could then move into rented accommodation, or buy a more modest property.

No pre-owned asset charges should arise as long as you never move back into the property. You must also be careful not to benefit from any other asset purchased with the proceeds of a subsequent sale of the original property.

## 12.3 SELL UP AND GIVE AWAY THE PROCEEDS

If you can't quite afford to follow the above strategy, you could, instead, sell your current home, buy a smaller one, and give away the surplus left over cash. All you need to do then is survive another seven years. If you're feeling really brave, you could even give away all the sale proceeds and move into rented property. While this is good IHT planning, it doesn't leave you with much security in your old age and it might cause some problems with the local authority if you ever need to go into a residential home.

## 12.4 RE-MORTGAGE AND GIVE AWAY THE PROCEEDS

If you would prefer to stay in your current home, another way to get most of its value out of your estate is to re-mortgage the property then give away or spend the borrowed funds.

The outstanding mortgage balance will be deducted from your estate when you die (subject to the rules explained in Section 2.11) and this will reduce your IHT bill as long as you have either:

- Given away the borrowed funds and survived seven years, or
- Spent the borrowed funds before you die

The major drawback to this method is the need to service the mortgage from your retirement income. Hence, a sensible refinement may be to buy an annuity with some or all of the mortgage proceeds. This will enable you to service the debt and give away or spend any surplus. The problem then, of course, is that in the event of a premature death shortly after purchasing the annuity, a lot of your home's value will have been lost – not to Her Majesty's Treasury but to the annuity provider.

## 12.5 SELL UP OR RE-MORTGAGE AND INVEST THE PROCEEDS

An even better approach might be to release equity in your property, either by selling or re-mortgaging it, and invest the proceeds in a discounted gift trust (Section 9.11) or loan trust (Section 9.12).

Alternatively, you could sell your property and invest the proceeds in AIM shares (Section 7.27). You would need to limit your investment to the amount you can genuinely afford, as any subsequent borrowings, including any mortgage on a new property, would be deemed to have indirectly funded the purchase (see Section 7.28).

Hence, while AIM shares provide the most complete shelter from IHT (after two years), they are probably only suitable where you sell the family home, buy something smaller and just invest the surplus.

A discounted gift trust or loan trust can be structured to provide an 'income' stream and will be more suitable in most other cases.

A final alternative, if you also have plenty of earned income, may be to invest some of your proceeds in a pension (see Section 10.15): although there are complex rules limiting the amount you are able to invest. See the Taxcafe.co.uk guide *'Pension Magic'* for more information.

All these investments have the advantage that your wealth is not lost in the event of a premature death.


## 12.6 SALE AT MARKET VALUE

If you sell your property to your children, or other beneficiaries, at full market value, no 'transfer of value' will take place and hence the property will immediately be excluded from your estate for IHT purposes.

### Wealth Warning
Actual payment of the sale proceeds by the purchaser will generally be necessary. Any prior arrangement to give any part of the sale proceeds back to the purchaser will also render this planning void, since the sale would not have taken place on 'arm's length terms', as required, and a transfer of value will have taken place.

Furthermore, there must not be any obligation on the purchaser to allow you to continue to occupy the property.

The second point above means you will subsequently only be able to live in the property under an informal 'licence to occupy', which is totally at the purchaser's whim. This will not suit everyone!

After the sale, you are free to spend the proceeds, perhaps to support yourself in your retirement. Any future growth in the property's value is also safely excluded from your estate.

As you spend the proceeds and the property grows in value, the reduction in your taxable estate starts to accumulate. These savings also start immediately after the sale and it is not necessary to survive for any period to benefit.

Alternatively, you could combine this method with the method in Section 12.5 and invest the proceeds in one of the IHT 'shelters' suggested there.

On the other hand, however, as time passes there is a danger that the adverse CGT considerations will outweigh any IHT savings. (As we saw in Sections 11.7 and 11.8, the purchaser will be subject to CGT on a sale of the property!)

Another important point to bear in mind is the fact that SDLT will be payable on the purchase of the property. The rates involved could be quite prohibitive in some cases (see the Taxcafe.co.uk guide *'How to Save Property Tax'* for full details).

## 12.7   THE WIDOW'S LOAN SCHEME & THE FAMILY HOME

The method described in Section 6.12 generally works just as well for the family home as for any other assets. Probably better, in fact, as there is an asset on which to secure the loan and thus give it the necessary commercial substance.

As explained in Chapter 6, however, this method is now only worth exploring in certain limited cases where one or both spouses already has a TNRB available.

### *Example*
*Oscar and Freddie are registered civil partners and equal joint tenants in common of a house worth £1.3m. Each of them already has a TNRB available from the death of a previous spouse.*

*Freddie dies in December 2020 and leaves an amount equivalent to twice the NRB, £650,000, to a discretionary trust. He leaves everything else to Oscar.*

*No IHT is payable on Freddie's death, since the legacy to the discretionary trust is covered by his NRB and TNRB and the rest of his estate is covered by the spouse exemption.*

*The trust takes a charge for £650,000 over the couple's house and then passes the title to Freddie's share of the house over to Oscar.*

*Oscar survives Freddie by just over two years and passes away in January 2023. At this time, the house is worth £1.4m.*

*The value of the house in Oscar's estate is, however, reduced to £750,000 by the £650,000 charge taken by Freddie's discretionary trust (provided the charge meets the necessary conditions explained in Sections 2.11 and 6.12).*

*After deducting the NRB of £325,000 and Oscar's TNRB from his previous marriage, just £100,000 of the house's value is subject to IHT at 40%, giving a charge of £40,000.*

*Without the widow's loan scheme, the whole value of the house would have been subject to IHT on Oscar's death. After deducting the NRB and his TNRB, a value of £750,000 would have been subject to IHT at 40%, giving a charge of £300,000.*

*The widow's loan scheme has thus produced a saving of £260,000.*

A widow's loan scheme incorporating a loan secured on the family home can usually be put in place for a cost of around £1,000 to £1,500, although this may be more in some parts of the country, or if there are additional complications. Further details of how to implement the scheme and some of the pitfalls that need to be avoided are given in Section 6.12.

## 12.8   LEAVE A SHARE TO THE CHILDREN

Another method that may be worth considering where one or both of a married couple are already entitled to a TNRB is to simply leave a share in the property to your children, who will then, after your death, own it jointly with your surviving spouse. See Section 6.8 for guidance on the value this share should ideally have in order to optimise the overall IHT position. Any RNRB to which you are entitled should also be taken into account. Remember, as explained in Section 10.5, a joint share in a property held as tenants in common may be any proportion and need not be an equal share.

If your surviving spouse and children sell the property immediately after your death, there should be no CGT liability – the children will benefit from the CGT uplift on death (see Section 11.2) and the surviving spouse should be covered by the main residence exemption.

Opinions differ, however, on the more common situation that arises when the property is retained and the surviving spouse continues to occupy it.

The surviving spouse's joint share in the property will give them a continuing right of occupation. Some IHT experts think this means the survivor can remain in the property without paying any rent and the children's share of the property does not need to be included in their estate on their subsequent death.

Hence, as planned, when the surviving spouse dies, their estate would only include their share of the property.

Other experts, however, believe the surviving spouse's continuing occupation amounts to an interest in possession and the children's share of the property would therefore fall into their estate unless they pay rent for their occupation of that share.

Still others consider a relevant property trust would come into being in respect of the children's share of the property. The consequences of this are explored in the next section.

Unfortunately, at present, it is not yet clear which set of experts is correct and HMRC has refused to comment. Personally, I've always favoured the view of the first set of experts, which means the IHT planning will work as intended, although it must be admitted the position is now far from certain.

If the method does work as intended, it still has the drawback that the children are exposed to CGT on the growth in value of their share of the property after the first parent's death. However, the resultant CGT liability arising will often be considerably less than the IHT saving. Furthermore, if the family intend to retain the property in the long term, CGT is often less of a concern anyway.

So, apart from the possible CGT exposure, everything should be fine as long as you are happy your children, and, more particularly, their spouses or partners, will all get along OK with your spouse after you're gone.

In practice though, this simple route often causes difficulty and families in this situation have been known to come to blows (both metaphorically and physically). The other joint owners have even been known to force the surviving spouse into selling the former family home against their wishes.

The best way around these practical problems is to use a trust and we will look at this more complex variation to this scheme in the next section.

## 12.9   CHILDREN PUT THEIR SHARE INTO TRUST

This variation to the method described in the previous section works as follows:

i)   After inheriting a share in the property, the children set up a trust, with the surviving spouse as both trustee and beneficiary, and transfer their share into it.
ii)  The provisions of the trust are that the property reverts to the children, as settlors, on the death of the surviving spouse.

The drawback to this scheme is that the trust set up by the children will be a relevant property trust (see Chapter 8) and will therefore be subject to anniversary and exit charges.

Nevertheless, these charges may well be substantially less than the amount saved by keeping part of the property out of the surviving spouse's estate. In many cases, where the children's share of the property is worth less than the NRB, the structure may, in practice, actually still avoid IHT on the property altogether.

The children will be unable to benefit from any CGT uplift (in respect of the trust's share of the property) on the surviving spouse's death. However, if the trust were then to sell its share of the property, the main residence exemption should be available as the property had been the main residence of the trust beneficiary (i.e. the surviving spouse). The trust could then pass the sale proceeds to the children.

Hence, while this scheme may be slightly flawed in theory, it will often work reasonably well in practice.

Note that, under this technique, the children need to be careful not to have any use or enjoyment of the property during the life interest of the surviving spouse. If they were to use the property while the spouse's life interest continued, they would face a pre-owned assets charge. Minor and incidental use of the property, such as limited social visits, is, however, permitted.

## 12.10   LEAVE A SHARE TO A DISCRETIONARY TRUST

In Section 6.11, we looked at the drawbacks to using a discretionary Will Trust and the possible problem of it being treated as an immediate post-death interest and thus falling into the surviving spouse's estate. As explained in Chapter 6, this is now only a problem for certain 'second time around' married couples.

A possible solution to this problem, where it still exists, is to leave an appropriate share in the family home (see Section 6.8 for what is 'appropriate') to a discretionary trust in which the surviving spouse is **_not_** a beneficiary.

As explained in Section 12.8, as a joint owner, the surviving spouse already has a right to occupy the property, so the fact they are not a beneficiary of the discretionary trust does not make any practical difference to them.

After an interval of at least two years and a day, the discretionary trust can be changed into an interest in possession trust in favour of the surviving spouse. This will be a relevant property trust and hence will not fall into the surviving spouse's estate. Anniversary and exit charges may apply but, as before, these may be avoided if the trust's share of the property is not worth more than the NRB.

This scheme is a fairly new idea and, as such, it is currently untested. Furthermore, even the experts are still debating whether it actually works in practice!

## 12.11   THE 'FULL CONSIDERATION' METHOD

The 'gifts with reservation' rules can be bypassed if, after giving the property to your children, you pay them a full commercial rent for continuing to live in it. Payment of the rent would also help to further reduce your estate for IHT purposes.

This method should also avoid the pre-owned assets charge. It is **essential**, however, that your rental payments are made under a formal lease and are reviewed every five years, in line with the pre-owned assets revaluation rules (see Section 10.21).

The major drawbacks to this method are the fact your children have to account for Income Tax on the rent they receive and are also fully exposed to CGT on the future growth in value of the property.


## 12.12   CO-OWNERSHIP

This method is popular with widows, widowers and other single parents who have mature, single, adult children. Quite simply, you put the property into joint ownership with one or more of your adult children and then live together with them there.

The transfer of one or more shares in the property is a potentially exempt transfer as long as the child or children are living there. It is the children's presence in the property that prevents the transfer from being a 'gift with reservation'. HMRC has also confirmed this method is not caught under the pre-owned assets charge.

However, if one or more of the donee children should subsequently move out of the property while the parent themselves is still in occupation, the 'gift with reservation' rules will come into play unless either:

a)     The parent pays a full market rent for their use of the child's share of the property, or
b)     The child rents their share of the property to another occupier

It is important that each party bears their own share of the household running costs. If any child were to pay the full household running costs, or even just part of the parent's share, a 'gift with reservation' would have taken place and the IHT planning will be undone.

While in practice this method works best when the children remain single, there is nothing in principle to prevent it from continuing to work when they marry, or even have children of their own (it just gets crowded).


## 12.13   SHEARING

IHT can be reduced by dividing up the legal interests in a property in such a way that there is no 'gift with reservation'. To use this method, the transferor must have owned the property for at least seven years and, if the property is held jointly by a couple, each of them must have owned their share for at least seven years.

This method is generally only effective when there is no intention of selling the property, i.e. it is to be retained in the family after the original owner's death.

To follow this method, you create a long-term lease over the property that becomes effective some years from now: say in 15 or 20 years' time. You then grant that lease to your children or other intended heirs. The grant of the lease represents a potentially exempt transfer and will escape IHT as long as you survive seven years.

The duration of the lease needs to be long enough to ensure you will never benefit from your freehold reversion. The strategy works best with a very lengthy lease, say for 999 years.

The start date for the lease needs to be chosen on the basis of the donor's life expectancy, but cannot be more than 21 years after its execution.

As the clock runs down towards the date the lease comes into effect, the value of your freehold interest reduces. Hopefully, if you time it right, at the date of your death your interest will have minimal value and will easily be covered by the NRB (plus any available TNRB or RNRB).

HMRC has confirmed this scheme avoids the 'gifts with reservation' rules. This is mainly so they can collect Income Tax under the pre-owned assets regime (see Section 10.21). Nonetheless, the scheme may still be worthwhile if the Income Tax cost is not significant, such as when the owner of the freehold has little or no taxable income.

The scheme may also be implemented by granting the lease to a trust with the transferor's heirs as the beneficiaries. The grant of the lease would, however, be a chargeable lifetime transfer (see Section 4.2) and the trust would be subject to anniversary and exit charges. Even so, the scheme may still produce significant savings in some cases.

### What If You Live Too Long?

If you are fortunate enough to still be around when the lease comes into effect then, in order to avoid the 'gifts with reservation' rules, you could start paying a commercial rent to your heirs (but see Section 12.11 above re Income Tax). Alternatively, by that stage, you may well be happy to move into something smaller!

### 12.14   THE THREE-WAY SPLIT

Following the introduction of the TNRB, most married couples should now be protected from IHT on a property worth up to twice the NRB. This scheme may exempt a property worth up to three times the NRB (i.e. £975,000 at current rates).

To follow this method we need to make an assumption about which spouse will die first. If we get this wrong, the survivor will have to think again (but should not get an immediate IHT bill). For the sake of illustration, let's assume it is a heterosexual marriage and the husband will probably die first (statistics would support us on this).

First, if the property is in England or Wales, we put it into a tenancy in common. Next, we divide the ownership so that two thirds goes to the husband and one third to the wife.

On the husband's death, he leaves half his share (i.e. one third of the total) to a life interest trust in favour of his wife, with the remainder to the children (or other beneficiaries). This will qualify as an immediate post-death interest (see Section 8.12) and hence fall within the wife's estate. Most importantly, it will also be an exempt transfer. Later, the wife allows an early termination of her life interest and passes that one third share of the property to the children. This will be a potentially exempt transfer, and will be exempt from IHT as long as she survives another seven years.

The husband leaves the other half of his share to a discretionary trust, thus utilising his NRB. At some convenient date more than two years later, this trust can be wound up and the property share will be passed to the children. Alternatively, to protect the widow, it may be better to keep the trust going and perhaps pay some modest anniversary charges.

When the widow dies, her NRB can be utilised against her remaining one third share of the property.

As discussed in Section 12.8, some experts would argue the widow has an interest in possession in the discretionary trust's share of the property and the scheme would therefore fail. Again, the position on this is not clear.

Before the introduction of the TNRB, many people took the view that this scheme was worth a try as there was nothing to lose. Now, however, the scheme generally represents something of a gamble since it means sacrificing the TNRB. It will certainly only be worth considering where the property is worth considerably in excess of twice the NRB, plus any available RNRB.

## 12.15   PRE-OWNED ASSET CHARGES ON THE FAMILY HOME

I have already discussed the most significant risks of pre-owned asset charges arising under the planning methods in this chapter. Just to complete matters, it is also worth noting:

- Methods that involve realising cash and giving it away (Sections 12.3 and 12.4) should not give rise to any charges as long as the donor does not benefit from the use of any asset purchased with the proceeds within a period of seven years after making their gifts.
- Methods that involve passing the deceased's share of the property to a trust or to someone other than their surviving spouse (Sections 12.8 to 12.10 and 12.14) could only pose a risk if the surviving spouse had originally given a share in the property to the deceased, or had given them the funds with which to purchase their share, and had done so before they were married.
- No pre-owned asset charges can arise under the methods covered in Sections 12.5 to 12.7 and 12.12.

## 12.16  DOWNSIZING

The RNRB may also be claimed against other assets or cash left to direct descendants, or certain types of trust for their benefit (see Section 8.6), to the extent these assets are covered by the sale proceeds of a former qualifying private residence sold after 8th July 2015 (see Section 3.4 for details of direct descendants and qualifying private residences).

Such a claim under the 'downsizing' provisions may be made when:
i)      An individual dies with no qualifying private residence, or
ii)     An individual had a more valuable qualifying residence at some time in the past, but after 8th July 2015

There is no need to actually trace the sale proceeds of the former qualifying private residence; it is simply a case of using the amount of those proceeds to derive the available exemption. Nonetheless, the relief may only be claimed against amounts, or the value of assets, which actually do go to qualifying beneficiaries or trusts. Furthermore, only actual sale proceeds (not deemed proceeds) may be used in the calculation of the relief available.

A widow or widower may include any RNRB transferred from their deceased spouse within their 'downsizing' claim. The maximum claim is derived as follows:

i)      Calculate the proportion of the individual's maximum available RNRB actually used against qualifying property on their death
ii)     Calculate the proportion of the individual's maximum available RNRB that could have been used if the individual had died immediately before selling the former qualifying residence, based on the assumption the actual sale proceeds received for the property represented its open market value
iii)    Deduct the proportion derived under step (i) from the proportion derived under step (ii)
iv)     The maximum relief available under the 'downsizing' provisions is derived by multiplying the individual's maximum available RNRB by the proportion derived under step (iii)

The amount of RNRB used for the purposes of the calculation at step (ii) is the actual amount of the RNRB at the time of the property's sale (or £100,000 in the case of a sale between 9th July 2015 and 5th April 2017) PLUS any RNRB transferred from the individual's deceased spouse: BUT the transferred RNRB is not the amount available at the time of the property's sale, but the amount available at the time of the widow or widower's death.

### Example 1
*Billie has been divorced for many years. In March 2017, she sold her house for £80,000 and moved into a nursing home. When she dies in March 2021, she does not own any qualifying property and leaves her entire estate to her son Duke. The sale proceeds for Billie's house amount to 80% of the RNRB deemed to have been available to her at that time (£100,000). The maximum amount of RNRB to which she would be entitled on her death is £175,000. Hence, she may claim an exemption of £140,000 (£175,000 x 80%) under the 'downsizing' provisions.*

### Example 2

*Frank is a widower whose wife died many years ago with only a very modest estate. In August 2018, he sold his home for £225,000 and moved into a small bungalow. When Frank dies in January 2021, he leaves his entire estate to his daughter, Nancy, including the bungalow, which is then worth £105,000.*

*If Frank had died in August 2018, he would have been entitled to a RNRB of £125,000. To this we must add a full RNRB entitlement transferred from his late wife, but we count this as £175,000, the amount applying at the time of Frank's death. This produces a total of £300,000, so the sale proceeds of £225,000 for Frank's former home are deemed to represent 75% of his maximum entitlement (£225,000/£300,000 = 75%).*

*When Frank dies in January 2021, his maximum RNRB entitlement is £350,000 (2 x £175,000). He therefore uses only 30% of his entitlement (£105,000/£350,000 = 30%).*

*Frank is able to claim 45% (75% less 30%) of his maximum RNRB entitlement under the 'downsizing' provisions. Hence, £157,500 (£350,000 x 45%) of other assets left to Nancy can be exempted under the RNRB, in addition to Frank's bungalow.*

Where an individual dies owning a qualifying private residence, but does not leave that property to a direct descendent, or a qualifying trust for their benefit, any RNRB available is effectively reduced by the value of that qualifying private residence.

For example, if Frank had left his cottage to his sister Ava, the RNRB available to exempt the assets left to Nancy would have remained £157,500, but there would be no exemption on the cottage itself.

### 12.17 MAKING THE MOST OF THE RESIDENCE NIL RATE BAND

Thanks to the 'downsizing' provisions described in the previous section, many married couples, widows, and widowers will be able to get the maximum benefit from the RNRB by ensuring they own a private residence worth at least £350,000 at some stage after 8th July 2015.

To get the maximum possible relief, they will also need to ensure that they:

- Actually have equity of at least this amount in the property (after deducting any mortgage against it),
- Sell the property for actual proceeds (rather than give it away, etc),
- Do eventually leave at least one of any qualifying properties that they own at the time of their death to their direct descendants, or a suitable trust for their benefit (see Section 8.6), and
- Also leave sufficient further sums to qualifying beneficiaries or trusts in order to fully utilise the relief available under the 'downsizing' provisions

The third and fourth steps can take place on the second death where the couple are currently both still alive. The third step becomes unnecessary where no qualifying properties are held at the time of death.

**Earlier Property Sales**

The maximum potential RNRB may also be obtained through earlier sales of qualifying property for at least the following amounts (net of any mortgage over the property):

Sales between 9th July 2015 and 5th April 2018:   £275,000
Sales during 2018/19:                             £300,000
Sales during 2019/20:                             £325,000

**Single People & Unmarried Couples**

Similar principles apply to single or divorced people, and unmarried couples, but each individual will need to own a share in a property, net of any mortgage, worth at least £175,000 at some stage after 8th July 2015, or to have sold a share in a property for at least the following amounts (again, net of their share of any mortgage):

Sales between 9th July 2015 and 5th April 2018:   £100,000
Sales during 2018/19:                             £125,000
Sales during 2019/20:                             £150,000

For an unmarried couple, the third and fourth steps described above will also need to take place on *each* death.

Note that an informal 'step-child', who is the child of a current or former unmarried partner, but is neither your own biological child, nor your legally adopted child, will not generally count as your child for the purposes of the RNRB, no matter how much you love them (sorry Michelle!)

# Chapter 13

# Family Investment Companies

## 13.1 INTRODUCTION TO FAMILY INVESTMENT COMPANIES

A 'family investment company' is a broad term used to describe companies set up to hold investments, including investment property, rental property, etc; and also used to pass wealth to, or share it with, adult children or other family members.

In addition to the IHT planning benefits we will explore in this chapter, holding investment or rental property through a company can also produce substantial tax savings on income and capital gains during your lifetime. These are explored in the Taxcafe.co.uk guide *'Using a Property Company to Save Tax'*, as well as tax issues around transferring property to a company.

Family investment companies come in a number of forms, with a variety of share structures, loan accounts, etc. In this chapter, we will explore some of the most popular structures.

## 13.2 SHELL COMPANIES AND LOAN ACCOUNTS

A simple method to create a family investment company is to start by setting up a new, 'shell' company with a small nominal value, say £100. New companies can easily be set up via an online service at a very modest cost (less than £50 in many cases, but more if you require a complex share structure).

The next step is to transfer the shares to your adult children or other intended beneficiaries. It is important to do this while the company is still an empty 'shell' as this means the transfer of value is very small, just the value of the nominal share capital and in most cases, covered by your annual exemption.

You now transfer your investments, rental property, etc, to the company in exchange for an interest-free loan account, repayable on demand. The loan account means you have received full consideration for the transfer, hence no transfer of value has taken place and no IHT charges can arise.

Let's look at an example of how this might work in practice.

### Example
*Joe and Katherine are a married couple with ten adult children and wish them all to benefit equally from their substantial residential rental property portfolio, worth £4m, and comprising twenty properties. They also have cash and other investments of £1m and a home of their own worth £800,000. At present, they have no other income apart from their rental property and a small amount of savings and investment income. In future, they will each receive a modest state pension, but they have made no other pension provision.*

They set up a family investment company ('FIC'), Gary Investments Ltd, with a nominal share capital of £100 and then give 10% of the shares to each of their children. These transfers are covered by their annual exemptions and are thus immediately exempt from IHT and cannot be subject to the pre-owned assets charge.

They now transfer their entire property portfolio to the company in exchange for an interest-free loan account of £4m. Unfortunately, while this is free from IHT (as no transfer of value has taken place) it must be treated as a sale at market value for the purposes of both CGT and SDLT (see the Taxcafe.co.uk guide 'Using a Property Company to Save Tax' for a full explanation of the rates, charges and reliefs applying under both taxes).

Let us suppose the portfolio was originally purchased for a total cost of £1.5m. This means the couple have capital gains of £2.5m, giving rise to CGT of £693,112 (£2.5m less two annual CGT exemptions of £12,300 each, taxed at 28%: I have assumed they are both higher rate taxpayers).

Additionally, the company has a SDLT bill of £150,000. Joe and Katherine lend this sum to the company to enable it to pay the SDLT. They also lend the company a further £50,000 to give it some working capital to get started, thus taking their loan account balance to a total of £4.2m.

The property portfolio yields an annual profit before tax of £250,000. After paying Corporation Tax at 19% and setting aside a small reserve, it is able to repay £200,000 to Joe and Katherine each year, giving them sufficient money to live on. While this is effectively an 'income' stream, it is tax free, as it is a loan repayment and therefore not subject to Income Tax.

Ten years later, the loan account balance has reduced to £2.2m; the rental property portfolio is worth £7.5m; Joe and Katherine's home is worth £1.5m; and the NRB and RNRB have increased to £391,000 and £211,000 respectively. Let's take a look at Joe and Katherine's IHT exposure at this stage:

|  | With FIC | Without FIC |
|---|---|---|
| Property portfolio | - | £7.5m |
| Home | £1.5m | £1.5m |
| Loan account | £2.2m | - |
| Cash and investments* | £0.107m** | £1m |
| Total assets | £3.807m | £10m |
| Less: Nil rate bands | £0.782m | £0.782m |
| Residence NRBs*** | £0.422m | - |
| Chargeable estate | £2.603m | £9.218m |
| IHT exposure at 40% | £1.041m | £3.687m |

* Assumed no growth as after tax income and capital gains used to pay living costs
** Reduced by payment of CGT, SDLT and loan of a further £50,000 to the company
*** Using the company, the couple's estates now amount to less than £2m each, so they should be able to benefit from their RNRBs if they plan things carefully. Without the company, however, the tapering provisions (see Section 3.4) will mean no RNRBs are available

After ten years, the family investment company has reduced Joe and Katherine's IHT exposure by over £2.6m. However, this has come at a significant cost, with a total of £843,112 in tax paid at the outset. As a result, the overall net saving, even after ten years, is only £1.803m.

You might wonder if Joe and Katherine could have achieved greater savings by simply giving properties directly to the children. Let's say they gave two properties to each child, so their total CGT bills would be the same. This would avoid the SDLT charges but, as the gifts to the children would be potentially exempt transfers, the value of the properties would remain in Joe and Katherine's estates, still exposed to IHT, for the next seven years. Furthermore, it is unlikely that all the properties would have an equal value, making it impossible to treat the children fairly as Joe and Katherine wish.

But the biggest problem with these direct gifts is they would leave Joe and Katherine with almost nothing to live on in their retirement!

Hence, to summarise, a family investment company provides the following advantages:

- There is no transfer of value and hence IHT savings begin to accumulate immediately
- There are no immediate IHT charges on transfers in excess of the NRB
- The loan account effectively provides a tax-free 'income' stream
- Profits and capital gains arising within the company are subject to Corporation Tax at just 19% instead of Income Tax at up to 45% (even more in some cases) and CGT at up to 28%
- Children or other beneficiaries can benefit equally, or in whatever proportions you wish (this can be difficult to achieve with direct transfers or bequests)

To further illustrate the benefits of a family investment company, the table below shows the overall saving achieved under the scenario set out in the example above, with the following additional assumptions and minor modifications:

i)      Property values remain static for the first year then grow at a compound rate of 7.5% per year
ii)     The first parent to die leaves their entire estate to the surviving spouse
iii)    Joe and Katherine spend all the cash they receive from the company, from pensions, and from their investments
iv)     Rental profits from the property portfolio remain at the same level
v)      Income Tax rates and thresholds remain at 2020/21 levels
vi)     The Corporation Tax rate remains unchanged at 19%

| Second Death After (Years) | Estate without FIC | Estate using FIC | IHT Saved | Overall Net Saving/(Cost)* |
|---|---|---|---|---|
| 1 | £5,800,000 | £4,906,888 | £357,245 | (£448,367) |
| 2 | £6,160,000 | £4,766,888 | £557,245 | (£210,867) |
| 3 | £6,547,000 | £4,631,388 | £766,245 | £35,633 |
| 4 | £6,963,025 | £4,500,726 | £984,920 | £291,808 |
| 5 | £7,410,252 | £4,375,263 | £1,213,995 | £558,383 |
| 6 | £7,891,021 | £4,255,391 | £1,454,252 | £836,140 |
| 8 | £8,963,436 | £4,034,127 | £1,971,723 | £1,428,611 |
| 10 | £10,202,746 | £3,840,679 | £2,544,827 | £2,076,715 |
| 12 | £11,634,923 | £3,679,375 | £3,182,219 | £2,789,107 |
| 15 | £14,211,731 | £3,508,843 | £4,281,155 | £4,000,543 |
| 20 | £19,967,149 | £3,468,080 | £6,599,628 | £6,506,516 |

* After accounting for 'up front' tax charges of £843,112; but also including the additional annual tax saving of £37,500 on rental profits from the residential property portfolio. This saving increases to £50,000 per year after the first death, although this potential increase is not accounted for in the table.

Taking the additional Income Tax savings into account, we can see it takes just three years before the family investment company starts to produce an overall saving. As this is based on the date of the 'second death', this means most couples would have a very good chance of benefitting from this method.

Unlike the example above, the table ignores any further savings that might be yielded if the RNRB becomes available. This will require some additional planning after the first death, but could lead to a further saving of up to £140,000 (at current rates).

**Problems and Limitations**

The major problem with this strategy is the 'up front' tax cost, which totalled £843,112 in Joe and Katherine's case. Furthermore, this needs to be funded, so the couple need to have sufficient liquid resources (cash and short-term investments) to cover this cost. As a very broad rule of thumb, if we say the value of your rental properties has roughly doubled since purchase, the 'up front' tax cost is likely to be around 20% of the value of your rental property portfolio (it was just over 21% for Joe and Katherine).

If you do not have enough liquid resources, you will need to sell some properties, which, in turn, will lead to more CGT. Selling a former home can be helpful, however, as some or all of the gain will usually be exempt from CGT, and an arm's length sale will usually preserve your RNRB entitlement (see Section 12.16).

Alternatively, a former home may be a suitable property to transfer to the company at a lower CGT cost, although this might jeopardise your RNRB. See the Taxcafe.co.uk guide *'How to Save Property Tax'* for further details on the CGT exemption for a former home.

In our example, I have also assumed the properties were debt-free. It may be difficult to transfer properties that are subject to a mortgage.

The loan account in the example will run out after twenty-one years. Hopefully, this is long enough for Joe and Katherine. Getting the duration of the loan account right is a matter of luck, or perhaps good timing – but the closer the second death is to the date the loan account is exhausted, the better.

If one or both parents survive for longer, they will need to use other resources to fund their living expenses. It is important that the children/company owners do not support them, as this could lead to problems under the 'gifts with reservation' rules (Section 4.9), effectively bringing the value of the company shares back into their estate. In a case like Joe and Katherine, this might be the time to sell the family home and downsize (see Section 12.16), perhaps putting some surplus funds into a suitable IHT shelter, as explained in Section 12.5.

Another potential problem, in some families, is the practical issue of running the company. Sibling rivalry may render this impossible and there may also be the worry of outside influences, such as the children's partners. Some of the children may also be less mature than others, which may be a cause for concern.

In the next section, we will look at some possible solutions to some of these issues.

**Not Limited**
An unmarried couple could use a family investment company in a similar way, except that IHT charges would arise on the first death. The loan accounts would need to be kept separate and it would be important to ensure both of the couple's NRBs and RNRBs (where appropriate) were fully utilised on their deaths. Similarly, a single parent could use a family investment company, but would only benefit from a single NRB, RNRB and annual CGT exemption.

A family investment company could be used to pass investment assets to other beneficiaries, such as nieces, nephews, siblings, or friends. The only difference to the figures given in the example above is that no RNRB would be available on the deceased's home.


## 13.3    OPTIONAL EXTRAS

There are a number of potential refinements or improvements to the strategy discussed in the previous section.

## Golden Shares

The parents may have a concern that their children will not be able to manage the company effectively together. To combat this, the parents can hold a 'golden share' that carries no rights to dividends, is non-transferable, and will be redeemed and cancelled on 'second death'. As such, the 'golden share' will have little or no value in its own right. However, the share will carry the power to appoint or remove directors and to block any resolution to remove a director appointed by the golden shareholders. Hence, the 'golden share' allows the parents to intervene, if necessary, and thus ensure the smooth running of the company (often the mere threat of intervention will be enough!)

## Shares in Trust

The family investment company's shares can be gifted to a trust rather than directly to the children, if desired. This could be used as a means to retain control over the shares allocated to a less mature (but adult) child until such time the parents feel they are responsible enough to participate directly in the company's management.

Alternatively, shares can be placed in a discretionary trust to benefit grandchildren or other family members (but not the donor's own minor children).

Provided the shares are held in the trust for less than ten years, no IHT charges should arise. Alternatively, it may be worth paying some anniversary or exit charges (see Chapter 8) to secure longer-term benefits (both practical and financial).

## Tax-Free Dividends

Each shareholder can receive up to £2,000 of tax-free dividends each tax year under the 'dividend allowance' (see Appendix A), so it may be worth paying these to the children. If there is insufficient cash available to also meet the parents' loan repayments, the dividends can be loaned back to the company and effectively 'stored up' until the children can take their own tax-free loan repayments.

## Reducing the CGT Cost

Spreading the property transfers across two or more tax years would enable the parents to use multiple annual CGT exemptions, saving up to £6,888 for each additional tax year involved (at current rates). The impact on the SDLT charges arising should be taken into account, however, as this will affect the multiple dwellings relief on the transfer (see the Taxcafe.co.uk guides 'How to Save Property Tax' or 'Using a Property Company to Save Tax' for details of this important relief).

Further savings may be achieved by delaying some or all of the transfers until a tax year when the parents' income is below the higher rate tax threshold, thus enabling some of the capital gains to be taxed at 18% instead of 28% (or 10% instead of 20% for assets other than residential property).

## Example Revisited

*Let's say Joe and Katherine transfer half their portfolio to the company on 5th April 2021 and the other half on 6th April 2021. As a result of the transfers, their taxable income for 2021/22 falls below the level of their personal allowances, meaning their basic rate bands are fully available for CGT purposes (see Section 11.1). Their CGT bills are now as follows:*

### 2020/21

| | | |
|---|---|---|
| Total gains | £1,250,000 (assumed equal split across two years) | |
| Less annual exemptions | £24,600 (£12,300 x 2) | |
| Taxable gains | £1,225,400 | |
| CGT @ 28% | | £343,112 |

### 2021/22

| | | |
|---|---|---|
| Taxable gains | £1,225,400 (as above) | |
| CGT @ 18% on | £75,000 (£37,500 x 2) | £13,500 |
| CGT @ 28% on balance | £1,150,400 | £322,112 |

| | |
|---|---|
| Total CGT suffered on transfers: | £678,724 |

I have assumed tax rates and allowances for 2021/22 remain at 2020/21 levels (see Appendix A) in this example.

Spreading the transfers has saved £14,388 (£693,122 – £678,724) in CGT: not a huge saving on gains totalling £2.5m, but an easy one to achieve. It is essential, however, that no contract or other fixed arrangements for the second transfer are in place before the end of the first tax year. Disposals are deemed to take place on the date of unconditional contract for CGT purposes.

Another way to reduce the CGT arising on the transfer may be to select properties giving rise to lower CGT bills, such as more recent acquisitions, or a former home (but bear in mind the potential impact on your RNRB).

### Avoiding the SDLT Cost

It might be possible to avoid, or reduce, the SDLT on the transfer by initially going into partnership with your children for a few years before forming the family investment company. This will mean delaying the formation of the company. It will also mean you need to retain some shares (although, with careful planning, your shareholding may be kept small). For more details on the tax-saving potential of using partnerships as a preliminary step to forming a company, see the Taxcafe.co.uk guide *'Using a Property Company to Save Tax'*.

### Accelerating the IHT Savings

If the parents reach the point where they feel they have sufficient personal resources outside the company to sustain them for the rest of their lives, they can gift the benefit of some or all of the remaining loan account to the children. This will be a potentially exempt transfer and the gifted amount will escape IHT if the donor parent survives seven years.

Note, however, that there may be CGT consequences for the donee on a subsequent repayment of the debt to them.

## 13.4    GROWTH SHARES

By creating a different share structure, incorporating 'growth shares', a family investment company can be used to pass on some or all of the future growth in value of your investments or rental property free from IHT. In many cases, the company can be set up with no 'up front' tax costs, or at least much less than using the technique in Section 13.2.

### *Example*
*James and Mary, a married couple, run a residential rental property business in partnership together. They each spend an average of more than twenty hours per week working in the business. The portfolio comprises ten houses purchased over several decades at a total cost of £1.5m and currently worth a total of £6m. Their only other significant asset is their home, worth £1.2m. They now wish to start passing on some of their wealth to their sons, Paul and Michael, but the cost of using the method set out in Section 13.2 would be £1.633m (£1.253m in CGT and £380,000 in SDLT), which they simply cannot afford.*

*Instead, they transfer their property business to a new company, Walton Investments Ltd, in exchange for 'Class A' Ordinary Shares. This transfer qualifies for 'incorporation relief' for CGT purposes, meaning their capital gains of £4.5m can be held over against the value of their shares and no CGT liability arises at this point. The transfer of partnership property to a company controlled by the same individuals is also exempt from SDLT. Hence, there is no 'up front' cost forming the company.*

*The company issues 'Class B' Ordinary Shares to Paul and Michael. These carry the right to any growth in value in the company in future, but the first £6m of the company's assets belongs to the 'Class A' shareholders. Hence, in effect, the 'Class B' shares are currently worthless, there is no transfer of value, and no IHT can arise.*

*While the current value of the 'Class A' shares, £6m, remains in James and Mary's estates, the future growth in the property portfolio's value will now effectively belong to Paul and Michael. Furthermore, if James and Mary are able to limit the dividends they withdraw from the company, any surplus after tax profits can either be paid to their sons, or accumulated within the company for their benefit.*

### Notes to the Example
i)      The transfer was only exempt from SDLT because James and Mary were operating as a partnership. In other cases, including joint ownership, SDLT will arise, and it would be necessary to operate as a partnership for a few years in order to obtain exemption.

ii)     CGT 'incorporation relief' is usually available where the business owners spend an average of at least twenty hours per week working in the business. In other cases it will depend on circumstances.

iii)    Whether the 'Class B' 'growth shares' have any voting rights is entirely up to you. If you wish to retain control over the company, the Class B shares can be non-voting.

iv)     Similarly, it is up to you whether the growth shares carry rights to dividends. My recommendation would be that they do, but this is at the discretion of the Class A shareholders (this is important to ensure the B shares have no value at the date of issue). Each shareholder can receive up to £2,000 of tax-free dividends each tax year.

See the Taxcafe.co.uk guide *'Using a Property Company to Save Tax'* for full details of the relevant CGT and SDLT reliefs applying to the transfer of a property rental business to a company, and the further benefits produced by 'incorporation relief'.

## Next Steps

In the example, I suggested the parents could allow surplus funds to accumulate within the company to benefit their children. Another strategy might be to take dividends to create a 'fund' to enable the parents to transfer some of their 'Class A' shares to the children at a later date.

### Example Continued
*Walton Investments Ltd makes annual rental profits of £375,000 before paying James and Mary salaries of £12,500 each. This leaves a profit of £350,000 which, after Corporation Tax at 19%, leaves after tax profits of £283,500, which are paid out to James and Mary as dividends.*

*James and Mary suffer Income Tax of £38,344 and NIS of £360 each, and are thus left with total after-tax income of £231,092 (£283,500 + 2 x £12,500 – 2 x £38,344 – 2 x £360). They require a little over £150,000 to cover living expenses, so they are able to put around £80,000 aside each year.*

*Let us say there are 1,000 'Class A' Ordinary shares, with James and Mary holding 500 each. A lifetime transfer of these shares will give rise to a capital gain of £4,500 per share (£4.5m/1,000). Let's say, after three years, James and Mary each transfer 135 shares to their sons. Each parent therefore has a capital gain of £607,500 (£4,500 x 135). After deducting their annual CGT exemption of, £12,300, they will each pay CGT at 20% on a taxable gain of £595,200, or £119,040, which they can pay out of the funds they have accumulated.*

*The transfer of the 'Class A' shares will be a potentially exempt transfer, which will escape IHT after seven years, and James and Mary's estate will have been reduced by £1.62m (£6m x 2 x 135/1,000), saving a further £648,000 in IHT.*

This process can be continued as long as the parents wish, although there are some limiting factors to be aware of:

a)    As the parents' shareholding reduces, the amount of income they are able to take from the company will also reduce. Hence, they cannot take this past the point where they have insufficient income to live on.

b)    If the parents wish to retain control of the company, they will need to keep more than 50% of the 'Class A' shares (and not allow the 'Class B' shares any voting rights).

c)    Salaries paid to the parents must not exceed a fair recompense for the work they do for the company. Excessive salaries will not attract Corporation Tax relief. Furthermore, once any 'Class A' shares have been gifted to the children, any excessive salary payments thereafter will give rise to a 'gift with reservation' and the IHT saving will be lost.

These additional steps are not essential and, as we can see, they come at a significant cost. In our example, to get a further £238,080 of after tax income over three years (as required to fund their CGT bills), James and Mary suffered a total of £166,746 in extra Income Tax. This effectively brings the total cost of the 'Class A' share transfers to £404,826 (£238,080 + £166,746). In other words, it has cost £404,826 to produce an ultimate saving of £648,000 that will take seven years to achieve (although some savings will arise as long as at least one of the parents survives at least three years).

In many cases, it might therefore be better for the parents to limit their withdrawals from the company to the amounts they need to live on, and allow the surplus to accumulate within the company, rather than try to make further IHT savings at the expense of other taxes.

See the Taxcafe.co.uk guide *'Using a Property Company to Save Tax'* for details of the most tax-efficient way to make salary and dividend payments to property company owners (I have assumed here that the employment allowance is available to exempt the company from employer's NIS on the directors' salaries). *'Using a Property Company to Save Tax'* also explains it is not generally tax efficient to use a company where rental properties are debt free and the owner intends to withdraw all the after tax profits every year: but we had other motives in this case!

## 13.5   PICK AND MIX

The method described in Section 13.2 produces the greater IHT savings, but comes at a significant 'up front' tax cost. The method in Section 13.4 can be implemented with no 'up front' tax cost in many cases, but only achieves IHT savings on future growth in value of rental property or other investments (unless further steps are taken, but then there are 'up front' tax costs again).

It is, however, possible to have a compromise solution that combines some of the benefits of both methods.

### *Example Revisited*
*Let's go back to the same opening position we had for James and Mary at the start of the example in Section 13.4. However, let's now assume they have cash and short-term investments of at least £413,112 available to fund any 'up front' tax costs.*

*As before, they transfer their rental property business to Walton Investments Ltd in exchange for 'Class A' shares but, this time, there is also 'cash' consideration of £2m in the form of an interest-free loan account repayable on demand. This means the value of their 'Class A' shares is now £4m (£6m – £2m).*

*Their 'incorporation relief' is restricted to the part of the gain attributable to their shares, £3m (£4.5m x £4m/£6m), and £1.5m of their gain is exposed to CGT. After deducting their annual CGT exemptions, this leaves £1,475,400 taxed at 28%, giving them a CGT bill of £413,112, which they are able to fund from their savings.*

The 'Class B' shares can then be issued to Paul and Michael in the same way as before (except it is now the first £4m of the company's net assets that belongs to the 'Class A' shareholders, rather than £6m).

However, instead of withdrawing salary and dividends, James and Mary can take tax-free loan repayments that will reduce their loan account, thus producing significant additional IHT savings, similar to those we saw in Section 13.2.

In fact, from an annual tax planning perspective, the most efficient strategy will be for James and Mary to take small salaries of £12,500 each, plus dividends of £2,000 each, in each tax year. The salaries provide Corporation Tax relief at 19%, are free from Income Tax (they are covered by the couple's personal allowances), and suffer just £720 in NIS (in total). The dividends are tax-free. Overall, these payments put a net £28,280 in the couple's hands while saving the company £4,750 in Corporation Tax at the same time.

Assuming they need a similar amount to that which we saw in Section 13.4 to cover their annual living expenses, they could therefore take a loan repayment of, say, £125,000 each year.

To see how this might work out, we will make the same assumptions we made in Section 13.2 (numbered (i) to (vi)), including the fact that Jim and Mary will spend all the cash they receive (after tax). This produces the following results:

| Second Death After (Years) | Estate without FIC | Estate using FIC | IHT Saved | Overall Net Saving/(Cost)* |
|---|---|---|---|---|
| 1 | £7,613,112 | £7,075,000 | £215,245 | (£126,337) |
| 2 | £8,153,112 | £7,040,000 | £445,245 | £175,193 |
| 3 | £8,733,612 | £7,011,750 | £688,745 | £490,223 |
| 4 | £9,357,650 | £6,990,756 | £946,757 | £819,765 |
| 5 | £10,028,490 | £6,977,563 | £1,220,371 | £1,164,909 |
| 6 | £10,749,643 | £6,972,755 | £1,510,755 | £1,526,823 |
| 8 | £12,358,266 | £6,990,859 | £2,146,963 | £2,306,091 |
| 10 | £14,217,230 | £7,050,686 | £2,866,618 | £3,168,806 |
| 12 | £16,365,496 | £7,158,731 | £3,682,706 | £4,127,954 |
| 15 | £20,230,709 | £7,427,933 | £5,121,111 | £5,780,949 |
| 20 | £28,863,836 | £8,741,787 | £8,048,819 | £8,930,752 |

* After accounting for the 'up front' CGT cost of £413,112; but also including the additional annual tax saving of £71,530 on rental profits from the residential property portfolio for the first sixteen years (when the loan account is exhausted), reducing to £37,641 per year thereafter.

The annual tax saving within the first sixteen years would increase to £84,515 after the first death, but would reduce to just £16,382 if the survivor continued to extract the same level of income from the company thereafter (these figures assume the employment allowance remains available to exempt salary payments to the surviving director from employer's NIS: see the

Taxcafe.co.uk guide *'Using a Property Company to Save Tax'* for more information).

As we can see, this hybrid 'compromise' solution still produces considerable tax savings at a more manageable 'up front' cost; although a significant amount of IHT will remain payable on the 'second death'.

Taking tax-free salary and dividends each year prolongs the period required to achieve the best IHT savings. In this example, the loan account lasts almost three years longer as a result, and there is a period when the couple's IHT exposure is up to £181,000 more than it might otherwise have been (although the same saving is achieved eventually).

However, over sixteen years, this strategy has saved £76,000 in Corporation Tax at a cost of just £11,520 in NIS. Furthermore, the additional Income Tax savings in the last three years of the loan's life total £101,070. Hence, overall, the strategy eventually produces an additional net **permanent** saving of £165,550 (£76,000 – £11,520 + £101,070) in return for a short-term, temporary risk of up to £181,000. Personally, I would generally go for that, but where the parents' life expectancy is short, it may make more sense to pay down the loan account as quickly as possible.

### An Alternative Approach

Rather than only pay the parents the amounts they need, the loan account could be paid down quicker. In the example above, assuming it continues to pay the salary and dividends already described, the company will have a further £279,500 available each year and could use this to make higher loan repayments. This would give Jim and Mary £154,500 more than they need each year (£279,500 – £125,000).

However, this strategy will only create an additional IHT saving if Jim and Mary:

a)    Spend this money (although this does not really benefit Paul and Michael),

b)    Give it away (this will be a potentially exempt transfer, and will only be exempt from IHT after seven years, or

c)    Invest it in some type of IHT 'shelter' such as a loan trust, discounted gift trust, or AIM shares

Assuming they follow one of these methods, their £2m loan account will now only last just over seven years. If they have followed (a) or (b) they will then have to start taking substantial dividends from the company to fund their living expenses, with a resultant Income Tax cost of £33,889 per year.

Following method (c) would have allowed them to invest £1,081,500 over the seven years the loan account lasted. If we say this produces a return of 5% (£54,075) this will still leave them £70,925 short for their annual cash requirements so, once again, they will need to take dividends from the company, although the annual Income Tax cost would now be only £7,853. Following this method, Jim and Mary's savings can be summarised as follows:

| Second Death After (Years) | Estate without FIC | Estate using FIC* | IHT Saved | Overall Net Saving/(Cost)** |
|---|---|---|---|---|
| 1 | £7,613,112 | £6,920,500 | £277,045 | (£64,537) |
| 2 | £8,153,112 | £6,731,000 | £568,845 | £298,793 |
| 3 | £8,733,612 | £6,548,250 | £874,145 | £675,623 |
| 4 | £9,357,650 | £6,372,756 | £1,193,957 | £1,066,965 |
| 5 | £10,028,490 | £6,205,063 | £1,529,371 | £1,473,909 |
| 6 | £10,749,643 | £6,045,755 | £1,881,555 | £1,897,623 |
| 8 | £12,358,266 | £5,990,859 | £2,546,963 | £2,703,867 |
| 10 | £14,217,230 | £6,300,686 | £3,166,618 | £3,450,876 |
| 12 | £16,365,496 | £6,658,731 | £3,882,706 | £4,294,319 |
| 15 | £20,230,709 | £7,302,933 | £5,171,111 | £5,773,755 |
| 20 | £28,863,836 | £8,741,787 | £8,048,819 | £8,969,850 |

* Assumes all surplus funds have been fully sheltered from IHT. In practice, this may not be the case, or may take a little longer to achieve (e.g. AIM shares are not 'sheltered' until after two years).
** After accounting for the 'up front' CGT cost of £413,112; but including the additional annual tax saving of £71,530 on rental profits from the residential property portfolio for the first seven years; £69,306 in the eighth year; and £63,677 per year thereafter.

As we can see, this alternative approach could lead to greater savings and could achieve them more quickly (although it is worth noting the savings arising where the second death occurs between fifteen and eighteen years after the company is set up are actually less).

However, this approach relies on investments that either carry a degree of commercial risk, or will take some time to achieve the full IHT savings anticipated in the table (see Sections 7.27, 9.11 and 9.12 for details).

## 13.6   MORE OPTIONAL EXTRAS

Once again, there are some potential refinements or improvements to the strategies discussed in Sections 13.4 and 13.5.

### Pension Contributions
Where the parents continue to run the business after the transfer, it may be possible for the company to make pension contributions of up to £40,000 per parent per year. These will attract Corporation Tax relief at 19% and will also provide an effective IHT shelter, as discussed in Section 10.15 (see the Taxcafe.co.uk guide 'Pension Magic' for further details).

As with salary payments, it is vital the parents do sufficient work in the business to justify the pension contributions made on their behalf, otherwise Corporation Tax relief may be denied and a 'gift with reservation' may arise.

## Golden Shares

If the parents may eventually wish to give 50% or more of the 'Class A' shares to their children, they may also wish to hold a 'Golden Share' (see Section 13.3) so they are able to retain control over the company. The Golden Share should ideally be issued at the outset before there are any concerns over values, voting rights, etc.

## Shares in Trust

The company's 'Class B' shares could be put in a trust rather than issued directly to the children, if desired. This could provide the same potential benefits as discussed in Section 13.3. If this is done at the outset, the shares would be virtually worthless, hence no transfer of value will have taken place, and no IHT charges can arise.

'Class A' shares can also be gifted to a trust and this will provide an opportunity to claim 'holdover relief' and thus avoid any immediate CGT liability (see Section 9.6). However, transfers worth in excess of the NRB will give rise to an immediate IHT charge at the 'lifetime rate' of 20%.

In a case like Jim and Mary (Sections 13.4 and 13.5), it will be possible to work out the maximum number of shares to transfer to get CGT holdover relief without giving rise to immediate IHT charges. With two settlors, transfers worth up to £650,000 in total (two NRBs) could be made free from IHT every seven years.

### *Example Revisited Again*

*Based on the revised version of the example in Section 13.5, the 1,000 'Class A' shares in Walton Investments Ltd would be worth £4,000 each (£4m/1,000).*

*Jim and Mary each transfer eighty-one shares to the Walton Discretionary Trust, with Paul, Michael, and their children (Jim and Mary's grandchildren) as beneficiaries. The total value of the transfer made by each parent is £324,000 (£4,000 x 81) and is thus covered by their NRB.*

*The couple have now passed a further £648,000 to their children free from both IHT and CGT and, provided they survive seven years, this will lead to an additional saving of £259,200 (£648,000 x 40%).*

Whatever class of shares are put in the trust, as long as the parents avoid any immediate IHT charges on the transfer (by limiting the value transferred by each parent to no more than their NRB), they can be held in the trust for up to ten years (less one day) without giving rise to any anniversary or exit charges (see Chapter 8). Alternatively, it may be worth paying some modest charges to secure longer-term benefits (both practical and financial).

## Accelerating the IHT Savings

If the parents have followed the method set out in Section 13.5, it may later be possible to create additional IHT savings by gifting some or all of their loan account to the children (subject, again, to the comments in Section 13.3).

# Chapter 14

# Other Advanced Inheritance Tax Planning Ideas

## 14.1 BUSINESS BUY BACK

Assets qualifying for 100% BPR or APR (see Chapter 7) can be transferred to a trust free from IHT. At some later stage, the transferor may decide to purchase the business back from the trust at market value. The end result would then be that funds equal to the value of the business (at the time of the buy back) have been passed into the relevant property trust regime (and are thus outside any individual's estate) without incurring any entry charge on the transfer.

### Example
*Sheridan and Smithy own an unlisted trading company, Two Pints Ltd, which they founded some years ago for an initial investment of £50 each; the company is now worth a total of £2,024,700.*

*They transfer their shares to the Barry Family Discretionary Trust to benefit their adult children, Gavin and Stacey. The transfer qualifies for BPR so no IHT arises.*

*The transfer also qualifies for entrepreneur's relief (see Section 11.5), so Sheridan and Smithy decide not to claim holdover relief for CGT purposes. Each of them has a capital gain of £1,012,300; their annual CGT exemption reduces this to £1m, on which they each pay CGT of £100,000 (at 10%).*

*A few years later (but more than two), Sheridan and Smithy buy the company back from the trust for its then market value of £3,030,850. As the trust has held the company for the benefit of Gavan and Stacey for more than two years, it may also claim entrepreneur's relief on its gain of £1,006,150 (£3,030,850 – £2,024,700). After deducting its annual CGT exemption of £6,150 (see Section 11.11), the trust pays CGT at 10% on its taxable gain of £1m, i.e. £100,000.*

*Sheridan and Smithy pay Stamp Duty of £15,155 on the purchase (£3,030,850 x 0.5%), bringing the total tax costs incurred to date to £315,155.*

*However, a net sum of £2,930,850 (£3,030,850 – £100,000) has now been placed in trust with no entry charge, leading to an eventual IHT saving of £1,172,340. Taking account of the tax costs incurred by Sheridan, Smithy, and the trust, (and the consequent reduction in their estates), the overall net saving achieved is £983,247 (£1,172,340 – £315,155 + £315,155 x 40%).*

*Furthermore, this saving will be achieved after two years not seven (i.e. once Sheridan and Smithy are eligible for BPR on the shares again) and no exit charges will apply to funds paid out to the trust beneficiaries within ten years of when the trust was set up.*

By way of comparison, a couple putting a net sum of £2,930,850 into a relevant property trust by way of a lifetime transfer would incur immediate IHT charges of at least £456,170 (£2,930,850 – 2 x £325,000 = £2,280,850 x 20% = £456,170). Furthermore, exit charges of at least 0.1167% would arise for each calendar quarter the funds were held in the trust, and it would take seven years before the funds were exempt from IHT on the couple's deaths.

## Some Provisos

There must be no fixed arrangement to buy the business back from the trust at the time of the original transfer. Even an intention to purchase the business back may be enough to require disclosure under the DOTAS regime (see Section 10.20).

The transferor must actually pay the funds required to purchase the business back from the trust. Any amount left outstanding as a loan would not be deductible from the purchaser's estate, as it would be deemed an 'artificially created debt' (see Section 2.11).

The purchaser will need to hold the business for another two years before they are eligible for BPR again. If they were to borrow to fund the purchase, those borrowings will be deducted from the value of the business for BPR purposes (see Section 2.11).

While the entry charge may be avoided under this technique, the trust will still be subject to anniversary and exit charges (see Chapter 8) if the funds (or assets purchased with them) remain in the trust for ten years or more.

Income accumulated within the trust (see Section 8.18) might also give rise to some exit charges, even within the first ten years, if this exceeds the NRB (or twice the NRB where there are two settlors). Such charges are likely to be very modest, however.

## 14.2    THE DOUBLE DIP

Where full BPR or APR is available on a business owner's death (see Chapter 7), the relevant assets can safely be left to a discretionary trust free from IHT. The deceased's spouse (or unmarried partner) can then buy the relevant property from the discretionary trust for full market value.

### Wealth Warning
Due to the rules on deduction of liabilities used to acquire relievable property (see Sections 2.11 and 7.11), the purchase will need to be funded from other existing assets and not by way of borrowing.

On the survivor's death, the chargeable value of their estate will effectively be reduced twice: through BPR or APR on the qualifying property; and then again by using other chargeable assets or funds for the purchase. This provides the effective 'double dip', illustrated by the following example.

***Example***

*On his death, Damon leaves the family business to the Parklife Discretionary Trust and the remainder of his estate to his widow, Justine. Justine buys the business from the trust for £1m, its current market value, using funds inherited from Damon.*

*On Justine's death, her estate comprises the family business, worth £1.2m, and other assets worth £650,000. Her IHT calculation is therefore as follows:*

| | |
|---|---|
| *Total estate value* | *£1,850,000* |
| *Less:* | |
| *Business property relief* | *£1,200,000* |
| | -------------- |
| *Chargeable estate* | *£650,000* |

*Justine's chargeable estate is covered by her NRB of £325,000 plus her TNRB received from Damon, leaving her executors with no IHT to pay.*

*If Damon had left the business to Justine rather than the trust, she would not have used £1m of other funds to purchase it. Those funds would then have been in her estate on her death, giving rise to an IHT bill of £400,000.*

Hence, as we can see from the example, this technique effectively enables a surviving spouse or partner to benefit from a double deduction in respect of qualifying business or agricultural property.

The purchase of the business shortly after the original owner's death should give rise to little or no CGT due to the 'uplift on death' (see Section 11.2). The same would apply to any inherited assets sold to fund the purchase of the business.

However, the major drawback is the purchase of the business must be funded from other existing assets: either assets already held by the surviving spouse or partner, or other assets inherited from the deceased spouse or partner. Funding the purchase through borrowing will not be effective. This restriction severely limits the usefulness of this technique, although it will still be possible to use it in some cases.

There are a few other little 'flies in the ointment' here:

i)      Stamp Duty or SDLT will be payable on the surviving partner's purchase of the business

ii)     Although inherited assets will benefit from the 'uplift on death', the surviving spouse or partner may suffer CGT liabilities if they have to sell any of their own existing assets to fund the purchase of the business

iii)    The discretionary trust will be subject to higher rates of Income Tax on income from the funds it holds; although the effects of this can be mitigated by paying income out to beneficiaries (see Section 8.21 for details)

iv)     The discretionary trust will be subject to anniversary and exit charges (see Chapter 8) if it holds assets with a value in excess of the NRB for ten years or more

Having said all that, it is worth bearing in mind the technique allows funds equal to the market value of the deceased's business to be put into a discretionary trust with no 'entry charge' (and no exit charges during the first ten years: subject to my comments in Section 14.1), so it is a very efficient way to set up a trust.

## 14.3 MONEY BOX COMPANIES

In one IHT case, a company with a business consisting of lending money to other associated companies was held to be carrying on a qualifying business for BPR purposes. It seems, therefore, that money lending can be a qualifying business.

However, an important factor in this particular case was the fact the loans were unsecured and repayable on demand. This meant the company's business comprised a business of 'making loans' rather than one of 'investing in loans' and this was enough to enable the company's owner to obtain BPR. The fact the loans were made to associated companies did not seem to affect the position. This is good news since it is doubtful whether many people will wish to make unsecured loans to non-associated companies.

This decision opens up some interesting planning possibilities. A person with a non-qualifying company, such as a property investment company, for example, could set up a money-lending company to make loans to the non-qualifying company.

The loans would need to be unsecured and repayable on demand and the volume of activity carried on by the money-lending company would need to be sufficient to make it a business (see Section 7.4). The money-lending company would also need to charge interest in order to provide the necessary 'profit motive'.

Under these circumstances, it would be possible to reduce the value of the non-qualifying company while the value of the money-lending company may be eligible for BPR, thus saving IHT on the death of the owner of both companies.

The non-qualifying business probably needs to be in a company in order to get the necessary reduction in value that saves the IHT. (See Section 14.4 for further benefits of putting non-qualifying businesses into a company)

## 14.4 CORPORATE DEBT

As we saw in Section 7.13, liabilities owed by a company reduce the value of that company and hence also the value of the shares in it.

When a person dies owning shares in a company, it is the value of those shares that is brought into their estate and there is no need to claim a separate deduction for the company's liabilities. Hence, there is also no need to meet the rules described in Section 2.11 regarding the payment of liabilities out of the assets of the deceased's estate.

It may therefore make sense if borrowings to finance investments not qualifying for any form of relief are made through a company.

### Example

*Phil has offered to lend his brother Don £500,000 to help him start a property investment business. The loan will be unsecured and interest-free.*

*If Don borrowed the money personally and later died still owing this money to Phil, his executors would need to repay Phil out of the assets of Don's estate in order to claim a deduction for this loan for IHT purposes (see Section 2.11).*

*Instead, Don sets up a company, Ever Lee Investments Ltd. He then gets Phil to lend the money to the company.*

*The debt to Phil will now automatically reduce the value of Don's shares in Ever Lee Investments Ltd for IHT purposes without having to worry about meeting the rules in Section 2.11.*

This technique solves the problem of having to repay a loan on the borrower's death but if such a loan was used to indirectly finance relievable property or excluded property, the other rules described in Section 2.11 would then apply.

# Chapter 15

# Domicile

## 15.1 WHAT IS DOMICILE?

In essence, your 'domicile' is the country you consider to be your permanent home. This does not necessarily equate to your country of birth, nor to the country in which you happen to be living at present.

Domicile should not be confused with residence, which is a far more transitory concept (but see Section 2.2 regarding deemed domicile).

At this point, it is worth noting that, technically speaking, you cannot actually have 'UK domicile' but will, instead, have your domicile in England and Wales, Scotland, or Northern Ireland. As we saw in Sections 10.10 and 10.11, this can be very important when it comes to intestacy or 'legal rights'.

However, it is usually safe to simply refer to 'UK domicile' for IHT purposes. Nonetheless, we will see some instances where the distinction between the different nations of the UK can be quite important later in this chapter.

It is also worth noting that the Channel Islands and the Isle of Man are not part of the UK for tax purposes, including IHT and domicile.

## 15.2 DOMICILE OF ORIGIN

At birth, each person acquires the domicile of the person on whom they are legally dependent at that time. That person will usually be their father, but it is their mother if their father is dead or their parents are living apart and they have a home with their mother, but not with their father. The domicile you acquire at this point is known as your 'Domicile of Origin'.

Throughout your minority, you continue to have the same domicile as the person on whom you are legally dependent. If that person changes their domicile during this period then your domicile also changes and you acquire a 'Domicile of Dependency'.

You only become capable of having your own independent domicile when you reach the age of 16 (or, in Scotland, 14 for a boy, 12 for a girl).

### *Example*
*Farrokh was born in Zanzibar in 1946 and lived with both of his parents at that time. His father was domiciled in India and his mother was domiciled in Zanzibar. Farrokh therefore acquired an Indian Domicile of Origin. In 1960, Farrokh's parents moved to England, taking Farrokh with them. They intended to remain in England permanently. At this point, Farrokh acquired a UK Domicile of Dependency.*

### Re-acquiring a Domicile of Origin

If it ever becomes uncertain which country you regard as your permanent home, your domicile will revert to your Domicile of Origin. Your domicile always reverts to your Domicile of Origin under these circumstances and not any Domicile of Dependency you may have had.

### Domicile and Marriage

Subject to the 'opt-in' election described below, marriage does not generally affect domicile. However, women other than US Nationals, who married before 1st January 1974, adopted their husband's domicile as a Domicile of Dependency.

Non-UK domiciled individuals with a UK domiciled spouse may elect to be treated as UK domiciled for IHT purposes. See Section 6.19 for further details.

### 15.3    DOMICILE OF CHOICE

In most cases, a person's Domicile of Origin remains their domicile for the rest of their life. A different domicile can only be acquired, as a 'Domicile of Choice', where a person emigrates and can prove their intention to reside permanently or indefinitely in their new home country.

Acquiring a new domicile for tax purposes, as a 'Domicile of Choice', can be very difficult. This is both good news and bad news since it cuts both ways and HMRC has had just as much difficulty proving a taxpayer has acquired the UK as their Domicile of Choice as taxpayers have had in proving they have acquired a domicile somewhere else.

To acquire a new domicile, as a Domicile of Choice, it is necessary to not only demonstrate an intention to adopt the new country as your permanent home, but also to follow this up by action and subsequent conduct.

If the taxpayer abandons their Domicile of Choice, without demonstrating a clear intention to adopt a new Domicile of Choice somewhere else, then their domicile automatically reverts to their Domicile of Origin.

### *Example*
*Brian has a UK Domicile of Origin. Twenty years ago, he emigrated to Spain and became Spanish domiciled. He declared this intention on form P85, which he lodged with the Inland Revenue (now HMRC) shortly before he departed for the Costa del Sol. In 2021, Brian gets a terrific offer to work in Los Angeles, so he leaves Spain and moves to California. Brian is uncertain, however, whether he wishes to remain in California permanently. As Brian's permanent home is now unclear, his domicile reverts to the UK!*

**Wealth Warning 1**

If you intend to emigrate to avoid UK IHT, make sure you pick the right country first time! Although Brian might eventually be able to establish Californian domicile, this will now be more difficult for him because he has established a 'track record' of abandoning his so-called 'permanent home' and it will be harder to prove he has no intention of returning to the UK.

**Wealth Warning 2**

Note that I referred to 'Californian' domicile above and not to US domicile. Strictly speaking, domicile relates to a 'territory' rather than a country (e.g. to a State in the USA). In countries with a federal system, like the USA, you will need to decide which territory you are adopting as your new permanent home, not just which country. This may severely restrict your freedom of movement. California may be big enough, but what about Rhode Island?

**Wealth Warning 3**

Another important point to note about emigrating to avoid IHT is you will continue to be ***deemed*** UK domiciled at the time of your death if you were still UK domiciled under general principles at any time in the preceding three years. As explained in Section 2.2, this may be affected by a Double Tax Treaty in some cases.

Emigrating to avoid IHT must therefore be done early and carefully.

## 15.4   A GUIDE TO EMIGRATION

There is no set procedure for establishing a Domicile of Choice through permanent emigration. Like many things in the tax world, each case will be examined on its own particular merits. Here are a few practical tips:

- Declare your intentions to HMRC on forms P85 and DOM1 before leaving the UK
- Buy a home in your new country
- Take your family with you (including the pets)
- Take whatever steps you can to establish citizenship, nationality, etc, in your new country
- Take up employment in your new country (or, alternatively, establish your own business there)
- Get on the electoral roll in your new country
- Buy a grave plot in your new country (this is given a great deal of importance by the tax authorities when looking at domicile)
- Try to visit the UK as little as possible
- Make sure your former home in the UK is not available for your use: preferably, it should be sold
- Ensure residential accommodation is not available to you elsewhere in the UK: if you must visit the UK, try to stay in hotels
- Sell as many UK assets as you can and close your UK bank accounts

- Resign membership of clubs, associations, etc, in the UK. Ideally, you should try to make a 'clean break' with your previous life in the UK
- Write letters or emails (e.g. to your solicitor) expressing your intention of never returning to reside in the UK
- Write a Will in your new country
- Try not to move on again to another territory

Following the above guidelines should generally ensure you become non-UK resident as well as non-UK domiciled. In fact, non-UK residence is generally a lot easier to achieve. Nevertheless, the statutory residence test (see the Taxcafe.co.uk guide *'How to Save Property Tax'* for details) could potentially lead to a few instances where an individual manages to achieve non-UK domicile, but remains UK resident for tax purposes.

An individual born in the UK with a UK Domicile of Origin, who has subsequently obtained an overseas Domicile of Choice, and who was UK resident in either of the previous two UK tax years, is deemed to be UK domiciled if they remain UK resident in the current tax year. Hence, for most people born in the UK, it remains essential to achieve non-UK residence, as well as non-UK domicile.

However, I must stress that, in the vast majority of cases, becoming non-UK resident is not enough to ensure you have become non-UK domiciled. The statutory residence test is merely an additional hurdle to overcome: there is a great deal more involved in obtaining a new Domicile of Choice!

For the reasons explained under Wealth Warning 2 in the previous section, you may need to think in terms of your new home territory, rather than country, when applying the above guidelines (e.g. Queensland rather than Australia).

If you really must retain any connections with the UK (and I don't recommend it), try to make it a different nation. For example, if you have an English Domicile of Origin and you wish to keep a UK bank account, make it an account with a Scottish or Northern Irish branch.


## 15.5    SHEDDING A UK DOMICILE OF DEPENDENCY

If you have a UK Domicile of Dependency, but a non-UK Domicile of Origin, it will be far easier for you to re-acquire your Domicile of Origin than to acquire a Domicile of Choice.

In this situation, you only need to leave your Domicile of Dependency for long enough to be in a position where the country that is your permanent home is uncertain in order to re-acquire your non-UK Domicile of Origin.

Remember also that England and Wales, Scotland, and Northern Ireland are all different territories for this purpose. Hence, for example, a person with an English Domicile of Dependency might be able to shed that domicile by moving to Scotland or Northern Ireland, even if they do not intend to remain there permanently.

Shedding a UK Domicile of Dependency will not, however, prevent you becoming deemed UK domiciled after 15 years of UK residence (Section 2.2).

## 15.6   RETAINING A DOMICILE OF ORIGIN

If you are lucky enough to have a non-UK Domicile of Origin it is far, far, easier to retain this as your domicile than to acquire a Domicile of Choice.

As stated above, it is very difficult for HMRC to prove an individual has acquired a new Domicile of Choice. This is especially true if the individual states it is their intention to return to their country of origin one day.

### *Example*
*Grace was born in Jamaica, of Jamaican parents. She has, however, lived in the UK for over 30 years, having moved here in her early twenties. Despite this, she has always stated she intends to return 'home' when she retires. She therefore remains domiciled in Jamaica.*

In **this** case, an 'intention' does not have to be backed up by action, but should be more than a vague notion that you would like to 'die in the land of your fathers'. Intentions such as 'to retire to your home country' or 'return home after your spouse's death' are the sort of thing that usually suffice.

To confirm your non-UK domiciled status, you should complete form DOM1, declaring yourself to be non-UK domiciled, and submit it to HMRC.

It may also be worth buying a grave plot in your Domicile of Origin. This is accepted as a strong indication of your intention to return to that country.

It's worth remembering you will keep your Domicile of Origin if there is some doubt about where you intend to make your permanent home. It might be enough to state you intend 'retiring abroad' if there is reasonable substance to your intentions. You might even retain a non-UK Domicile of Origin by expressing doubt about whether you intend to live in England or Scotland!

Sadly, as explained in Section 2.2, none of this may actually save any IHT if you are deemed UK domiciled from being UK resident for 15 or more of the previous 20 tax years (subject to any applicable Double Tax Treaty).

So that you don't end up with deemed UK Domicile, you should try to spend six years out of every 20 abroad (not necessarily in your Domicile of Origin).

### Wealth Warning
Non-UK domiciled individuals resident in the UK for seven or more of the previous nine UK tax years may be subject to punitive Income Tax charges unless they elect to pay UK tax on foreign income and gains.

# Chapter 16

# The Inheritance Tax Planning Timetable

## 16.1    IT'S NEVER TOO EARLY TO START

Most tax advisers will tell you it's never too early to start IHT planning, but when you're struggling to pay a mortgage and make some headway at the beginning of your working career, IHT will probably be the last thing on your mind.

Nevertheless, as we saw in Section 9.3, the earlier you start, the more effective your planning will be, and if you are lucky enough to have the wealth to follow the kind of planning in that section, long term planning will help to pass on more family wealth to the next generation, or even the one after that.

Even if you have little wealth, your first step should be to ensure any life policies are written in favour of other family members.

## 16.2    MARRIAGE

First of all, marriage is a good time to remind the family to do their IHT planning by making the exempt gifts set out in Section 5.4. This is also a good time to put money into trust for your children, even before they're born!

Next, remember to make a new Will. An existing Will is rendered void on marriage unless it was made in contemplation of your union.

Once you are married, it may be worth taking steps to ensure your NRB is fully available to transfer to your spouse on your death. As we saw in Chapter 6, this may not always be the best course of action but is certainly something you should at least consider.

## 16.3    BECOMING A PARENT

This is the one that focuses the mind and gets most people thinking about IHT planning.

It's time to step up the ante and begin thinking about tax efficient trust structures for your children (see Section 10.17). Get your parents to give money directly to your children instead of you (if you can afford to do without it).

It's time to re-write your Will again as well; you will need to think about how to provide for your children if you die prematurely. Consider what kind of structure you would like to put in place from the choices available (see Chapter 8). Don't forget to appoint a guardian too!

Now you're a parent, the RNRB comes into play and you should start to factor it into your planning (see Sections 3.4, 12.16 and 12.17).

## 16.4    ADULT CHILDREN

You can now start giving assets directly to the children without the need for any trust structures. Making use of the annual exemption may make sense, although most of us seem to have little choice anyway!

Normal expenditure out of income can be established to pass on substantial sums to the children and when they marry, you can use the exemptions in Section 5.4.

You may want to consider putting a 'family debt scheme' in place (see Section 6.16), or using a family investment company (see Chapter 13).

## 16.5    YOUR FIRST GRANDCHILD

Time to start looking at trust structures again; as we saw in Section 10.17, gifts to grandchildren are much more tax effective. Bare trusts for grandchildren are useful and avoid the problems you get with your own minor children.

You may want to re-write your Will again. Think about 'skipping a generation'. What's the point of leaving money to the children if they're already well established? It might be better left to the grandchildren, so IHT doesn't come up again for another two generations.

## 16.6    GRANDCHILD'S EIGHTH BIRTHDAY

Your grandchild's eighth birthday is a key date. From the next day onwards, you will be able to put money into a relevant property trust for their benefit and pass it to them absolutely within less than ten years, i.e. before any anniversary charges can arise (see Section 8.18). This opens up a number of additional planning opportunities, as we have seen in previous chapters.

## 16.7    RETIREMENT

As pensions or other savings income starts to come in, you may now be able to afford to pass on income-producing assets, perhaps by using a trust (see Section 9.6). Alternatively, a family investment company may be a good vehicle to allow you to retire and still enjoy a tax-free 'income' stream (see Chapter 13).

If you decide to downsize your home, you may be able to benefit from some of the planning strategies considered in Section 12.5, while still preserving your RNRB entitlement (see Section 12.16).

If you have assets qualifying for BPR or APR (see Chapter 7), consider how to preserve the relief after your retire (see Sections 7.20 and 7.30). Consider also whether it is better to pass these on now or to hold on to them so your children (or other beneficiaries) can obtain a tax-free 'uplift on death' for CGT purposes when you pass away.

## 16.8   LOSING A PARENT

If one of your parents dies intestate or with a Will that isn't tax efficient, a deed of variation (Section 17.1) can be used to put IHT planning into place retrospectively.

When your first parent dies, you should consider whether it is better for them to use their NRB on assets that might be appreciating in value (see Section 6.7) or for it to transfer to your surviving parent (assuming they are still married).

If you don't need the money, get your legacies transferred to your children (or even grandchildren) instead. Gifts to charity may also reduce the IHT bill (see Sections 3.5, 3.6 and 17.1).

## 16.9   STILL TOGETHER

Elderly married couples face a bit of a dilemma. If you're both getting older, it may make sense to start giving away surplus wealth as potentially exempt transfers that will hopefully become exempt if you survive seven years.

However, if you die within seven years of making any potentially exempt transfer or chargeable lifetime transfer, this will restrict the proportion of your NRB that transfers to your spouse. As we saw in Chapter 6, this may have adverse consequences, although there are also times when such transfers will be advantageous, especially when assets appreciating in value are gifted.

You need to weigh up these conflicting factors before making any lifetime transfers that are not immediately exempt. While such transfers may sometimes be beneficial for elderly married people, any potential impact on your surviving spouse's TNRB should also be considered.

If you do decide to make lifetime transfers that are not immediately exempt, it will generally make sense for these to be made by the spouse with the longer life expectancy.

## 16.10  LOSING A SPOUSE

You have two years to put a deed of variation into place to make sure your late spouse's estate is dealt with tax efficiently. Obviously, the key point is to maximise the benefit of their NRB, either by having it transfer to you, or by using it to pass on appreciating assets free from IHT (see Section 6.7).

If your spouse leaves any property qualifying for BPR or APR, it may make sense to pass this directly to the children (or other beneficiaries) in case the relief is later lost. This is often particularly important in the case of a family farm where the surviving spouse may no longer be able to run it. Alternatively, you may want to put a 'double dip' in place (see Section 14.2).

Generally, your spouse's RNRB will transfer to you and should form part of your own subsequent planning. However, there will be some instances where it will be better to utilise your spouse's RNRB at this stage, if you can (e.g. if their estate was less than £2m, but you now expect yours to significantly exceed this level).

This is also a good time to assess your own financial needs and start making plans to give away any surplus. Consider your own life expectancy and review the appropriate action set out in Sections 16.12 to 16.14.

## 16.11  REMARRIAGE

Remarriage provides another opportunity to make some of the exempt gifts outlined in Section 5.4. On this occasion, the ability to make tax-exempt transfers into trust for the benefit of your children may be particularly useful.

If either or both of you are a widow or widower, you may have an existing TNRB entitlement (see Section 6.8). If so, you should now consider taking steps to maximise the benefit of your existing TNRB. The methods discussed in Sections 6.9 to 6.12 and 12.7 to 12.10 are available to save your family up to £260,000.

This is also a good time to consider your new combined estate and decide whether there are surplus assets that can be given away. If your spouse already has an existing full TNRB entitlement, you will be able to make lifetime transfers without risking any loss of relief. If they have an existing partial TNRB entitlement, some lifetime transfers may still be made without risk.

Once again, you should re-write your Will, as any previous Will not made in contemplation of your new marriage will be rendered void.

## 16.12 LIFE EXPECTANCY OVER SEVEN YEARS
### (Per Office for National Statistics: men under 83, women under 85)

There's still time to make potentially exempt transfers that should hopefully have time to become fully exempt. Ending the 'reservation' on a 'gift with reservation' will give it time to become exempt also. Remember, if you are single and survive at least three years, some savings may still be made. If you are still married, however, some caution may be required (see Section 16.9, but also Section 16.11 if this is not your or your spouse's first marriage).

Longer-term planning strategies, such as family investment companies (see Chapter 13) may still be viable but, after this, it's probably too late (although they would still have worked for Tom Moore; Vera Lynn; Joan Graham; the Queen Mother; Kirk Douglas – if he was British ... and many others!)

## 16.13 LIFE EXPECTANCY THREE TO SEVEN YEARS
### (Men aged 83 to 94 and women aged 85 to 95)

Transfers made now should still benefit from tapering (see Section 4.5), so some tax may be saved if you are single. Transfers by married people at this stage carry a strong risk of having an adverse impact on your spouse's TNRB unless they are immediately exempt (see Section 16.9 but also Section 16.11 if this is not your or your spouse's first marriage).

Whether you're married or not, it's time to really start making the most of the annual exemption, the small gifts exemption, and normal expenditure out of income (these are all immediately exempt).

A loan trust or discounted gift trust may make sense at this point, and possibly also gifts of appreciating assets not qualifying for BPR (but see Chapter 11 regarding the CGT implications).

You may be able to save IHT by emigrating. If you survive at least three years after establishing non-UK domicile, you can avoid IHT on any non-UK assets.

## 16.14 LIFE EXPECTANCY TWO TO THREE YEARS
### (Men aged 94 to 100 and women aged 95 to 101)

Now's the time to think seriously about those AIM shares, but never forgetting 'Dodgy Dave' (see Section 10.2).

Anything that gets your money into qualifying business property (see Chapter 7) may still save IHT if you can survive two years. Rights issues and transfers of assets into a company under your control may provide immediate savings.

Loan trusts and discounted gift trusts may still save you money even now, as well as other transfers of appreciating property (but watch the CGT position).

## 16.15   LOSS OF CAPACITY

If you expect to lose the ability to take care of your own affairs in the near future, it will make sense to appoint a power of attorney. A power of attorney, or next of kin, can apply to the Court of Protection to make a Statutory Will on your behalf.

The Court of Protection can also authorise your power of attorney to make lifetime gifts on your behalf for IHT planning purposes and is generally sympathetic to applications made for this purpose.

However, despite this, it is generally sensible to put as much IHT planning as possible in place before you lose 'capacity'; as everything becomes considerably more difficult once an 'attorney' has been appointed. There is also some risk they might not act as you may have wished.

Write a new Will, make appropriate gifts, and consider the actions set out in the next section. A disabled trust may also be a good idea at this stage (see Section 8.11). Do as much as you can before it's too late!


## 16.16   DEATHBED PLANNING

So, if you've really left it far too late, what can still be done?

Some of this may seem a little flippant, and I have no wish to cause any offence to anyone: particularly, as I said in the Foreword, at this difficult time. Tax planning may be the farthest thing from your mind at this point and who could really blame you. Nevertheless, here are some of the things you could think about if time is running out:

### Deathbed Marriage

The biggest deathbed planning point, if you're still single at this stage, is to marry your partner. No point trying to hang on to your freedom now, just get on with it!

It will almost always be worth marrying at this stage, even if you have very few assets, as any unused proportion of your NRB or RNRB will transfer to your spouse.

### Last Gasp Gifts

If you haven't used your annual exemption (see Section 5.2) for this, or the previous, tax year, get gifting. If you've made no previous gifts, one simple £6,000 payment to one of your nearest and dearest will save your family £2,400.

For the rest of your family and friends, there's the Small Gifts Exemption (see Section 5.3). Every person you can find to give £250 will save your estate £100 in IHT.

Remember, however, as explained in Section 4.7, if made by cheque, these gifts will not be effective unless the cheque clears through the transferee's bank account before you pass away. Online banking may therefore be better if you feel up to it.

## What About the House?

Although your family may be able to sort things out with a deed of variation (see Section 17.1), it may make things easier for them if you change the title to a tenancy in common now.

## Maximising the Residence Nil Rate Band

As explained in Section 3.4, some or all of the RNRB is withdrawn if your estate is worth more than £2m at the time of your death.

Hence, while potentially exempt and chargeable lifetime transfers made shortly before your death will not usually save IHT, it may be possible to use them to reduce the value of your estate and thus prevent your RNRB from being withdrawn.

### *Example*
*It is March 2021 and Nelson, a widower, is dying. His late wife Sheena died some years earlier, leaving her modest estate to him.*

*Nelson's estate is worth £2.7m, including his home, worth £1m, which he plans to leave to his children, and various cash and savings totalling £700,000.*

*As things stand, Nelson's RNRB will be completely withdrawn by tapering and the IHT on his estate will total £820,000 (£2.7m - £650,000 = £2.05m x 40% = £820,000).*

*Instead, Nelson gives all his cash and savings to his children shortly before he dies. These transfers become chargeable on his death and IHT of £20,000 (£700,000 - £650,000 = £50,000 x 40% = £20,000) will be payable on them.*

*However, the gifts reduce the value of Nelson's estate to £2m, meaning he will be entitled to a RNRB of £350,000. IHT of £660,000 (£2m - £350,000 = £1.65m x 40% = £660,000) will now be payable on his estate.*

*The total IHT arising on Nelson's death is thus £680,000 (£20,000 + £660,000), meaning the lifetime gifts have led to a saving of £140,000 (£820,000 - £680,000).*

A married person could easily reduce the value of their estate to £2m by giving the excess to their spouse shortly before they died. This would generally be an exempt transfer (unless the couple had 'mixed domicile': see Section 6.18) and would have no impact on the TNRB; but it would mean the deceased's RNRB was available to transfer to their widow or widower.

Where assets other than cash are transferred, the CGT consequences will need to be considered. We looked at these in detail in Chapter 11. However, in some cases, it may be worth taking a CGT hit to save more in IHT.

### Example Revisited

*The facts are exactly as set out above, except Nelson transfers various assets worth £700,000 to his children rather than cash. The transferred assets stand at an overall capital gain of £500,000 and do not include any residential property. Nelson is a higher rate taxpayer and has used his annual CGT exemption already, so CGT of £100,000 arises on the transfer. Nelson's CGT liability is deducted from his estate, so this increases the total IHT saving to £180,000 (£140,000 + £100,000 x 40%). Overall, the family still remains £80,000 better off (£180,000 - £100,000).*

For transfers to a spouse (as defined for CGT purposes: see Section 11.6), there would be no immediate CGT cost but the 'uplift on death' (see Section 11.2) would be lost and this may eventually lead to a higher CGT cost that should therefore be taken into account.

Transfers of assets qualifying for BPR or APR may also help to reduce your estate, as these are still counted for the purposes of the RNRB tapering rules (see Section 3.4). Where CGT 'holdover relief' also applies (see Section 11.4), the transfer can be made free of CGT. However, once again, the 'uplift on death' will be lost and you need to consider whether this may be more valuable to your heirs in the end.

If you are married, it is important to remember, apart from transfers that qualify for 100% BPR or APR, other transfers at this stage that are not immediately exempt, will affect your spouse's TNRB, so you need to bear this in mind.

### Remember Your Normal Gifts

The exemption for normal expenditure out of income (see Section 5.7) applies to lifetime gifts only. To get that final year's exemption, you need to make sure you've made that expenditure before you go.

### Consider Setting up a Disabled Trust

As explained in Section 8.11, it may make sense to set up a disabled trust during your terminal illness. This may make things easier for your beneficiaries.

### Spend!

'There are no pockets in shrouds,' they say, so why not spend it before HM Treasury gets hold of it.

Any money you spend that qualifies as 'maintenance of family' (see Section 5.5) will escape IHT. For example, you could spend £1,000 buying clothes for your teenage daughter instead of leaving her a legacy of £1,000 that produces an IHT charge of £667 (see Section 2.9).

You could also think about buying depreciating assets. "How will that help my family?" you may ask, but think about this:

### Example

*Ian knows he has only a few months to live and wants to give his friend Chas a last gift. What Chas would really like is a new car and the model he has his eye on, a 'Rhythm Stick Blockhead', costs £50,000 new.*

*Ian therefore buys a 'Rhythm Stick Blockhead' but doesn't give it to Chas straight away. Instead, Ian leaves the car to Chas in his Will. When Ian dies a few months later, the car, now second-hand, is worth only £35,000 and this is the value to be used for IHT purposes. If Ian had simply given the car to Chas brand new, a sum of £50,000 would have been included in his estate. Hence, by leaving the car in his Will instead, Ian has saved up to £6,000 in IHT.*

### Contractual Obligations

The liabilities under any contractual obligations existing at the date of your death will be deductible from your estate provided they meet the rules set out in Section 2.11. Hence, if your beneficiaries would like something done to an asset that is about to pass to them under the terms of your Will, why not contract for the work to be done at your expense?

### Review (or Make) Your Will

While you're still of sound mind, there is still time to change (or make) your Will. Maximising the value of your NRB should be top of the list if you are married (see Chapter 6 for full details) and you should consider the RNRB if you have children or grandchildren.

As we shall see in Section 17.1, your beneficiaries can enter a deed of variation within the next two years as long as all affected parties agree. What you might need to consider at this stage, however, is whether any beneficiaries in your current Will are likely to stand in the way of IHT saving measures by refusing to agree to a deed of variation.

Furthermore, as we shall see in Section 17.1, deeds of variation do have some significant drawbacks that can be avoided by making the relevant provisions in your Will instead.

The easiest way to save IHT at this stage is to change your Will to leave some or all of your estate to charity (see Section 3.5). Your existing beneficiaries may not be happy but it's your decision (mostly – see Section 10.11).

If you wish to benefit from the additional relief for charitable legacies we examined in Section 3.6, you may wish to include the relevant provision in your Will as, again, one of your beneficiaries might not agree to the necessary deed of variation. Furthermore, as explained in Section 3.6, there have been some doubts over whether deeds of variation can be used for this purpose. There are also a few technical hurdles to be overcome.

All in all, while deeds of variation are an extremely useful IHT planning tool, it will generally make sense to put as much of your IHT planning in place via your Will as you can.

**Go Home or Stay Away**

In Chapter 15, we looked at the issues of retaining a foreign 'Domicile of Origin', shedding a UK 'Domicile of Dependency', or obtaining a foreign 'Domicile of Choice'.

In borderline cases, the outcome will be heavily influenced by your final actions. To keep or re-acquire a foreign Domicile of Origin, it may be wise to go home to die.

To maintain a foreign 'Domicile of Choice' it will be best if you remain in your adopted country. Buying a grave plot and arranging your funeral in your new adopted country will also be helpful to your cause.

**Maximise Your Business Property**

While, as explained in Section 7.17, the business property itself needs to have been held for at least two years to qualify for BPR, you can enhance the value of existing business property at any time. This might, for example, include:

- Paying business debts from private resources
- Paying off liabilities incurred to finance the acquisition, enhancement, or maintenance of business property (again from private resources)
- Buying additional assets for use in your business (as long as these are funded from existing private resources, not from borrowing): for example, could you buy the business premises you currently rent?
- Rights issues of shares by a qualifying private company
- Transferring assets into a qualifying private company (Section 7.21)

Transferring assets to a company may also have CGT or SDLT consequences.

Remember, if you have disposed of qualifying business property within the last three years, you can restore full BPR by buying replacement property (see Section 7.18), including qualifying AIM shares.

**Deathbed CGT Planning**

What you generally should **not** do at this stage is make disposals that give rise to CGT liabilities. (Although there are exceptions, as we have seen.)

If you sell assets before you die, your estate will be liable for the CGT arising based on your original base costs for those assets. Subject to this liability, the net proceeds of the sale will remain in your estate and will be subject to IHT.

If you hang on to those assets, the IHT may be a little greater (as there is no CGT liability to deduct) but, as we saw in Chapter 11, your personal representatives or beneficiaries will be able to sell them later with little or no CGT liability. Conversely, therefore, the best deathbed planning for CGT purposes might be to accumulate more assets – especially from your spouse! (See Section 11.6)

# Chapter 17

# Planning After Death

## 17.1 DEEDS OF VARIATION

Perhaps the 'last resort' in IHT planning is the deed of variation. This is an essential planning tool where a family finds the terms of the deceased's Will (or intestacy) have an undesired effect. Where all affected beneficiaries are in agreement, it is possible to vary the Will in order to create a better result.

As the deed of variation is a legally binding document, it is wise to consult a lawyer when completing it. Strictly speaking, the IHT rules only require the document to be a written instrument, although a formal deed is generally recommended.

### Conditions

i)  The required variations must be recorded in writing within two years of the death (this is the deed)
ii) All existing beneficiaries affected by the variations to the Will or intestacy should sign the deed. (New beneficiaries benefitting from the variations do not need to sign, although this does no harm)
iii) The deed should include a statement that the signatories intend the deed to have effect for IHT purposes
iv) Where the deed results in additional IHT being payable on the deceased's death, a copy must be sent to HMRC within six months of the date of the deed. At the same time, HMRC must also be notified of the amount of additional tax due
v)  The variation must not be made for any consideration in money or money's worth, except in the case of other compensatory variations to the deceased's Will or intestacy

It is also common practice for the deceased's personal representatives to sign the deed, although this is not required by law.

Variations made by such a deed are treated for IHT purposes as if they had been made by the deceased. This treatment also extends to the pre-owned assets regime (see Section 10.21).

This means a beneficiary who becomes a party to a deed of variation and, as a result, gives up a right to all or part of their inheritance, is not themselves regarded as having made any transfer of value (neither chargeable nor otherwise).

Deeds of variation may be used to create any type of trust or implement many of the other planning techniques described throughout this guide.

**Deed of Variation Drawbacks**

Variations made under a deed of variation effectively rewrite history and are treated as if they had been made by the deceased – *but only for IHT purposes!*

For CGT and Income Tax purposes, the original beneficiary (under the deceased's Will or the laws of intestacy) is regarded as having made a transfer to the new beneficiary, or to any trust that receives property under the deed of variation.

This could result in the creation of a settlor-interested trust (see Section 9.8) or may invoke the settlements legislation where the new beneficiary is a minor child of the original beneficiary (see Section 10.17).

Where a deed of variation is used to make, or increase, charitable legacies, there are a few additional formalities that need to be observed. It is essential the charity (or trustees of a charitable trust) is notified of the existence of the deed. HMRC will look for evidence that the charity or trustees are aware assets or funds are being redirected to them under the deed. Copies of an exchange of letters between the parties involved should be sufficient for this purpose.

As explained in Section 3.6, there have been doubts over whether it is possible to use a deed of variation to increase charitable legacies in order to benefit from the reduced IHT rate. This may no longer be the case, so it will certainly be worth a try, but it is better to make the appropriate provisions in a Will.

## 17.2    DISCLAIMERS

Under a simpler procedure a beneficiary can disclaim their inheritance. Only conditions (i) and (v) in the previous section need to be satisfied. The deed should only be signed by the person making the disclaimer.

The disclaimed inheritance will generally fall into the residue of the estate and will be dealt with accordingly.

This procedure will be particularly useful where NRB legacies have been included in Wills made prior to October 2007 and the family decide it would now be more sensible for the surviving spouse, as the residuary beneficiary, to receive the entire estate.

In addition to its simplicity, a disclaimer has the added advantage that the disclaimed legacy is treated as passing directly from the deceased to the new beneficiary for Income Tax purposes. This is therefore a much better way to pass a legacy directly to the original beneficiary's minor child.

**Disclaimer Drawbacks**

A disclaimer is not possible where the original beneficiary has received any benefit from their legacy since the deceased's death (e.g. by living in an inherited property). However, it will often remain possible to use a deed of variation to achieve the same result – for IHT purposes at least!

## 17.3    TRANSFERS OUT OF TRUSTS WITHIN TWO YEARS OF DEATH

Transfers of property placed into a relevant property trust on the death of the settlor that take place within two years of the settlor's death, are treated as if they were legacies made by the deceased directly. Such transfers are exempt from the exit charge (see Section 8.19).

Where the transferee is another trust, it will be treated as if it had been established under the deceased's Will. This provides scope to set up an immediate post-death interest, a bereaved minors' trust or an '18 to 25 Trust'. In effect, this enables testators to create a discretionary trust under the terms of their Will that can be converted, as appropriate, within the two years following their death.

### Wealth Warning

Once again, these provisions only apply for IHT purposes. Hence, the transfer out of the original relevant property trust will be subject to CGT in the normal way (see Section 11.11). Furthermore, holdover relief is not available under these circumstances.

The relevant property trust will also be liable for Income Tax on any income received prior to the transfer.

## 17.4    SECOND CHANCES

One might say the procedures outlined under Sections 17.1 to 17.3 already provide a 'second chance' to get the IHT planning right. However, only one variation under the procedure in Section 17.1 is allowed in respect of any item of property. Similarly, only one transfer of any item of property can fall under the rules explained in Section 17.3.

Nonetheless, it is possible for the same item of property to be subject to a deed of variation and later transferred out of a relevant property trust within the rules set out in Section 17.3 (or vice versa). The variation and the transfer must take place within two years of death to be effective for IHT purposes.

## 17.5    MORE PET PROBLEMS

Where property is passed to a new beneficiary under either a deed of variation or by way of a transfer out of a relevant property trust within two years of the settlor's death, and the new beneficiary makes a potentially exempt transfer of that same property shortly afterwards, there is a strong chance HMRC will apply the associated operations rules (Section 10.19). This would mean the deceased is treated as having left the property directly to the ultimate recipient which, in most cases, is likely to make it fully chargeable to IHT.

## 17.6    PROPERTY APPOINTMENTS

Where real property (land and buildings) is to be passed (appointed) to a beneficiary subject to a mortgage, it will generally be better for them to take on the existing debt, as this will be exempt from SDLT, rather than buy the property from the estate, or take out a new mortgage.

As long as there is an 'arm's length' commercial mortgage provider involved, the original debt should still be deductible from the deceased's estate (see Section 2.11).

## 17.7    POST-MORTEM RELIEF

Where a beneficiary sells certain types of inherited assets for less than their probate value, they may claim 'post-mortem' relief for their effective loss. The relief decreases the value of the deceased's estate for IHT purposes and a refund of the IHT already paid may be claimed where appropriate.

The relevant assets must be sold to an unconnected person (see Appendix B for a list of connected persons) on arms' length terms within a specified period after the deceased's death. The specified period depends on the type of asset sold, as follows:

- Quoted shares: twelve months
- Land and buildings: three years
- Related property (see Section 10.4): three years

A claim is not possible in respect of any other assets.

When making a claim, the beneficiary must take account of all sales within the relevant period. Hence, when some inherited assets have also been sold at a profit, it is only the beneficiary's overall net loss that may be claimed.

In effect, the values of all the inherited assets sold by the beneficiary within the specified period are adjusted to their sale price. This is to prevent 'cherry picking', i.e. only claiming for losses without taking account of profits.

### Tax Tip
A form of 'cherry picking' can still be achieved by leaving the relevant assets to a discretionary trust in the first instance and then appointing all loss-making assets to one beneficiary prior to sale, and within two years of the deceased's death. As explained in Section 17.3, the beneficiary is treated as if they had inherited these assets absolutely, thus enabling them to make the post-mortem relief claim.

# Chapter 18

# The Future of Inheritance Tax

## 18.1 CRYSTAL BALL GAZING

Most of the more effective IHT planning measures involve planning for the long term. However, this necessarily involves making some assumptions about the future and, if there is one thing any of us can predict about the future, it is that it will not be exactly as we predict!

Nonetheless, it is worth me looking at some of the proposals about the future of IHT we know of, as well as adding some speculation of my own. The measures outlined in this chapter are not firm Government proposals, but are the sort of thing they might consider.

None of this may actually happen. Indeed, many past proposals have failed to come to fruition. But, when carrying out your own long-term IHT planning, you should be aware of these possibilities.

Two recent high profile reports may give us an idea of where IHT could be heading. I will look at these in the next two sections then give you my take on them in Section 18.4. Lastly, in Section 18.5, I will add my own personal thoughts – but I stress that is all they are, personal thoughts, albeit backed by over thirty years experience watching the behaviour of the UK Government.

## 18.2 OFFICE FOR TAX SIMPLIFICATION RECOMMENDATIONS

For those who've never heard of the Office for Tax Simplification, or 'OTS', as it is sometimes known, it really is an actual Government department and not something out of George Orwell's '1984'.

The OTS published a report on the structure of IHT in July 2019. Their key recommendations included (my numbering):

**OTS1:** Replace the current annual exemption, the exemptions for gifts in consideration of marriage, and the exemption for normal expenditure out of income (Sections 5.2, 5.4 and 5.7) with a single, annual personal gifts allowance. No figure for the allowance was recommended, but £25,000 was mentioned in the report.

The small gifts exemption (Section 5.3) should be increased substantially. A figure of £1,000 was mentioned, but not specifically recommended.

**OTS2:** Reduce the seven year period prior to death, for which lifetime gifts become chargeable to IHT on the donor's death (Section 4.5) to five years, but abolish taper relief.

**OTS3:** Abolish the CGT 'uplift on death' on assets that are exempt from IHT, or subject to relief, on the owner's death. The person inheriting the assets would 'inherit' the deceased's original base cost for the assets instead.

**OTS4:** Restrict BPR (Chapter 7) to businesses that would qualify for entrepreneur's relief: i.e. where the trading element accounts for more than 80% of business activities, rather than the current need to merely be over 50%. However, the relief should be extended to furnished holiday lets to align it with the CGT and Income Tax treatment of these businesses.

**OTS5:** Review the availability of APR on farmhouses (Section 7.30) and extend it to cases where the farmer has had to go into care, or for long-term medical treatment.

**OTS6:** Blanket exemption for all death benefits under term life insurance, whether written in trust or not (see Sections 10.12 and 10.13).

**OTS7:** The pre-owned assets regime (Section 10.21) should be 'reviewed': this seems to be code for 'abolished'.

### 18.3 ALL PARTY GROUP RECOMMENDATIONS

In January 2020, the All Party Parliamentary Group ('APG') on 'Inheritance and Intergenerational Fairness' published its report on the 'Reform of IHT'. Being politicians instead of civil servants, like the OTS, they were able to be a bit more radical. The key points are summarised below (my numbering again).

**APG1:** Replace IHT with a 10% 'Death Tax', rising to 20% on taxable amounts (after exemptions) in excess of £2m. Something similar to the NRB (including the TNRB) would be retained (and at a similar level) but the RNRB would be abolished.

**APG2:** Abolish the current annual exemption, small gifts exemption, exemption for normal expenditure out of income, and exemption for gifts in consideration of marriage (Sections 5.2 to 5.4 and 5.7) and replace them with a single annual allowance of £30,000 per tax year. A single, flat rate, 'Gift Tax' at 10% would apply to any amounts in excess of the allowance.

**APG3:** The spouse exemption and exemption for gifts to charity would be retained for the purposes of both the 'Death Tax' and the 'Gift Tax'.

**APG4:** No further tax would apply to lifetime gifts on the donor's death and the 'gift with reservation' rules would be abolished (effectively, they would no longer be needed).

**APG5:** Trusts would be subject to an annual charge (instead of the current ten-year anniversary charge) and a fixed, flat rate charge on capital distributions to beneficiaries (instead of the current exit charges).

**APG6:** BPR and APR would be abolished. Beneficiaries would have ten years to pay the 'Death Tax' arising on business assets (similar to the current rules for payment of IHT relating to land and buildings: see Section 2.8).

**APG7:** Deemed domicile (see Section 2.2) would arise after ten years of UK residence (out of the previous fifteen). Excluded property trusts (Section 9.13) would be taxed the same as any other trust where any UK resident was able to benefit from the trust and any settlor has deemed UK domicile.

**APG8:** 'Death Tax' would apply to balances held in pension funds on death.

**APG9:** The 'uplift on death' for CGT would be abolished and beneficiaries would inherit the deceased's original historic base cost for the assets instead. They would also be entitled to principal private residence relief (see the Taxcafe.co.uk guide *'How to Save Property Tax'* for details) for any periods the deceased occupied a property as their main residence.


## 18.4    MY TAKE ON THE RECOMMENDATIONS

The reports covered in Sections 18.2 and 18.3 were issued before the Coronavirus crisis, so we must appreciate things have changed somewhat: especially when we consider the Government's future revenue requirements.

Governments of all persuasions are balancing two conflicting objectives:

- To raise enough revenue from tax to run the country
- To win the next election

As far as the first objective is concerned, this is going to be a tough job over the next decade, due to the huge amount of additional national debt caused by the Coronavirus crisis. This means that recommendations will only be taken seriously if they are at least tax neutral or, better still (from the Government's point of view) raise more revenue.

Having said that, things that make life easier for HMRC are also appealing to the Government, and can save more in costs than might perhaps be lost in tax, so some degree of simplification is possible.

For this reason, I think the abolition of some of the exemptions for lifetime gifts and their replacement with a single annual allowance is a strong possibility. Hence, I think the recommendation at 'OTS1' in Section 18.2 may well be adopted.

Personally, I'd say the idea of reducing the period for the taxation of lifetime gifts made prior to death to five years ('OTS2') has a 50/50 chance. In itself, it is a reasonable simplification measure and should be broadly tax neutral, but HMRC will fear it may open up a lot more scope for IHT planning as it would mean the ability to use your NRB every five years instead of every seven.

In the current climate, I think there is a good chance the Government might adopt recommendations that raise additional revenue, like abolishing the CGT 'uplift on death' where assets are exempt or relieved from IHT ('OTS3' and 'APG9'); restoring IHT on pensions ('APG8'); and both reducing the period for deemed domicile and tightening the rules on excluded property trusts ('APG7').

Restrictions on BPR to align it with entrepreneur's relief ('OTS4') will also appeal to the Government. Some relaxation in APR on farmhouses to deal with some of the current unfairness ('OTS5') also seems probable. My personal view is that these changes are more likely than the abolition of these important reliefs ('APG6').

A blanket exemption for death benefits ('OTS6') seems unlikely in the revenue hungry environment we will have over the next decade and, while abolition of the pre-owned assets charge ('OTS7') would be sensible , HMRC won't want to give up their 'safety net', so I think this idea will be quietly forgotten.

The APG's most radical proposals for a 'Death Tax' and 'Gift Tax' to replace IHT ('APG1' to 'APG4') may have had a good chance if it hadn't been for the Coronavirus crisis. Now, however, I think the Government is unlikely to have the appetite for such radical change as it will lead to too much uncertainty over future revenue streams, taxpayer behaviour, and, of course, the impact on the next election. Nonetheless, if someone can convince them it will raise extra revenue without losing votes, they could go for it. More likely, I think we may see this in the Opposition's manifesto at the next election.

However, the reforms to IHT on trusts recommended in 'APG5' look pretty sensible and could be made either tax neutral or could increase the tax take a little without haemorrhaging votes too badly. Having said that, if I had a pound for every proposal to reform the IHT treatment of trusts that's been abandoned over the last few years... well, I'd have a few quid, I can tell you.

## 18.5   WHAT ELSE MIGHT WE SEE?

Finally, I will add my own thoughts on what we might see ahead for IHT. But please remember, all this, and the comments in the previous section, is just my personal view!

## The Short to Medium Term

Over the coming decade, the Government will have to raise revenue where it can. We are likely to see tax increases across the board, especially in taxes that will predominantly fall on people who enjoy little sympathy from the majority of the electorate. In short, this makes IHT increases falling on the wealthier members of society highly likely.

The Government is also very fond of stealth tax. By freezing bands and allowances, there is little headline news to damage their election prospects but they can leave inflation to do their dirty work by quietly eroding away the value of tax reliefs.

Hence, as already predicted in Section 3.2, I would expect a further freeze in the NRB, as well as a freeze to the RNRB and its taper threshold. I have predicted three years in my forecasts in this guide, but it could be longer.

I also think we could see a higher rate of IHT applying to larger estates. Say a 50% rate on amounts in excess of £2m.

The OTS has proposed, broadly, to exempt lifetime gifts made more than five years prior to death. However, the Government could go the other way and tax all gifts made up to ten years prior to death. This has been suggested before, after all.

The IHT charges on trusts may be another prime target. The Gov could increase the rate of anniversary and exit charges to a maximum of 10%, or even a flat rate of 10% instead of the current maximum of 6%. There will be little sympathy for those affected in the environment we will be living in and the political will may be strong enough to overcome the objections that have blocked previous attempts at reform.

## Longer Term

The longer term position depends very much on which political party is in power. When the economy has recovered from the Coronavirus crisis (and we have no idea how long that will take), a future Conservative Government might consider abolishing IHT (perhaps accompanied by an abolition of the CGT 'uplift on death' along the lines of 'APG9').

However, a future Labour Government might be more likely to adopt all the APG's proposals, including a 'Death Tax' and 'Gift Tax', along the lines set out in Section 18.3.

## A Final Personal Note

Personally, I think taxing death, or personal gifts between family members, is completely immoral and just plain wrong. If it was up to me, IHT would be abolished tomorrow. However, what I have done in the last two sections instead is to give you my view, not of what **should** happen, but what **could** happen. None of this may happen at all. But something will.

# Appendix A

## UK Tax Rates and Allowances: 2018/19 to 2020/21

| | Rates | 2018/19 £ | 2019/20 £ | 2020/21 £ |
|---|---|---|---|---|
| **Income Tax (1)** | | | | |
| Personal allowance | | 11,850 | 12,500 | 12,500 |
| Basic rate band | 20% | 34,500 | 37,500 | 37,500 |
| Higher rate/Threshold | 40% | 46,350 | 50,000 | 50,000 |
| | | | | |
| Personal allowance withdrawal | | | | |
| Effective rate/From | 60% | 100,000 | 100,000 | 100,000 |
| To | | 123,700 | 125,000 | 125,000 |
| Additional rate/Threshold | 45% | 150,000 | 150,000 | 150,000 |
| | | | | |
| Starting rate band (2) | 0% | 5,000 | 5,000 | 5,000 |
| Personal savings allowance (3) | | 1,000 | 1,000 | 1,000 |
| Dividend allowance | | 2,000 | 2,000 | 2,000 |
| Marriage allowance (4) | | 1,185 | 1,250 | 1,250 |
| | | | | |
| **National Insurance** | | | | |
| Primary Threshold | 9%/12% | 8,424 | 8,632 | 9,500 |
| Secondary Threshold | 13.8% | 8,424 | 8,632 | 8,788 |
| Upper earnings limit | 2% | 46,350 | 50,000 | 50,000 |
| Employment allowance | | 3,000 | 3,000 | 4,000 |
| Class 2 – per week | | 2.95 | 3.00 | 3.05 |
| Small profits threshold | | 6,205 | 6,365 | 6,475 |
| | | | | |
| **Pension Contributions** | | | | |
| Annual allowance | | 40,000 | 40,000 | 40,000 |
| Lifetime allowance | | 1.030m | 1.055m | 1.0731m |
| | | | | |
| **Capital Gains Tax** | | | | |
| Annual exemption | | 11,700 | 12,000 | 12,300 |
| | | | | |
| **Inheritance Tax** | | | | |
| Nil rate band | | 325,000 | 325,000 | 325,000 |
| Main RNRB | | 125,000 | 150,000 | 175,000 |
| Annual Exemption | | 3,000 | 3,000 | 3,000 |

### Notes
1. Different rates and thresholds apply to Scottish taxpayers (except on interest, savings and dividend income, and on capital gains)
2. Applies to interest and savings income only
3. Halved for higher rate taxpayers; not available to additional rate taxpayers
4. Available where neither spouse/civil partner pays higher rate tax

# Appendix B

# Connected Persons

The definition of 'connected persons' differs slightly from one area of UK tax law to another. Generally, however, an individual's connected persons include the following:

i) Their husband, wife or civil partner

ii) The following relatives:
   - o Mother, father or remoter ancestor
   - o Son, daughter or remoter descendant
   - o Brother or sister

iii) Relatives under (ii) above of the individual's spouse or civil partner

iv) Spouses or civil partners of the individual's relatives under (ii) above

v) The individual's business partners

vi) Companies under the control of the individual or of any of their relatives under (i) to (iv) above

vii) Trusts where the individual, or any of their relatives under (i) to (iv) above, is a beneficiary

Additionally, for the purposes of the pre-owned asset charge (see Section 10.21), 'connected persons' also include:

- Aunts and Uncles
- Nephews and Nieces
- Companies under the control of any of these relatives
- Trusts where any of these relatives are a beneficiary

# Appendix C

# Sample Documentation

<u>1. Memorandum recording a gift (IHT liability remains with transferor in the first instance)</u>

MEMORANDUM OF GIFT FROM

Roger Meadows of 3 Taylor Street, Penzance

TO

Ian Deacon of 4 Queen Street, Belfast

MEMORANDUM that on 15th August 2020 Roger Meadows transferred by way of gift to Ian Deacon the sum of one million pounds (£1,000,000)

Dated:   20th August 2020

Signed by Roger Meadows:

Signed by Ian Deacon:

**Note:** Any IHT arising at the time of the transfer will be the transferor's liability. In practice, however, most transfers to other individuals will be potentially exempt transfers, meaning no IHT actually arises at that stage. Any further IHT arising in the event of the transferor's death within the next seven years will usually be the transferee's liability. If this is not desired, a memorandum along the lines of Item 3 below will be appropriate.

<u>2. Memorandum recording transferee's liability for IHT on a lifetime transfer</u>

MEMORANDUM OF GIFT FROM

James Stewart of 15 Castle Street, Stirling

TO

Mary Stewart of 42 Palace Road, Linlithgow

MEMORANDUM that on 16th November 2020 James Stewart transferred by way of gift to Mary Stewart (subject to the payment of any Inheritance Tax) the assets listed in the schedule below to the intent that they have become and are the absolute property of Mary Stewart and IN CONSIDERATION of such transfer Mary Stewart undertook to pay any Inheritance Tax in respect of such gift assessed upon James Stewart or his personal representatives and indemnifies James Stewart and his personal representatives accordingly.

SCHEDULE

- Property at 87 Flodden Avenue, Berwick upon Tweed
- Ten thousand Ordinary £1 Shares in Darnley plc
- The sum of five thousand pounds (£5,000) in cash

Dated:   21st November 2020

Signed by James Stewart:

Signed by Mary Stewart:

3. Memorandum recording a gift (all IHT to be borne by the transferor)

MEMORANDUM OF GIFT FROM

Noddy Hill of 6 Slade Street, Wolverhampton

TO

David Holder of 9 Flame Avenue, Birmingham

MEMORANDUM that on 28th February 2021 Noddy Hill transferred by way of gift to David Holder the sum of two million pounds (£2,000,000). The said Noddy Hill hereby further undertakes that he or his personal representatives shall pay any Inheritance Tax assessed in respect of such gift out of the assets of his general estate and indemnifies David Holder accordingly.

Dated:   28th February 2021

Signed by Noddy Hill:

Signed by David Holder:

# Appendix D

## Abbreviations Used in this Guide

| | |
|---|---|
| AIM | Alternative Investment Market |
| APG | All Party Parliamentary Group |
| APR | Agricultural Property Relief |
| BPR | Business Property Relief |
| CGT | Capital Gains Tax |
| CPI | Consumer Prices Index |
| DOTAS | Disclosure of Tax Avoidance Schemes |
| EEA | European Economic Area |
| FIC* | Family Investment Company |
| GAAR | General Anti-Abuse Rule |
| HMRC | HM Revenue and Customs |
| IHT | Inheritance Tax |
| ISA | Individual Savings Account |
| Ltd | Limited (i.e. a limited company) |
| NRB | Nil Rate Band |
| OTS | Office for Tax Simplification |
| PET* | Potentially Exempt Transfer |
| RNRB | Residence Nil Rate Band |
| SDLT | Stamp Duty Land Tax |
| TNRB | Transferable Nil Rate Band |
| UK | United Kingdom |
| VAT | Value Added Tax |

\* Only used in headings, titles, footnotes, etc.